THE RAILWAY ENTHUSIAST'S
BEDSIDE BOOK

The Railway Enthusiast's
Bedside Book

Edited by
H. A. VALLANCE

B T BATSFORD LTD   LONDON

First published 1966

© B. T. Batsford Ltd, 1966

Set in 11 pt. Bembo (Series 270) 1 pt. leaded
Made and printed in Great Britain by
William Clowes and Sons, Limited, London and Beccles
for the publishers
B. T. BATSFORD LTD
4 Fitzhardinge Street, Portman Square, London W.1

CONTENTS

Contents

EDITOR'S NOTE

THIS BOOK has been written by enthusiasts for enthusiasts. Of some two dozen contributors, more than half are keen amateur students of railways, experts whose knowledge has been acquired through profound personal interest. The remainder are professional railwaymen of the type that may well be called enthusiasts, because they are obviously in love with their work and enjoy telling others about it.

The essays cover a wide field. On the practical side, you may read of the preparation of timetables; of minor mishaps, some of which might have had far more serious results; of the operation of a special traffic; and some points of railway law. For the historian, there are articles on railway archives; the pioneer Stockton & Darlington Railway; and a biographical sketch of a famous chief mechanical engineer. Pictorial records are covered in an article on railway photography. In reminiscent vein are railway recollections of six decades, and a retrospect of a country junction 40 years ago. Topography and scenery are represented in descriptions of journeys from London to the Highlands of Scotland, and across the mountains of Norway. Unusual notes are struck in essays on monorail systems, railway names, and private stations.

Except for those received from official sources, the illustrations have come from the cameras of photographers whose names have long been familiar to their fellow-enthusiasts. In selecting the illustrations, the emphasis has been laid on steam-hauled trains, to provide a varied pictorial record of an aspect of railways that is fast passing away.

No attempt has been made in the text or the illustrations to delve deeply into technicalities. The aim has been to present as many facets of the railway as possible in a light and interesting way that will be welcomed at the close of a long day, just before the light is switched out.

The Railway Club   H.A.V.
320 High Holborn
London, W.C.1
December 1965

ACKNOWLEDGMENT

THE EDITOR and Publishers wish to thank the following for permission to reproduce the illustrations appearing in this book:

W. J. Verden Anderson, for page 28 lower.
P. J. Bawcutt, for page 214 upper.
Derek Cross, for pages 113, 160 lower, 177, 195, 224 and 233.
Elizabeth Cross, for page 132 lower.
John R. Day, for pages 98 and 142.
M. W. Earley, for pages 107, 159 and 160 upper.
H. C. Hughes, for page 214 lower.
B. H. Jackson, for page 132 upper.
Charles E. Lee, for page 196 upper.
London Transport Board, for page 196 lower.
The Rev. A. W. V. Mace, for pages 17, 75 and 76.
Henry D. Narvarte, for page 97.
Ivo Peters, for pages 108 lower, 114 upper, 178 and 251.
Eric Treacy, for pages 18, 27, 58 lower, 114 lower, 131, 141, 223, 234 and 252.
P. B. Whitehouse, for pages 57, 58 upper, 108 upper and 213.

They also acknowledge with thanks permission of the following to include the quotations:

The Daily Telegraph, for the quotations from "Peterborough" on pages 32, 117, 170, 182, 192, 203, 237 and 264.
The Evening News, for the quotations on pages 85 and 264.
Robert Hale Ltd., for the quotation from *Under a Suffolk Sky* by Allan Jobson, on page 93.
Rail News, for the quotations from the *Eastern Region News* on pages 70, 155 and 237.
The Railway Magazine, for the quotations on pages 126, 146, 155, 161, 170 and 192.

The text decorations were designed by Peter Winding.

THE ILLUSTRATIONS

The Illustrations

Thoughts on the Bull

ELMER T. RUDD

ALREADY THERE HAD BEEN ONE COLLISION, but it had been at fairly low speed, achieving little but a loud bang. The next one—it was on the Dublin-Cork main line near Mallow—was to be a real smasher. Furthermore the Bull was determined to see all he could of it, at close quarters.

"What's *that*?" he asked abruptly.

That was an old goods wagon, its planking pierced by just such slots as would suit snipers spraying bullets on a wrecked train. The Bull's companions assured him that it was the thing from which they were to watch the collision. But not only was the Bull a thorough man; he trusted in his Maker, and he said peremptorily: "Take it away! Take it *away*!"

So they took it away. Some of them, thus assisting in a fine piece of deliberate wrecking, then awaited the inevitable smash, perhaps nervously and not too near. But the Bull stood close to where he knew the point of impact would be, alert, quite avian, like a thrush about to give the rising worm the bird, with his hat on the back of his head.

At 40 miles an hour, the collision was admirably ample. In one thunderclap, a huge old teak-bodied dining car, several other vehicles, and the Bull, were engulfed in a great brown cloud of dust, rust and flying wreckage.

But the cloud dispersed, as clouds do, and there was the Bull, himself quite undamaged, rushing forward to inspect the results of his machinations.

By now you may have assumed that this was a Commandant of Irregular Forces making mischief during the Irish Troubles, and, if so, you will be wrong. This was Oliver Vaughan Snell Bulleid, C.M.E. of Coras Iompair Eireann, sometime C.M.E. of the Southern Railway of England, last Apostle of Steam, and one of the greatest, ascertaining the efficacy of the Fischer automatic coupler under conditions of serious accident.

He was satisfied. The Fischer coupling had behaved as it was claimed to behave. The great old dining car, which in more than half a century had served so many Irish chops and steaks between Dublin and Galway, was still in one piece. Now I knew that dining car well in its time. The elderly girl who used to polish all the door-handles of the trains at Westland Row Station, said it was a darling car, so it was! Perhaps that was its finest hour!

That smash at Mallow was characteristic of the Bull, and long before the Irishmen at Inchicore gave him that name, still it would have been characteristic. Before ever he commanded the senior Irish Locomotive Department; before he commanded that of the Southern Railway; when he was still one of Nigel Gresley's people on the Great Northern Railway (the English one of that name) he was capable of such pranks, and because he was Bulleid, an able man and clever, he got away with them. The next story has already appeared in print, so it should not be censored, but let me tell it as it was told to me.

Our scene is the flat, green, apparently limitless expanse of Eastern England, where the skies are immense and Lincoln Cathedral stands up from the fens as St. Kilda stands up from the ocean beyond the Hebrides. Steadily across that vastitude rumbles a long, long Great Northern goods train, and on the engine footplate are three men, one of them Bulleid.

"I want you to make a full emergency brake application!" he says.

The driver jumps, though drivers are, and have to be, cool men.

"Did you *mean* that, Mr. Bulleid?"

"Yes. I want to see what happens."

"Is that an *order*, sir?"

"Yes. I'll take full responsibility."

So the driver makes his F.E.B.A., with the results that might be expected from a long train of goods empties with no continuous automatic brakes. The train comes to a stand, on the rails but divided. Bulleid is instantly down on the ballast, looking for skid marks and so forth, making notes in a neat little book. The enginemen mop their brows. From the rear come increasingly loud gusts of abominable words. They are uttered by the guard. What, he wishes to know, is the meaning of this (flaming) trick? The (physiological) train is divided. He has been thrown from one end to the other of his (crimson) goods brake, which but for him would have been set on fire when the (obscene) stove was upset by the shock—and a great deal more that would go down well in a contemporary kitchen-sink drama.

Thoughts on the Bull

Our scene shifts to the Chief Mechanical Engineer's carpet at Doncaster. Gresley's carpet, like those of many C.M.Es., could be an uncommonly warm one at times, and so it was now. The fireworks concluded with a reminder that Mr. Bulleid was *not* the C.M.E. of the Great Northern Railway.

Bulleid was withdrawing from the Presence when the Presence gently called him back.

Exactly *what* happened when one made a full emergency brake application on a loose-coupled, unbraked goods train weighing so-many tons and travelling at such-and-such speed?

Bulleid told him. It was quite an academic occasion. At last, and for the second time that morning, Bulleid was again withdrawing from the Presence, and once more Jove thundered.

"Bulleid! You are *not* the Chief Mechanical Engineer of the Great Northern Railway!"

He never was so, nor of the London & North Eastern; but of the Southern he was, and no British railway had ever before seen the like of him, or of the things he made. Bulleid was the last of the great originals among British locomotive engineers; perhaps indeed the greatest of them, at any rate in the eyes of those who love mechanical and experimental engineering for its own fascinating sake. That is how *I* love engines, and people who make engines. I am an artist, and I have generally found that where an engineer has no art in him, there is little imagination in his engineering. Odsfish, what deadly dullness have we seen in much work highly esteemed in the past! And in British work at that, so that certain Frenchmen, and Austrians, and Germans, and occasionally even Americans, have made one feel ashamed! When I feel like that, it is comforting to recall the work of Bulleid, a worthy last hope of that science which G. J. Churchward, F. W. Webb (repellent man, but what a man!), Joseph Beattie, T. R. Crampton, and Richard Trevithick had served in the course of a century and a half, the science of straight steam locomotion.

Does Bulleid, in his house at Exmouth, like to think he has been a rebel? It would be impertinent to try and answer this question for him. But never would he make a sacred cow of Tradition. When he was going to Dublin, somebody there asked what to expect, and was told that he would probably require that the chimney of the next engine should be placed on the tender. And so indeed he did, for a reason he had. There in Ireland was a country with beggarly coal, no native oil, and not enough water-power to go round. How should a man work a railway in such a country? There had been precious little coal during the war when Ireland had stayed neutral, and that neutrality seems to have irritated the Americans, so many of whom had been so whole-hearted and wide-pursed when certain Irishmen had risen against the British in the course of their previous quarrel with the Germans.

What had Ireland got, to make a locomotive go? Well, there was plenty of turf (peat, to the British). If anyone could make a railway engine run on turf, Bulleid could. His first essay was with an old mogul goods engine, and sure enough, the smokebox gases were led aft!

There were some rummy stories about that conversion. During the engine's trials, a friend of mine in County Kildare wrote to me that she had got as far as Thurles, and was presently standing there in a pool of oil. Some time later, he reported, she was as far as Mallow. But then came *The Quiet One*. This was a very advanced locomotive, yet simpler, and presently for the better, than her forerunner, the *Leader* on the Southern Railway in England. One feels that, with much money and much patience, *The Quiet One* might have gone far. The men of C.I.E. gave her that name because of the way she sailed up, rather than steamed up; even more silent than a Swiss electric running light.

But one suspects that already the combined interests of Standard Oil and General Motors (who rule the Western World) had thoroughly done their work. Nothing shall prosper among us without the blessings of the oil and motor companies, and it was one of the many ironies of history that the Bull, before he went into retirement, initiated the great substitution of diesel for steam power in the Republic of Ireland and so, it may well be, saved her main-line railways.

It was an eminent Southern officer who told me that Bulleid was a rebel. At the worst stage in the war, in 1940, he sent his senior-officers'-issue tin hat into his paint shop at Eastleigh, requiring that it should be painted in malachite green, with a picture of a cat on the front of it. My distinguished friend thought this very shocking indeed. But why? It did not make a ha'porth of difference to what was happening in Northern France! Somebody was the Cat-Who-Walked-By-Himself; for Inchicore had not yet dubbed him The Bull.

When Bulleid went from the London & North Eastern to the Southern in 1937, some of us wondered what was coming, though the Turgid Many were quite sure that there would be something like a light Gresley Pacific, just strong enough to hoist the Atlantic Coast Express to Honiton Tunnel, or to take single-handed, and not very fast, the Night Ferry on the English lap of its progress between London and Paris. The Turgid Many did not know that the Southern's New Man was a rebel, who, like all the best rebels, had served faithfully under an autocrat beforehand.

We got a whiff of what was coming when he became President of the Institution of Locomotive Engineers (1939-44). There was going to be

A Bulleid Pacific huffs and puffs its way out of Dover with the "Golden Arrow"

Stanier Pacific No. 46210, Lady Patricia, *climbing out of Euston with a train for Holyhead*

Bristol train leaving Newcastle with Gresley Pacific No. 60080, Dick Turpin

something odd. Not until 1941 did it appear. Certainly the first of the Merchant Navy class, *Channel Packet*, was outwardly quite unlike anything else in Europe (apart from its general dimensions) or America (apart from its peculiar wheels). Certainly, it was a Pacific. It was cased, but not stream-lined—and Bulleid knew something about streamlining; his ideas on the subject had certainly helped to produce the aerofoil shape on Gresley's last Pacifics, six years before. But the valve gear? We could not see it. We were told that it was a radial gear, and that it involved chains and sprockets within an enclosed oil-bath. But not until sometime later did we get a diagram, in the course of a masterly paper, and understand more or less what went on inside *that box*, as someone called it at Question Time.

Later, we were given a run to Exeter, in an immense train of rather shabby coaches which could be briefly spared from the Southern Railway's contri-bution to the British War Effort. Apart from Sir Eustace Missenden and his Southern Railway staff, there were several journalists and suchlike aboard the train. W. A. Willox, then of *The Railway Gazette*, and in one's experience never a man to gush unduly, went almost starry-eyed over the train's acceleration out of Waterloo. We got away from Waterloo, he said, like the wind. In his entourage was John Skelton, who suddenly stopped talking about South America, giving his eye to his stopwatch and evidently loving her like a mother. Even Hamilton Ellis had a stopwatch, saying with a smirk of half-shame that it was borrowed, and that he never used such a thing unless, as now, he was being paid to do it. The truth was that all these people wanted to see what happened when you had a Pacific locomotive, with a big firebox apparently full of thermic siphons and things, and a work-ing pressure of 280 lb. per sq. in., on a train of unprecedented length, pointed towards Exeter by the London & South Western line.

We were not disappointed. Willox had been quite right about "getting away like the wind", and then, somewhere around Winchfield, a person best left nameless came out with his "I told you so!" For clouds of smoke, and an abominable odour, were coming from the front of the train, and someone else said he was sure that both came from *that box* with the works in it. When we pulled up in the environs of Basingstoke, it seemed that the only Southern Railway face neither red nor elongated was Bulleid's. He was down on the ballast, as on a long-ago occasion in Lincolnshire or some-where, apparently fascinated by the fault and its possible causes, and wearing that mild grin which, like his feline handshake, many men will remember for a long time.

Two old engines, one South Western and the other more or less South Eastern & Chatham, took us on to Salisbury, where there was another of Bulleid's new babies waiting to take us to Exeter.

I have said that the train was immense, also that the carriages were oldish and shabby. Evidently the brakes were in like case with the awful green-jazz moquette we sat on, for, after the manner of senile vacuum brakes, they leaked on. It was therefore against a susurration of brake-blocks in slight but troublesome contact with indignant tyres, that the great train climbed up the Nadder Valley towards Semley. It might have brought two of my beloved "T 9s" to a dead stand about Tisbury, but the Pacific was not to be put out by a collection of tired Maunsell coaches. And when, having been brought to a stop at Seaton Junction (required, I was told, by Bulleid in the interests of science), she lifted that train up the hill and was accelerating before the summit inside Honiton Tunnel, one knew that *here indeed was an engine*!

Amateurs—and myself has already confessed to being an artist—had already been restive at the appearance of Bulleid's Pacifics. But when he brought out his wartime goods engines, all hell was let loose, except among Southern Railway people who had to work a railway always overloaded and often under fire from our far-from-loving German cousins. An engine had been required which should combine a maximum of power and manoeuvrability with a minimum of weight. Bulleid provided it, in the "Q 1" 0–6–0. Given his head, he could have worked all the Southern Railway on three or four classes of steam locomotive, plus the electric multiple-units and some electric freight engines which (a masterpiece of collaboration by improbable partners!) he produced with Alfred Raworth.

Surely that was the most important thing! A useful locomotive that could go anywhere, with any sort of train, probably the most powerful locomotive that ever ran on six wheels only! From the amateurs came a scream in harmonic chorus, at this engine which looked so rum! Even a Russian engineer, emerging with other people from the northern end of the Guildford tunnel, stared and said: "Remarkable! Remarkable!" (Acknowledgements to John F. Parke, who was there.) But then, in the nineteen-forties, Russians were still accustomed to steam locomotives which not only had platforms all round, but something like a ship's rail protecting their enginemen.

Some of the amateurs, I say, were furious. Rixon Bucknall wrote: "Beauty of form is a matter of opinion, but the verdict of a press-sponsored inquiry promotes belief that machinery of such grotesque appearance is doing as much to arouse in travellers a loathing and contempt of the railways as did all the dirt, the dishonesty, the discourtesy and the delay of the recent overcrowded and difficult times." As an old-lag journalist (as well as artist) the present writer could have told him a thing or two about the value of press-sponsored inquiries. A voice crying in the wilderness was that of Hamilton Ellis, anonymously; for this, as remarked, was the time when he was being paid, now and then, to carry a stopwatch on trains. He wrote, in *Modern Transport*: "Much derision has been aroused, for instance, by the absence of running plates on the 'Q 1' and the consequent exposure of the wheels. Now the running plate is a survival of the days when it was a common practice, owing to primitive means of lubrication, for the fireman to make somewhat precarious journeys to and from the front end while travelling at speed. It may reasonably be claimed that to a great extent platforms are retained on modern engines for the same reasons as buttons survive on the back of morning or dress-coats—because they have been there for generations and once upon a time served a useful purpose. . . .What is needed is a new aesthetic style, suited to the structural peculiarities of the modern engine, and it would appear that Mr. Oliver Bulleid has begun to evolve just such a style."

Alas, the "modern engine" is now of a very different sort, at its best electric, and, in its common form, something that stinks. But had Bulleid been two years earlier in all his doings (Lord! If only oneself had been born in 1907!) he might have given steam locomotion on railways quite ten years' respite keeping oil at bay for just long enough. Those two years would have given time for full and proper trials of his "Leader" class steam locomotives, which the dead hand of British Railways, under, but little supported by Government, dropped like the wrong end of a poker.

The "Leaders"—a design conceived on grand heroic lines—were to have been, and ought to have been, revolutionary. There was a double-bogie locomotive, each bogie driven by a three-cylinder simple engine with sleeve valves, which was expected to develop a torque comparable in uniformity with that of a nose-suspended electric motor, but superior to it in speed range, and of lighter unsprung weight. Bulleid had decided on sleeve valves after examining a Sabre aircraft engine belonging to a Hawker Typhoon fighter flown by his son in the R.A.F. (How very Bulleid!) There was much more to the "Leader". To many of us she was the *Machine Incroyable*, and it was not surprising that when she appeared, there were infant ailments galore. So have there been with every revolutionary machine since the first wheel broke against a rock. The time, further, was out of joint for such mechanical adventures, and this was a very expensive one, not likely to be favoured by a newly nationalized undertaking committed to doing things (not very successfully it seemed) on the cheap. Furthermore, Bulleid was much against State meddling, and his political persuasion was unequivocally blue.

So he went to Ireland. The "Leader" died, and her sisters were stillborn. Some time later, Steam itself began to die on railways.

Scotland's Mountain Barriers

ROBERT M. HOGG

THE RELIEF OF A COUNTRY has a powerful determining influence on the routes followed by the railway lines, and river valleys assume great importance in facilitating communications in hilly areas. The mountainous nature of Scotland, both north and south of the Central Lowlands (or Midland Valley) has rendered her railways peculiarly dependent on river valleys and other natural gaps for their crossings of the intervening mountain and hill ranges by the easiest routes available. To the student of railway construction, as to the interested geographer, there is a fascination in correlating the layout of the railway routes with the valley approaches to the upland areas.

The most notable example of the control that relief exercises over the direction of our railway routes is afforded by the great barrier of the Grampian Mountains. Stretching across Scotland from Ben Nevis to the Cairngorms, this block of high ground presents a serious obstacle to railway communications between north and south. The two main routes from Central Scotland to the north are accordingly forced to bend either towards the coast, *via* Aberdeen, or westward, to take advantage of the proximity of the headwaters of the Tay and Spey river systems.

The route from Perth to Inverness is, nevertheless, an extremely difficult one, with long, heavy gradients to be negotiated on either side of the summit at Druimuachdar Pass, 1,484 ft. above sea-level, the highest point reached by any British main-line railway. At this altitude, the line is constantly liable to snow blocks in winter, necessitating unceasing vigilance and immediate precautions to keep the route open.

On leaving Perth, an obvious route northwards is afforded by the lower section of the River Tay, past Stanley to Dunkeld. From Dunkeld, the railway continues to follow the narrowing valley of the Tay as far as Ballinluig, where the main valley turns westward. The northward continuation of the valley is, however, maintained by the tributary River Tummel, to slightly beyond Pitlochry, where it also turns to the west. Yet another tributary stream, the Garry, gives access north-westward, through the deep and narrow Pass of Killiecrankie, to Blair Atholl, and so up to the open moors leading towards the summit. The real hard climbing begins at Blair Atholl, whence a stretch of 16 miles up Glen Garry, the greater part of which is on a gradient of 1 in 70, has to be surmounted before the Druimuachdar Pass is gained, and the summit passed, two miles beyond Dalnaspidal station. The descent also is rapid, by the River Truim, a tributary of the Spey, to the wider valley at Newtonmore, and thereafter down Strath Spey to Aviemore.

The direct line from Aviemore to Inverness crosses the intervening Monadhliath Mountains by the Slochd Mhuic Pass (1,315 ft.) and reaches Inverness *via* the Findhorn Valley, Strath Nairn, and Culloden Moor. The gradients are as severe as 1 in 60 on each side of the summit, and are particularly formidable for southbound trains on account of their longer continuous stretches. The older route from Aviemore to Inverness, *via* Forres, attains a height of 1,052 ft. above sea-level three miles south of Dava. The summit is approached from Grantown-on-Spey by over four miles of 1 in 80 and 1 in 84, and from Forres by a long climb of 18 miles, most of which is at 1 in 70 and 1 in 75. On the other hand, the main line from Perth to Aberdeen avoids the Grampian massif by making use of the easy run along the wide valley of Strathmore to Forfar, and is joined near Montrose by the East Coast route into Aberdeen.

Two other lines make long penetrations from the Central Lowlands through the western fastnesses of the Grampian range, making full use of river valleys, lochsides, and passes to assist in the negotiation of these highlands. They are the West Highland Railway from Glasgow to Fort William, and the winding route from Stirling north-westwards to Oban. These two routes, both famous for their scenic grandeur, cross each other at the little Highland village of Crianlarich, and run thence for some five miles, on opposite sides of the sparsely populated Strath Fillan, to Tyndrum, with the consequent anomaly of two railway stations at each of these small remote hamlets.

The West Highland Railway, after leaving the Clyde, hugs the hillsides high above the shores of the Gareloch, Loch Long and Loch Lomond, to Ardlui, whence it climbs steeply up the narrow Glen Falloch to Crianlarich. Still climbing up Strath Fillan, it attains a local summit beyond Tyndrum, and descends sharply to Glen Orchy at Bridge of Orchy Station. After the lonely crossing of the desolate Moor of Rannoch, the summit level (1,350 ft.) is reached at Corrour. A steep descent of six miles at 1 in 67 brings the train alongside Loch Treig, from high above the loch down almost to water level, near Tulloch. Glen Spean is then followed to Spean Bridge, and Fort William is approached through easier country.

The Stirling-Oban line has an even more sinuous course, as it winds hither and thither to obtain a passage through the depths of the mountains. A continuous valley occupied successively by the rivers Teith and Leny, Loch Lubnaig, and the little River Balvag, is followed through Callander and Strathyre; and the railway then crosses a low divide to the head of Loch Earn. Passing the end of the loch, the line ascends Glen Ogle on a long gradient of 1 in 60, and crosses another watershed 941 ft. above sea-level into Glen Dochart, a transverse valley formed by the River Dochart, a branch of the Tay system. Glen Dochart conducts the line westward to Crianlarich, whence it continues along Strath Fillan and Glen Lochy to the head of Loch Awe. The River Awe is then followed through the deep and narrow Pass of Brander to the shores of Loch Etive, and along the coastal strip to Connel Ferry. In the final six miles to Oban, the railway passes over Glencruitten Summit (301 ft.) which is approached on each side by long gradients of 1 in 50.

South of the Midland Valley, the Southern Uplands present another physical interruption to easy railway communication. Although of lower mean height than the Highlands, they also constitute a broad, dissected plateau with the highest ground stretching in a wide belt from Loch Ryan (Wigtownshire) across the entire country to St. Abbs Head on the Berwickshire coast. Were it not for the deep river valleys which penetrate and divide these uplands, they would form a great obstacle to railway communication. The maintenance of adequate railway connections between industrial Scotland and England has required the provision of four main routes from Edinburgh and Glasgow, one passing through Berwick, and three through Carlisle; the position of these lines in relation to the coastal fringe or the valleys through the hills is therefore important.

The East Coast route from Edinburgh to Berwick skirts the northern rampart of the Southern Uplands, the Lammermuirs, by following an easy route along the coastal plain of East Lothian, but on entering Berwickshire, is confronted by the eastern prolongation of this range towards the coast. At Cockburnspath, therefore, the line bends inland and climbs steeply up the valley of a little stream, the Pease Burn, for four miles on a gradient of 1 in 96 to reach the miniature pass at the summit near Grantshouse. Thereafter, the descent is more gradual down the wooded valley of the Eye Water.

The railway regains the coast at Burnmouth, and passes along the cliff-tops to Berwick.

The next line westwards is the Waverley Route from Edinburgh to Carlisle, *via* Galashiels and Hawick. This difficult line crosses the Southern Uplands where they are cut in two by the transverse valley of the River Tweed, and consequently has two watersheds to cross. After an easy run over the Midlothian Coalfield, the first climb starts at Hardengreen (near Dalkeith), and continues in turn by the valleys of the South Esk and the Gore Water, and the headwaters of the Scottish River Tyne, to reach the 900-ft. pass between the Moorfoots and the Lammermuirs at Falahill. More than eight miles of the ascent are on a gradient of 1 in 70. Then follows a more gradual descent down the pastoral vale of Gala Water, a tributary of the Tweed, to Galashiels. The line continues with an undulating run over open country to Hawick, where the second climb commences. The barrier ahead, an area of bleak and desolate moorland, is formed by the high ground connecting the Southern Uplands with the Cheviot range. The ten-mile climb, with an average gradient of 1 in 80, takes advantage of the valley of the Slitrig Water, a tributary of the Teviot, to reach the summit at Whitrope Tunnel, nearly 1,000 ft. above sea-level. On the southern slopes, the line drops steeply for nearly eight miles at 1 in 75 down Liddesdale, following the windings of the River Liddel to the Solway Plain and into Cumberland.

The remaining two routes connect Glasgow with Carlisle. The first, the main line of the former Caledonian Railway, follows the valley of the Clyde almost to the river's source, to reach the famous Beattock Summit (1,014 ft.). An abrupt ten-mile descent, with the gradient varying between 1 in 69 and 1 in 88, takes the train down the Evan Water, a tributary of the Annan, to Beattock, whence it continues down Annandale to the Solway Plain. The Caledonian main line from Carstairs to Edinburgh (Princes Street) reaches a height of 880 ft. above sea-level at Cobbinshaw, whence there is an unbroken descent for 16 miles, practically into Edinburgh; the first 5½ miles are at the ruling gradient of 1 in 100.

The most westerly main line from Glasgow into England (the former Glasgow & South Western Railway) passes from the plain of the lower Clyde to the Ayrshire plain through the Barrhead Gap in the Renfrew Heights, and subsequently reaches the summit of the line, some 600 ft. above sea-level, near New Cumnock. The train then descends Nithsdale, to the Solway plain at Dumfries, road and rail running side by side in the narrow valley of the River Nith.

In addition to these main-line routes into and through Scotland, many minor cross-country and branch lines owe their very existence to the presence of river valleys and other natural routes by which they are enabled to negotiate mountainous terrain to reach their destinations. In this category, the most obvious and most heavily-affected routes are the lines radiating north and west from Inverness, to Wick and Thurso in the far north, and to Kyle of Lochalsh on the west coast. The northward line in particular is forced to make three enormous detours, partly due to the long coastal indentations, penetrating far inland on this coastline, and partly to the necessity of following the available valley routes through the high moorland counties of Sutherland and Caithness.

Shortly after leaving Inverness, the River Ness and the Caledonian Canal are crossed, and the line has thereafter an easy run westward for the next ten miles along the southern shore of the Beauly Firth to the town of Beauly, where the River Beauly is crossed as it enters the head of the Firth. Proceeding northwards from Beauly, the line surmounts a miniature summit a mile beyond Muir of Ord, in crossing from the Beauly valley to the valley of the River Conon, feeder of the Cromarty Firth. Thence, after rounding the head of the Cromarty Firth, the line reaches Dingwall, County Town of Ross-shire, on its northern shore, under the frowning shoulders of 3,400-ft. Ben Wyvis. The railway has thereafter an easily-graded run north-eastward along the entire northern shore of the Cromarty Firth to Invergordon, a war-time naval base (13 miles from Dingwall), and inland across the low neck of the intervening Tarbat Peninsula to Tain, on the southern shore of the Dornoch Firth. Here, the second great detour commences, involving, for example, a 40-mile rail journey to reach Dornoch, terminus of a branch (now closed) from The Mound Station on the north side of the Dornoch Firth, but scarcely five miles distant in a straight line from Tain.

After an easy undulating run of 13 miles north-westward along the southern shore of the Dornoch Firth from Tain to Bonar Bridge, and another three miles beside the Kyle of Sutherland, the wide basin forming the inland extremity of the firth, the railway reaches Culrain, and immediately leaves Ross-shire, crossing the River Oykell by a masonry arch viaduct with a central girder span, to reach Invershin Station, half a mile distant in the adjoining county of Sutherland. Beyond Invershin, the line leaves the estuary and runs due north up the valley of the River Shin to Lairg, an important livestock centre and railhead for several road services to remote villages on the far north-west coast of Sutherland. This portion of the journey commences at Invershin by a three-mile climb up the Shin valley at a gradient of 1 in 72, which, beyond Lairg, steepens to 1 in 70 for almost another three miles as the line turns east again and climbs to the 488-ft. summit amidst wild and bleak moorland country over the watershed from the Shin drainage area to that of the River Fleet. Then follows an eight-mile descent to Rogart with gradients mostly of 1 in 80 and 1 in 95 by heather-covered moorland,

A heavy load on Beattock Bank: "The Royal Scot", hauled by Stanier Pacific No. 46250 City of Lichfield, climbing to Beattock Summit, with rear-end assistance

Glasgow-Carlisle train, hauled by a Caledonian 4-4-0, at Beattock Summit in pre-grouping days

Special train near Ardlui, West Highland Railway, in 1959, headed by N.B.R. 4-4-0
Glen Loy *and* Glen Falloch

scarred by deep and narrow gullies and rushing streams. An easy run of 24 miles follows, down Strath Fleet to The Mound and north-eastwards along the coast by Golspie and Brora to Helmsdale, the only severe gradients being the short but sharp rise of 1½ miles at 1 in 60 from Golspie to Dunrobin and the corresponding descent on the north side.

At Helmsdale, the railway finally leaves the coastline on its most circuitous detour of all, inland over the high and windswept Caithness moors, the most grim and forbidding part of the journey. The line is forced to adopt this long and difficult route because the Ord of Caithness and other rocky headlands of the coastline preclude any possibility of a line along the narrow coastal fringe; this detour thus involves a 60-mile rail journey to reach Wick from Helmsdale though they are only 30 miles apart along the coast.

Turning inland at Helmsdale along wooded Strath Ullie, the valley of the River Helmsdale, the line faces a long but broken ascent of 28 miles to the summit (708 ft.), on the County March of Sutherland and Caithness, midway between Forsinard and Altnabreac stations. In this vicinity, there are snow fences on both sides of the railway for long distances over the open moors, an indication of the heavy wind-driven snowfalls occurring here in the winter, which necessitate these additional precautions to keep the line open. The approach to the summit from the south includes several stretches as steep as 1 in 60, while the equally rapid descent on the north side extends for some 17 miles, practically continuously, almost to Georgemas Junction. At Georgemas, Britain's farthest north junction, the branch lines to Wick (14 miles) and to Thurso (6½ miles) on the extreme north coast diverge to follow the valleys of the Wick Water and River Thurso respectively to their destinations; the climax to a most diversified but interesting journey by coast and moorland to the two most northerly towns on the Scottish mainland.

The branch to Kyle of Lochalsh leaves the north line at Dingwall, and bends sharply west, to follow a tortuous and devious route (64 miles long) through the rugged heart of Ross-shire, from the grey north sea on the country's eastern seaboard to the blue Atlantic beating on the western shore.

Leaving Dingwall, the line runs round the flat lands on the north side of the town and has an easy 2½-mile course to Fodderty Junction where it diverges from the Strathpeffer branch (now closed), which continued along the level valley to this northern spa. The Kyle line, however, rises steeply on a four-mile gradient of 1 in 50, along the northern slope of the valley, overlooking Strathpeffer, and past Achterneed Station, to reach the summit of this portion of the line at the Raven Rock, at a height of 458 ft. Here the railway runs through a picturesque gorge between the immense precipitous rocks, awe-inspiring in their massiveness, and so passes from the valley of the Peffery to that of the upper River Conon. A rapid descent follows, including over a mile at 1 in 50, to the level of Loch Garve, the line skirting its wooded southern shore to Garve Station at the western end of the loch.

Soon after leaving Garve and crossing Corriemuillie summit at 429 ft. the line descends again by gradients of 1 in 50 and 1 in 75 to the level of Loch Luichart and to Loch Luichart Station. The level of the waters of the loch was raised early in 1954 to meet the needs of a new hydro-electric scheme in that area, and a new station and adjoining length of line had to be built at a higher level, to replace the original station, the site of which was submerged in the loch when its level was raised.

Leaving Loch Luichart, the railway soon enters Strath Bran, and climbs steadily past the isolated and lonely station of Achanalt, to the head of the strath, amid the wildest and bleakest of mountain scenery. Still rising gradually, the line passes Achnasheen Station, and in another three miles reaches the highest point, Luib Summit, 646 ft., surmounting the ridge between Strath Bran and Glen Carron. A rapid descent of almost eight miles follows, down the narrow valley of the River Carron, to Achnashellach Station, surrounded by a variety of forest and mountain scenery, wild but majestic. Continuing down the widening valley, the line soon passes Strathcarron Station and reaches the shores of Loch Carron, close along the eastern edge of which the train runs by Attadale to Strome Ferry Station, the original terminus.

From Strome Ferry to Kyle of Lochalsh the line has a more level run, but a very curving one along the narrow ledge between the placid waters of Loch Carron and the lofty mountains rising steeply from the water's edge. In curving in and out round the rocky hillsides, the train passes through many steep rock cuttings, some of which rise perpendicularly to heights of 70 ft. Even the site of the station at Kyle of Lochalsh and the immediate approach to it had to be blasted out of the solid rock. The Dingwall to Kyle of Lochalsh line is indeed one of the most scenic routes in Scotland, giving unforgettable views of the rugged Highlands in their wildest and most awe-inspiring moods.

In the extreme south-west, two long and difficult routes call for attention—the lines to Stranraer from Dumfries and from Ayr. The Dumfries-Stranraer line is 73 miles in length, and traverses from east to west the entire counties of Kirkcudbright and Wigtown, together known as Galloway. Topographically, this area may be divided into Upper Galloway, the hilly northern portion forming the western end of the Southern Uplands of Scotland, and Lower Galloway, the lower southern portion. Although the railway from Dumfries to Stranraer keeps well south of the mountainous north of Galloway, it does have to negotiate the southward extension of the hilly area projecting into the lowland belt between the Rivers Dee and Cree. Even the lower parts of Galloway, however, do not entirely facilitate railway construction or operation, as the east-west direction of the railway is criss-crossed by the transverse valleys of the many rivers flowing southward from the upland areas to the Solway Firth and Irish Sea, necessitating frequent descents into their valleys, and corresponding ascents, often for long stretches and on severe gradients.

Immediately after leaving Dumfries, the River Nith is crossed, and the railway enters the Stewartry of Kirkcudbright, and soon passes Maxwelltown, a mile beyond which the first climb is encountered—$3\frac{1}{4}$ miles at 1 in 73, up to Lochanhead Station, well among the hills. From this elevation, there follows a more gradual descent of $8\frac{1}{2}$ miles into the "Dalbeattie Dip", the first of the transverse valleys, that of the Urr Water, which is crossed by the railway near Dalbeattie. The corresponding climb out of the valley of the Urr extends for $5\frac{1}{4}$ miles to Castle Douglas, the most important market town in Galloway, but with no gradient worse than 1 in 100. The succeeding nine miles from Castle Douglas to New Galloway Station are level or very slightly undulating. This part of the line meets the Dee Valley at Crossmichael, and follows it northwards until it widens into Loch Dee and Loch Ken. The line runs up the eastern shore of Loch Dee to Parton Station, near which the loch is crossed by the Ken Viaduct, consisting of three bowstring girder spans, the biggest engineering work on the line, and so into New Galloway Station.

At New Galloway, the line begins to penetrate the southward prolongation of the hills of Upper Galloway, the most difficult part of the route, extending for 20 miles almost to Newton Stewart, but also the most picturesque and wildest. The first great ascent is the four-mile stretch at 1 in 80 from New Galloway Station by the Black Water of Dee to Loch Skerrow Platform adjoining the loch of that name in a desolate moorland. Thence to the summit at Gatehouse of Fleet Station, the gradient profile resembles a saw-edge, with dips at 1 in 76 on both sides into the valleys of the two tributaries of the River Fleet, namely the Little Water of Fleet and the Big Water of Fleet. Having attained the summit at Gatehouse of Fleet Station, there follows a long and steep descent from this windswept height to the valley of the River Cree, near Palnure, comprising over seven miles at 1 in 80 (the Creetown Bank), a formidable undertaking for eastbound trains.

Beyond the Cree Viaduct, near the head of Wigtown Bay, there is a variable but more gradual climb for $2\frac{1}{2}$ miles to Newton Stewart Station. Thereafter there follows an undulating but steady rise to a minor summit midway between Kirkcowan and Glenluce stations, and a five-mile drop at 1 in 85/90 to the lofty Luce Viaduct over the Luce Water, at the head of Luce Bay. Thence, an easy seven-mile run to Stranraer Station and Harbour brings to an end this winding and difficult route to the most south-westerly Scottish town, with its harbour on the sheltered waters of Loch Ryan, from which the ferry to Larne operates.

The 58-mile route from Ayr, through Girvan, to Stranraer, besides crossing several transverse valleys and watersheds, has enormous climbs to surmount, through the belt of high ground at the western end of the Southern Uplands, forming the Ayrshire-Wigtownshire county boundary. The first miniature summit over the watershed between the Rivers Ayr and Doon is reached in 3½ miles from Ayr Station, and includes gradients of 1 in 88 and 1 in 70. The next is at Maybole Station, 310 ft. above sea-level, and the highest point on the Ayr-Girvan section, reached by gradients of 1 in 75 and 1 in 80. Thence to Girvan, on its narrow coastal ledge, the course is undulating but mainly falling by gradients ranging around 1 in 70, down to the Water of Girvan Valley.

Southward from Girvan the first great climb is met, with four-mile gradients of 1 in 54 and 1 in 56, almost uninterruptedly to a summit tunnel one mile north of Pinmore Station. The descent from Pinmore to the next station, Pinwherry, is also rapid down grades of 1 in 69 and 1 in 65, into the valley of the River Stinchar. Here there commences the second climb, eight miles in length, from Pinwherry Station to a lonely spot on the moors, four miles south of Barrhill Station, over gradients of 1 in 67 and 1 in 73. This summit, 600 ft. above sea-level, and the highest on the line, is in wild hill country of heather and rocks, peat and black mountain streams. There follows a steep 14-mile descent by Glenwhilly and New Luce stations to Challoch Junction, where the Dumfries-Stranraer line is joined for the final run into Stranraer.

PIONEERS

A replica of Stephenson's famous locomotive "Rocket" is to be seen outside the Historic Transport Museum at Clapham, as an invitation to the public and a symbol of the museum's contents.

"What's that?" demanded an elderly woman passing the place the other day. She was told.

"Really?" she exclaimed. "I didn't know they had rockets in those days."

"Peterborough", in "The Daily Telegraph"

Timetable Science

G. E. WILLIAMS

TO THE PASSENGER who travels but seldom, or who has to work out the details of an unfamiliar journey, a railway timetable may appear to be a needlessly complicated maze of figures and footnotes, through which he finds his way with difficulty. However, it must be obvious that the timetable is an absolute necessity, and that without it there would be at least uncertainty, if not chaos. Even when this has been admitted, probably many people take the timetable for granted, and do not pause to consider how much has gone into the making of this foundation of the pattern of services.

The first essential is the preparation of the actual working schedules, as it is from these that the information contained in the timetables issued to the public is compiled. The public and the working timetables are complementary, but the accuracy of the working schedules is of paramount importance, to ensure that the services advertised to passengers are basically sound. As its name suggests, the public timetable shows only the passenger services. On the other hand, the working timetable also contains a host of correlated details, such as the time at which trains pass certain stations or junctions, notes on the classification of trains, and the working of empty coaches and light engines. This additional information is essential to give the staff responsible for the day-to-day working of a railway as complete a picture as possible of the operating requirements.

Nowadays, it is the general practice for the working timetables to be divided into passenger and freight train services and issued as separate books. In certain instances, however, where services are infrequent, as on some branch lines, the need for this does not arise and they are combined in one timetable. The acceleration of the freight services envisaged in the plans for modernizing the railways may make it desirable to discontinue this separation of the passenger and freight train services, and issue the working timetables as one publication. Improvement of the freight services probably will necessitate finding paths for these trains during the peak hours, something which is not the practice at the present time. There is much to be said for the combination of the passenger and freight services, as it obviates the need to refer to two publications, and presents in a more concise form the train services in operation.

Let us now consider the work involved in the compilation of both the working and public timetables. On British Railways the timing of train services is done on the train-graph principle, and the first stage is the preparation of these diagrams, in which the progress of a train throughout its journey is shown as a line joining the points obtained by plotting the time at which it reaches stations or junctions. The graphs can vary in size considerably according to circumstances, but for main-line routes a size of 40 in. by 30 in. is the most convenient. These sheets of fairly heavy-weight paper are squared off in approximately one-eighth-inch feint rules, with slightly heavier rules placed every ten or fifteen squares horizontally and vertically.

The time scale to which it is proposed to work is inserted above the horizontal line at the top of the sheet. This is variable according to the circumstances; where intense services are in operation, it is usual to have a time scale of half a minute per square, but for general practice one-minute squares are quite sufficient and meet most conditions. The distance scale is shown on the vertical plane, and can be varied according to circumstances. Quarter-mile squares are suitable for main lines, but in congested areas this may have to be subject to adjustment, so as not to "cramp" the graph.

It is preferable to have prepared lists of stations, and so on, for the various routes to be covered to affix to the graphs as necessary, which saves a great deal of time in the preparatory work. It is also an advantage to fix the list of stations on both sides of the graph in order to facilitate production. An abridged diagrammatic plan of the running lines as well as the gradients of the route can also be included alongside the station names if required; but this is not really essential, as the staff are usually well acquainted with the geographical features of their particular region.

Whether or not the passenger and freight services are combined in one working timetable, the graphs must include them both, the passenger trains being inserted first and the freight and ancillary services common to both added later, but, as mentioned previously, if freight trains are accelerated to such an extent as to run at speeds comparable to those of passenger trains, the graphing of both types of service will have to be timed concurrently, particularly if freight trains have to run in turn with the passenger services. To keep the graphs down to a reasonable size, capable of easy reference, it is desirable to have separate graphs for Mondays to Fridays, Saturdays only and, of course, Sundays. This is the usual method, except on routes not heavily used; in these cases it is usual to have separate graphs for weekdays and Sundays.

No particular significance is attached as to whether the down trains or the up are inserted on the graph first. This is left to the discretion of the timing clerk responsible, but having completed one way, the addition of the reverse direction will reveal any adjustments necessary to either, as the case may be. Some special indication has to be made on the graph of routes with main and relief lines, if a train has to be diverted from one to the other in the course of its journey. This can be countered by using a continuous line for trains running on the main line and a broken line for those running on a subsidiary line. Where there are electric train services involved, such as in suburban areas, and these run in between hauled trains over the same line, it is helpful to use a line of another colour.

When the time scale, the stations and junction points on the route have been inserted on the graph, a start can be made in timing the train services proposed. The type of service to be operated is based largely on previous experience, but amendments brought about by changing circumstances are taken into consideration as necessary. In this connection, meetings are held from time to time with district traffic departments, and where inter-regional trains are involved, with the other regions concerned. At these meetings various suggestions are put forward, such as omitting or including certain stops on trains, running of additional trains or discontinuing others, and speeding up or slowing services. At the preliminary discussions, alterations of this sort may appear to be practicable, but they must be proved by applying them to the graph. Sometimes adjustments are necessary. That is the great advantage of the graphical method of timetable preparation; it shows at a glance what changes and additions can be made, and what alterations to the schedules of other trains would be necessary.

In timing train services, a host of advance information is necessary, and while this is readily available, it has to be constantly kept in mind to ensure accuracy on the graph. Briefly, the main considerations are as follows:—

Sectional running times for each type of train;
Time to be allowed at stations for traffic purposes;
Type of locomotive or power unit employed;

Timetable Science

Form of signalling on line of route;
Geographical layout of the line;
Connectional facilities at junction stations.

With the developments in train services now taking place as the result of the modernization plans, these considerations are being constantly adjusted as the plan is implemented. Whereas the principal power unit has been the steam locomotive, the introduction of diesel locomotives, diesel multiple units, electric locomotives, and electric multiple units, as the case may be, has radically changed the structure of the services in many parts of the country over the last few years, and will continue to do so for some time to come. Although the number of adjustments to the train service from one issue of the timetable to another formerly were comparatively few, this is not so at the present time, and to keep pace with the introduction of the modern forms of power, services have to be completely revised as these become available.

When a line is electrified, a large number of temporary schedules have to be prepared to cover the interim period while the engineering work is being carried out, in addition to adjustments necessary at week-ends, when lines are sometimes given over completely to the contractors to enable work on a major protect to be carried out. The same position arises to some extent where dieselization is taking place; the schedules have to be adjusted from time to time as units are coming into traffic. The whole concept of the services has been changed. For example, the sectional running times have been accelerated, signalling adjusted correspondingly, station layouts simplified, and so on, to take full advantage of the improvements brought about. Speed restrictions have been raised to limits hitherto unknown on British Railways, and the whole timetable structure radically changed on a large number of routes.

This brings us back to the complexity of the changes confronting those responsible for the preparation of the working timetables, not just a few alterations but more often than not a completely revised timetable. Nevertheless, the method of compilation remains the same, but as the modern trend is to provide a pattern service as far as possible on a regular sequence, the graphing, once the service laid down is established, will remain constant for some time to come, apart from, perhaps, some seasonal adjustments and changes resulting from the experience gained after the service has been in operation for a time.

There is no doubt at all that a regular service between various large centres where the traffic justifies it is the correct way of handling the situation. This has been proved in the past, for example in the service between London and

Brighton at regular hourly intervals, and on the Eastern Region between Liverpool Street and Norwich on a similar basis; also the use of standard departure times on other services where, perhaps, the service does not demand such frequency. This not only assists in the compilation of the time-tables but is greatly appreciated by the public for obvious reasons.

Coming back to the actual graphing, the train paths are inserted on the diagram by making a small dot at the commencing point of the journey, and a similar dot at the next scheduled stopping or passing place. The dots are then joined by a straight line, and the graph is continued in this way until the destination of the train is reached. Throughout the journey, due regard must be paid to the operating conditions and restrictions to which reference has already been made.

A transparent ruler or a large set square is used to make the train paths on the graph. Probably a set square is the better, because it is less likely to slip and spoil the work; but whatever form of straight-edge is used, it must be really transparent, so that it does not obstruct the view of the graph in any way. This stage of timetable work is most interesting, and as the construction of the graph proceeds, the pattern of the service begins to come to light. This may not appear easy to recognize, but with practice and care, a completed graph presents in no other way possible a definite picture of the line occupation of any particular route.

When the train service has been proved practicable in this way, the preparation of the printed timetable can be undertaken. The graphing and drafting of the working timetable can be carried out concurrently if necessary; it is largely a matter of which is best in the circumstances. The printed time-table includes a deal of information which cannot be shown on the graph, such as working notes to cover varying circumstances, restrictions on loading, connectional margins at junction stations, and so on. It is necessary for these to be included in the working timetable for the information of the train crews and station staffs.

The public timetable is prepared from the completed draft of the working timetable. When the basic details of the train times have been extracted, relevant information, such as the class of accommodation provided, through carriage workings, and refreshment car facilities, is added. Supplementary pages, designed for quick reference, are also included. These show sum-maries of the principal services between important centres, trains in which seats can be reserved, sleeping car facilities, and continental services.

The provision of the coaching stock required for the passenger trains has also to be considered in the timetabling of the services. Where "named" services are concerned, regular train formations are maintained, and work on a fairly permanent schedule, which allows for adequate turn-round facilities for maintenance, cleaning, and so on, to be carried out. On the other hand, suburban services work to a much closer margin, and are diagrammed to operate over their various routes as necessary. These generally are also of a permanent formation, but to conserve energy, coaches are detached during non-peak hours and the workings diagrammed in such a way as to ensure a balanced working throughout the day.

The modern trend is to dispense with trains of non-regular formations as far as possible, as these are costly in operation, and very often are unbalanced, which means that empty carriage working has to be incurred. The amount of rolling stock available is limited, and it is not regarded as economic to hold a large number of coaches in reserve over and above those required to meet normal needs. It is, of course, possible to run additional trains at certain times to meet traffic requirements or for special excursions, but these can only be arranged up to certain limits from a "pool" of coaches held for this purpose.

The introduction of diesel multiple units has resulted in a large reduction of branch-line coaching stock. These diesel trains are formed of various combinations of vehicles to cover the requirements of the district where they are used, and work to and from diesel depots on a fixed roster. While due allowance is made to cover maintenance periods, the number of units available for strengthening trains is limited, and it is not always possible to provide units for this purpose.

The essential part of operating train services is to avoid as far as possible the running of empty coaching stock trains. These are not only unprofitable but take up train paths which could be used to advantage for other services, particularly around London and other congested places. A move in this direction in some Regions has already taken place whereby incoming mainline trains remain at the terminus, and form outgoing passenger trains, thus avoiding the running of empty carriage trains to and from a local carriage depot. This could with advantage be extended in many directions, to obtain a more economic use of the rolling stock, with a consequent improvement in train operation.

The neatly-tabulated columns of figures presented to the public are an inadequate testimony of the complexity of the work of a branch of the railway service of which but little is heard. Such are present-day economic conditions that the compilation of a timetable for a route on which traffic is both heavy and varied in type is comparable with a science in which a very high standard of accuracy is absolutely essential.

Commenting on the work involved in making alterations, the general manager of one of our largest railways once likened a train service to a house of cards, which has to to be rebuilt if the bottom card is disturbed. "Remembering all this," he added, "and the pressure under which the work must be done, the wonder is not so much that an occasional error creeps into a timetable as that such marvellous accuracy is arrived at." That opinion was expressed more than 70 years ago. The greater complexity of present-day traffic lends additional weight to it.

"THE SILVER JUBILEE"

Written by a member of the Railway Club in admiration of "The Silver Jubilee", the first streamline train in Great Britain. Inaugurated in October 1935, this train ran between London (King's Cross) and Newcastle, 269 miles, in 4 hr., with an intermediate stop at Darlington, in each direction. It was withdrawn at the outbreak of the Second World War, but the 4-hr. schedule between London and Newcastle has been restored.

By power of speed you win the right,
Of speed and comfort, and the skill
That rules your course and guides your will
With shrewd surveillance day and night;
By right of these, from Thames to Tyne
You bear the guidon of the line.

One second for a double chain,
Faster than ball was ever bowled,
Eighteen score tons in weight all told,
Salute with arrogant disdain
The reeling miles: "From Thames to Tyne
We bear the guidon of the line."

Yet, should the "distant" warn, you glide—
The rail joints rippling 'neath your tyres—
Securely curbing rash desires,
With prudence tempering your pride.
For to your faith from Thames to Tyne
Is pledged the honour of the line.

Then far across the minstered plain,
By field and coppice, mere and mead,
With wheels a-whirl in spokeless speed,
Exultant wheels that vaunt amain:
"From Thames to Tees, and Tees to Tyne,
We bear the guidon of the line."

London & North Western Railway.

THE LONDON AND NORTH WESTERN RAILWAY COMPANY'S Through Booking and Carrying arrangements extend over the greater portion of the United Kingdom, the Company's Railway being the

ROYAL MAIL ROUTE

TO

SCOTLAND, IRELAND, and all the PRINCIPAL TOWNS

In the Midland and Manufacturing districts of England and Wales.

FREQUENT EXPRESS TRAINS RUN BETWEEN

London and Birmingham in $2\frac{3}{4}$ Hours.
London and Manchester in $4\frac{1}{4}$ Hours.
London and Liverpool - in $4\frac{1}{2}$ Hours.

Mail trains are run in connection with the Mail Steamers to and from Kingstown (for Dublin). The Company's New Express Steamers sail between Holyhead and North Wall, Dublin, connecting with Express Trains to and from London, Birmingham, Liverpool, Manchester. and all parts of the London and North Western system.

The Irish Mail Service via Holyhead, Kingstown, Cork, and Queenstown is arranged in connection with the American Steamers.

DAILY TRAIN AND STEAMBOAT SERVICE to and from GREENORE for DUNDALK, NEWRY, ARMAGH, ENNISKILLEN, AND THE NORTH OF IRELAND, ALSO TO FLEETWOOD AND STRANRAER FOR BELFAST, LONDONDERRY, &c.

DRAWING-ROOM CARRIAGES

Fitted with Lavatory Accommodation and provided with every modern convenience, are run by certain Express Trains between

LONDON AND LIVERPOOL, LONDON AND MANCHESTER, AND LONDON AND EDINBURGH, GLASGOW AND PERTH,

And many of the 1st Class Carriages on the through trains are provided with Lavatories.
No Extra Charge beyond the ordinary 1st Class Fare.

SLEEPING SALOONS AND CARRIAGES, provided with Pillows, Rugs, and Lavatory accommodation are attached to the Night Express Trains. The fare for each Berth is 5/- in addition to the ordinary First Class fare.

Third Class Passengers conveyed by all Trains except the Irish Mails.
For information respecting Trains, Fares, &c., apply to Mr. G. P. NEELE, Superintendent of the Line, Euston Station, London.
Full particulars as to Merchandise Rates and arrangements can be obtained of Mr. THOMAS KAY, Chief Goods Manager, Euston Station, London.

HOTEL ACCOMMODATION

Is provided at the principal stations on the railway. The following are first class Hotels, and will be found to afford every convenience and comfort for passengers.

Station.	Name of Hotel.	Station.	Name of Hotel.
LONDON	Euston.	LIVERPOOL	North Western.
ALDERLEY	QUEEN.	KINGSTOWN	Royal Marine.
BIRMINGHAM	Queen's.	KESWICK	Station.
BUXTON	Palace.	LANCASTER	County.
CARLISLE	County.	LEEDS	Queen's.
CHESTER	Queen.	STAFFORD	London & North Western
CREWE	Crewe Arms.	WARRINGTON	Patten Arms
GREENORE	Station.	WATFORD	Clarendon.
HOLYHEAD	Prince of Wales.	WINDERMERE	Rigg's.

Telegraph and Postal Services specially provided for at the North Western Hotels.

GEORGE FINDLAY,
General Manager.

EUSTON STATION,
LONDON, N.W., April, 1885.

Rival routes . . .

Midland Railway Company.

THE PICTURESQUE ROUTE BETWEEN LONDON & MANCHESTER & LIVERPOOL
THROUGH MATLOCK AND THE PEAK OF DERBYSHIRE.

THE TOURIST ROUTE
BETWEEN
ENGLAND and SCOTLAND
Is via SETTLE and CARLISLE.

A Special Service of Express Trains has been established by this Route between

LONDON, EDINBURGH, AND GLASGOW

Pullman Parlour Cars by Day Express Trains, and Pullman Sleeping Cars by Night
Express Trains, in both directions.

Passengers holding First Class Tickets may now travel in the Pullman Parlour Cars attached
to the Day Express Trains WITHOUT EXTRA PAYMENT.

A Special Service of Express Trains is run between

LONDON AND LIVERPOOL AND MANCHESTER,
(VIA MATLOCK, AND THE PEAK OF DERBYSHIRE).

**Passengers travelling by this Route pass through the most picturesque
portion of the Peak of Derbyshire, and the Vale of Matlock.**
Pullman Parlour Cars by Day Trains, and Sleeping Cars by Night Trains.

Passengers holding First Class Tickets may now travel in the Pullman Parlour Cars attached
to the Day Express Trains WITHOUT EXTRA PAYMENT.

A SPECIAL SERVICE OF EXPRESS TRAINS HAS ALSO BEEN ESTABLISHED BETWEEN
LONDON, NOTTINGHAM, SHEFFIELD, LEEDS, & BRADFORD,
AT CONVENIENT HOURS DAILY.

The Company run a service of well-appointed Omnibuses between the St. Pancras Station
and Hotel, and the Charing Cross and Waterloo Stations. Passengers holding through Tickets
between the Midland and South Eastern and London and South Western Lines are conveyed
across London by these Omnibuses free of charge.

Small one-horse Omnibuses are also provided by the Company to meet the Trains at St.
Pancras, when previously ordered, to convey Passengers and their Luggage to any part of
London, or on an order being sent to the Station Master at St. Pancras, they will be sent to
Private Residences, Hotels, or Railway Stations in London to convey Passengers to St. Pancras.
The charge is one shilling per mile, minimum, three shillings; for distances over six miles
where two horses are required, the charge is one shilling and sixpence per mile; minimum,
six shillings.

All the Trains of the Midland Company convey First and Third Class Passengers at
ordinary Fares, and First Class Passengers may avail themselves of the Pullman Parlour Cars
attached to Day Express Trains *without extra payment.* For Berths in the Sleeping Cars a small
additional charge is made.

The Trains of the Midland Company run to and from:

The St. Pancras Station, in London ;
The St. Enoch Station, in Glasgow ;
The Waverley Bridge Station, Edinburgh ;
The Central Station, Ranelagh Street, Liverpool ;
The New Street Station, in Birmingham ;
The Central Station, in Manchester, and
The Wellington Station, in Leeds.

The Official Time Tables of the Company, and every information respecting their Trains
and Arrangements, may be obtained at any of the above-mentioned Stations, and the other
Stations on the Line.

In London, Tickets and all information can be obtained at the Company's West End Office
445, STRAND, 10A, NEW BOND STREET ; 5, TRAFALGAR BUILDINGS ; "GLOUCESTER
BOOKING OFFICE," 495, OXFORD STREET, the London, Brighton, and South Coast Company's Offices, 28, REGENT CIRCUS, and 8, GRAND HOTEL BUILDINGS, TRAFALGAR
SQUARE, and at the Office of the Company's Agents, THOS. COOK & SON, LUDGATE CIRCUS.

THE MIDLAND GRAND HOTEL (one of the largest Hotels in Europe), containing upwards
of 400 Bed Rooms, with spacious Coffee Room, Reading Room, and numerous Drawing
Rooms, has been erected by the Company at the ST. PANCRAS TERMINUS, and will be
found replete with every accommodation ; the Company are also owners of
THE QUEEN'S HOTEL, LEEDS, and THE MIDLAND HOTEL, DERBY, adjoining the
Midland Railway Station in each of these Towns. Both First Class Hotels for Families and
Gentlemen.

DERBY, April, 1885. **JOHN NOBLE, General Manager.**

LONDON, BRIGHTON & SOUTH COAST RAILWAY.

LONDON, PARIS, AND THE CONTINENT.

Via Newhaven, Dieppe, and Rouen.

The Shortest, Cheapest, and most Picturesque Route.

Through Tickets, including all charges, issued between London and Paris, Dieppe, Rouen, Fécamp, Havre, Bordeaux, Pau, Lyons, Geneva, Neuchatel, Lausanne, Marseilles, Hyères, Cannes, Nice, Mentone, Turin, Genoa, Milan, Verona, Venice, Bologna, Florence, Rome, Naples, Brindisi, Aix les Bains, Berne, Biarritz, Ancona, and Reggio.

Also for the Anglo-Norman Tour and the Swiss and Italian Tours, &c.

The commodious and powerful Paddle Steamers employed in this service are acknowledged to be the best crossing the Channel between England and France, and are provided with Private Quarter Deck and Paddle Box Cabins.

The Trains run to the Harbour alongside the Steamers at Newhaven and Dieppe.

The Trains between London and Newhaven, and also between Paris and Dieppe, are fitted with a communication between Passenger, Guard, and Driver, and are provided with the Westinghouse Automatic Continuous Brake.

For particulars see " Bradshaw's Continental Guide."

THE ROUTE for Express Merchandise between London, Paris, Lyons, and all parts of the South of France, Switzerland, Italy, &c.

A Grande Vitesse Goods and Parcels Service daily between Paris (St. Lazare Station) and London Bridge Station.

HONFLEUR Via NEWHAVEN.—Steamers run regularly between these ports conveying Passengers and Merchandise.

LONDON STATIONS:—Victoria, London Bridge, Kensington, Chelsea, West Brompton, Clapham Junction, &c.

WEST-END GENERAL BOOKING and INQUIRY OFFICES:—28, Regent Circus, Piccadilly, and 8, Grand Hotel Buildings (under the Grand Hotel) Trafalgar Square.

PARIS STATION:—Rue St. Lazare, near the Madeleine.

OFFICES IN PARIS for Tickets and Information:—10, Rue du 4 Septembre (near the Bourse), and 4, 6, and 8, Rue St. Anne.

J. P. KNIGHT, General Manager.
London Bridge.

. . . and Rival routes . .

SOUTH EASTERN RAILWAY

(LONDON, FOLKESTONE, AND DOVER).

ROYAL MAIL & SHORT SEA ROUTES.

FOLKESTONE AND BOULOGNE,
DOVER & CALAIS, DOVER & OSTEND.

SIX CONTINENTAL SERVICES DAILY.

TERMINI IN LONDON.

Charing Cross } AND { Cannon Street
(WEST END). } { (CITY).

LONDON & PARIS IN 8 HOURS.

BY SPECIAL EXPRESS,

Daily Tidal Trains viâ Folkestone and Boulogne

(The Quickest, Shortest, and Best Route);

AND BY THE

MAIL TRAINS AND PACKETS,

Viâ Calais and Dover,

IN 9 HOURS.

The Trains at Boulogne and at Dover run to and from alongside the Steamers.

SEA PASSAGES 90 MINUTES.

Brussels, Cologne, Berlin, St. Petersburgh, Vienna, Munich, Naples, Turin, Venice, Rome, Brindisi, Marseilles, and most of the chief Continental Cities and Towns, with equally quick travelling.

THROUGH TICKETS ISSUED AND BAGGAGE REGISTERED.

Parcels and Goods forwarded at reduced through rates.

ITALIAN, SWISS, AND OTHER CONTINENTAL TOURIST TICKETS, &c.

All particulars of Fares, Times of Trains, &c., on application to H. FARMER, Quai Bonaparte, Boulogne; C. ZWINGER, 4, Boulevard des Italiens, Paris; E. UTYBORCK, 46, Montagne de la Cour, Brussels; and 1, Friedrich Wilhelm Strasse, Cologne; Imorbersteg Frères, Bâle; or at the Offices of the Company.

(By Order) **MYLES FENTON, General Manager.**

LONDON BRIDGE STATION.
Season, 1885.

Locomotives on the Ganges

"HOOGHLY"

IN HIS *History of Railway Locomotives down to the End of the Year 1831*, C. F. Dendy Marshall referred to an interesting episode in the career of the Hedley locomotive *Wylam Dilly*. In 1822 this engine, with paddles attached, was used as the motive power for a makeshift steamboat which towed coal barges on the Tyne during a strike of keelmen. Thirty-six years later, and 5,000 miles away, locomotives were again being used in this unorthodox fashion, but so far this interesting event seems to have escaped the attention of railway historians.

The East Indian Railway Company had been incorporated in 1845, but after protracted financial negotiations its efforts were at first restricted to an "experimental" section from Howrah, on the Hooghly, opposite Calcutta, to Raneegunge. This was completed in 1855, and work then proceeded on the main line towards Delhi. The latter included a large bridge over the Jumna at Allahabad, and it was decided to push ahead with the comparatively easy section westward from that point at the same time as work was proceeding on the line in Bengal.

This arrangement necessitated the transport by local contractors of large quantities of stores up the Hooghly, Bhaugeerutty and Ganges rivers from Calcutta to Allahabad and various places *en route*. The tortuous 900-mile journey to Allahabad took even the Government steamboats at least three weeks. Moreover in the dry season, from November to June, the Bhaugeerutty became too shallow to take boats with a draught greater than 2 ft.

6 in., and the route from Calcutta was then *via* the Soonderbunds, a labyrinth of winding creeks at the delta mouth, and the Barashee and Goraee rivers; this added another 300 miles to the journey.

By 1857 the East Indian Railway had discovered that it was losing far more stores on the journey up the Ganges than were being lost on the long trip from England to Calcutta *via* the Cape of Good Hope. A Transport Department was then inaugurated to supervise the contractors' arrangements, and two wooden cargo boats were ordered locally from Brown & MacNicol for the railway company. Then suddenly, in May 1857, the Mutiny broke out. The Government urgently required steamboats for the movement of troops and military stores—but existing resources were inadequate, and marine engines took a long time to import from England.

On September 1, 1857, Colonel Arthur Cotton, of the Madras Engineers, suggested that this problem could best be solved by building boats, 200 ft. long and about 20 ft. wide, powered by locomotive engines fitted with long axles and 7¼ ft. paddle wheels. At that time, the East Indian Railway had a number of unerected locomotives surplus to immediate requirements; these had been ordered for the new lines under construction, and had been sent out in good time to avoid congestion in the small erecting shops.

The Government acted promptly, and on September 9 asked the railway company to fit locomotive engines into the two Brown & MacNicol boats, at Government expense, and also to fit out as soon as possible two further boats, one of which was to have *two* locomotive engines. In addition two more locomotives were required to power a large vessel being built by the Government.

The first Brown & MacNicol boat went into service in December 1857, and was known as "Locomotive Steam Boat No. 1, *Surprise*"—all things considered, this was probably a suitable name. It was quite small, only 85 ft. long, with the locomotive fixed amidships so that the smokebox faced the rear. The width was 16 ft., excluding the paddle-boxes, and the light draught was given as 3 ft. 6 in.

No. 2, *Success*, went into service in April 1858, and was 120 ft. in length. She was soon followed by No. 3, *Mechanic*, which was probably similar in dimensions. Then came No. 4, *Sir Henry Lawrence*, a much larger vessel built of iron, and powered by two locomotive engines. The Government boat, named *Sir William Peel*, also went into service during 1858 with two locomotives purchased from the East Indian Railway. All these vessels were used by the Government for the transport of troops and stores, and at the end of the emergency period only *Surprise* and *Success* were returned to the railway company.

Meanwhile, in February 1858, the East Indian Railway had terminated the arrangements with the contractors, and had decided to build up its own fleet of sailing boats, steamers and barges ("flats"). Up to that date 73,000 tons of stores had been despatched up the river, but of that total 700 tons had been lost in various wrecks, and nearly 11,000 tons were "unaccounted for".

Accordingly, in April 1858, the railway company indented for a 220 ft. iron steamboat, to be built in India, incorporating two locomotive engines (side by side) working 12 ft. paddle wheels. This vessel started work in March 1860 as No. 5, *Queen of the Ganges*, and was followed in September of that year by No. 6, *Excelsior*, of the same type. Both were built by Brown & MacNicol, and were in fact 228 ft. in length and 27 ft. in width (excluding paddleboxes). The light draught was 2 ft. 9 in., or 3 ft. 6 in. with cargo, and they towed one or more large flats filled with stores. The total load was usually 200 to 250 tons, but on one occasion the *Queen of the Ganges*, towing three flats, transported 585 tons of stores from Calcutta to Dinapore.

No. 7, *Kasheejee*, was a 162 ft. vessel purchased second-hand in 1860 to work the Caragola ferry service. It had two ordinary marine engines, but it is interesting to note that in 1862 it was fitted with two locomotive boilers, apparently taken from E. B. Wilson 0-4-2 engines of 1854–5 (E.I.R. Nos. 317 and 329).

The next eight steamboats, numbered 8 to 15, were steel-plated vessels built in England and also had marine engines, but they deserve brief mention because they were supplied by the well-known locomotive builders Robert Stephenson & Co., the hulls being built by C. Mitchell & Co. They were named *Queen Victoria, Prince Albert, Prince of Wales, Princess Royal, Princess Alice, Prince Alfred, Princess Helena,* and *Sir James Melville,* the last named gentleman being an ex-officio director of the railway company who died in July 1861. All were shipped out in sections, except the last one which was sailed out to India *via* the Cape of Good Hope carrying 400 tons of coal as freight; this must have been a hazardous voyage for a river steamer, even though it was fitted with a false bottom for the journey. The dimensions varied somewhat from boat to boat, but in general they were about 210 ft. long, 35 ft. wide, and 7 ft. 6 in. deep, with a registered tonnage of 330.

The first two Stephenson vessels started work in 1861, and the next two in the following year, but by the end of 1862 the construction of the railway had progressed to such an extent that the company decided to discontinue its transport department. All the boats were gradually sold, or converted into flats, with the exception of the *Kasheejee* which remained on the Caragola ferry until it sank there in 1887. *Prince of Wales, Princess Alice,* and *Prince Alfred* were sold to the Eastern Bengal Railway, and survived for many years on that company's river services.

Excelsior, one of the locomotive boats, was retained in use as a ferry at Allahabad from 1864 until the Jumna bridge was opened on August 15, 1865. Its companion was a smaller vessel named *Monghyr*, of unknown origin, put into service in 1863; here again a locomotive engine was used as motive power during its short life in railway service.

Thus altogether 12 East Indian Railway engines were used in the river steamboats; of these, six were salvaged and put into service during 1865–7 as part of the company's locomotive stock. The five engines used in the boats sold to the Government were not returned to the railway, and presumably continued their aquatic career. The fate of the remaining engine is not clear, but this may well have been the one used in the *Success*; this boat had the misfortune to run aground in December 1862, and was probably a total loss.

There is little direct evidence regarding the individual locomotives used in these exploits, but a comparison of the records of engines ordered by the East Indian Railway with the earliest locomotive list of that company gives a reasonably accurate overall picture. There were two main classes, one for passenger and the other for goods traffic, which were generally similar in design and followed good contemporary English practice. The wide (5 ft. 6 in.) gauge encouraged the use of inside frames and cylinders, although it is noteworthy that the E.I.R. soon afterwards changed to outside cylinders for ease of maintenance with the limited workshop facilities available.

The passenger engines were of the 2-2-2 wheel arrangement, with 6 ft. 6 in. driving wheels, and 15 in. by 22 in. horizontal cylinders. The boilers were 10 ft. 7 in. long, and 4 ft. $0\frac{7}{8}$ in. in diameter (inside), with a working pressure of 120 lb. per sq. in. The grate area was 18 sq. ft., the heating surface totalled 1,156 sq. ft., and each engine weighed about 27 tons in working order.

Five were built in 1853, by Tayleur & Co. at the Vulcan Foundry, and the remainder in 1854–5—ten by Tayleur & Co., five by Slaughter & Co., and ten each by E. B. Wilson and Beyer Peacock. There was also a similar Fairbairn engine, built for the Madras Railway, which was diverted to the East Indian Railway because of the difficulty in landing a heavy engine at Madras.

Only two of these engines did not appear in the East Indian Railway list; they formed part of the second Tayleur order, and the available evidence suggests that these were the engines used for the Government steamer *Sir William Peel*. One engine, built by E. B. Wilson, was not put into service on the railway until 1865, and is identified as the one used in the *Monghyr*; it was No. 86 on the North West Provinces section, becoming No. 80 shortly afterwards when the N.W.P. and Bengal sections were combined, and was withdrawn from service in 1881.

The goods engines were of the 0-4-2 wheel arrangement, with 5 ft. driving wheels and 16 in. by 22 in. cylinders, slightly inclined to clear the leading axle; the boilers were similar to those used for the passenger engines. As with the previous class, five were built in 1853 by Tayleur & Co., and the remainder in 1854–5—25 by E. B. Wilson, 25 by Kitson & Co., ten each by Slaughter & Co. and R. & W. Hawthorn, and five by Tayleur & Co. In addition, there was again a solitary Fairbairn example from the Madras Railway.

Eight of these engines (four by E. B. Wilson and four by Kitson) had an unexpectedly early demise. They were shipped aboard the *Anne Rose*, which sailed from Liverpool but was lost at sea *en route* to India. In addition to the locomotives, this 1,130-ton vessel was carrying 54 sets of carriage ironwork, and 371 tons of rails; in view of the long journey round the Cape of Good Hope it is perhaps surprising that more of these little ships were not lost.

One of the Kitson engines seems to have become No. 57 in the North West Provinces list in 1865, and later No. 298 in the combined list, but as it was withdrawn in 1873, very little definite information is available; it may well have been the locomotive salvaged from the *Surprise*. Two other Kitson engines, and three built by E. B. Wilson, do not appear in the locomotive lists at all; three of these must have been the ones used in the Government boats *Mechanic* and *Sir Henry Lawrence*. One was probably lost in the *Success*, and there is on record a reference to one locomotive being lost on the journey from Howrah to Allahabad.

In 1856, E. B. Wilson and Kitson & Co. each built four more engines of the same type to replace those lost in the *Anne Rose*. Those from E. B. Wilson were used in the large steamers *Queen of the Ganges* and *Excelsior* and in 1866–7 they were put into service on the railway as Nos. 332–335. In 1881, they became Nos. 626–629 in the duplicate list, and No. 629 was withdrawn in 1882. The other three, however, survived long enough to become "H", "I" and "J" in a new and somewhat novel duplicate list adopted by the East Indian Railway about 1885, and the last survivor ("J") was not withdrawn until 1892.

Some idea of the general appearance of the locomotive steamboats can be gleaned from a sheet of small and somewhat indistinct plan and elevation drawings preserved among the India Office Records. No mechanical details are shown, but it seems clear that the engines were simply fixed centrally in the flat boats with the wheels removed and a minimum of additional fittings. However, the chimneys were extended to a more suitable height above the deck.

The *Surprise* is shown with a flat barge on either side, each 85 ft. long and carrying a locomotive and tender as cargo, and this appears to have been the usual method adopted for the transport of the locomotive stock up river by these smaller steamboats; it was argued that this made the vessels easier to manœuvre in the tricky river channels. In contrast, the *Queen of the Ganges*, which had two engines (rated at 90 h.p. each) side by side in the centre, is shown towing a long 175-ft. flat. An interesting footnote, headed "Extract from *Newcastle Guardian* from its own Correspondent at Calcutta, 20th Octr. 1860", reads as follows:

> "A few days ago one of the East Indian Railway Co's Flats was sunk in going up the River by the Steamer 'Queen of the Ganges' which she had in tow. It appears the Steamer had been backing, and her stern struck the Flat, made a large hole in her and she sunk. It was supposed to contain £20,000 worth of Iron-work part of which was the Sone Bridge, made at the works of Sir W. G. Armstrong, Newcastle-on-Tyne."

Thus the East Indian Railway's steamboats did not solve entirely the problem of losses on the journey up the Ganges, but they certainly justified their existence by helping to speed up the construction of the trunk route to Delhi. Altogether they conveyed 21,000 tons of stores and equipment, compared with nearly 150,000 tons carried by the railway company's much more numerous, but slower, sailing fleet. Their career was comparatively brief, but the novel use of locomotive power entitles them to a place, however small, in railway history.

The steamboat diagrams, and most of the documents on which this account has been based, are Crown copyright material in the India Office Records, and are used by permission of the Secretary of State for Commonwealth Relations.

A SCHOOLBOY'S FIRST IMPRESSION

The railway [from London Bridge to Croydon] is most glorious and delightful travelling. I went in the first class, being the farthest from the engine, although contrary to Mr. Hunter's wishes, as it was sixpence more than the other, yet only 1s. and 9d. Far superior in comfort, and built like a coach. Five of them, one behind another. It started at the rate of the trotting of a horse, then faster and faster, until it goes at the rate of 10 miles and a half in 22 minutes, over the top of houses up to the first station, then hills on each side. After having gone by the Railway, the Omnibus seems mere child's play.

From a letter from Vincent Leigh Hunt to his parents, 1840

Unusual Mishaps

G. O. HOLT

WHATEVER MAY BE SAID about the law of averages, there would seem to be good grounds for the old saying that misfortunes never come singly. Just as someone may have a most unfortunate run of bad luck so, as many people have noticed, a railway accident may be quickly followed by another. Evidently there is nothing new in this: as long ago as August 1845 a leading article in *Herapath's Railway Journal* drew attention to what was described as "not only a sort of congregation of accidents at about the same time, but, at various periods, a crowding together of accidents of a similar character".

Yet on turning to a table of notable railway accidents which used to be published in the *Railway Year Book* one finds no trace of accidents in 1845 to justify this observation, indeed such details as Herapath went on to relate in his article suggest that the incidents he had in mind would seem rather trifling today. Nor does the *Year Book* table of accidents show that serious mishaps were frequent in the early days for, after the fatal accident to Huskisson (when the Liverpool & Manchester was being opened on September 15, 1830) the next thought to be worthy of a place in the list came ten years later (August 7, 1840) when a casting fell from a truck on the Hull & Selby Railway.

No doubt many occurrences in the intervening years seemed alarming enough at the time but, viewed in perspective, they should not have seemed any more disturbing than other perils of travel. Accidents to carriages on the roads were frequent; shipwrecks were quite commonplace; and it is rather surprising to find that in Victorian times as many as 150 pedestrians a year might be killed in the streets of London.

The Liverpool & Manchester, the world's first railway in the full sense of the term, evidently carried its passengers with exemplary safety, and the worst disaster in its early years came in 1833. The failure of an engine caused a train to stop unexpectedly, and three passengers, who got out and wandered on the line, were killed by a passing coal train. The Railway Age, it will be remembered, came in with gloomy predictions of death and destruction, and this period of freedom from serious accidents is greatly to the credit of the first generation of railwaymen, who had so much to learn about their way of life and little experience to guide them. The speed of trains was, of course, quite slow and personal injuries from mishaps were not serious as a rule.

In the year 1840, some 500 miles of new line were opened, more than double the figure in any previous year, and one result of this was a shortage of competent railwaymen. The newly constituted Railway Department of the Board of Trade lost no time in recognizing its duties, and sent out inspectors to enquire into the more serious accidents.

On November 12 of that year, a series of calamities on the London & Birmingham disturbed the public, and aroused the critics. The story is little known and throws light upon the working of a most important main line. That morning, a London & Birmingham locomotive, No. 90, was working a down goods train near Harrow when the crank axle broke: a happening by no means unusual on the Birmingham line at that time. A message was sent back to Camden, and two locomotives (Nos. 15 and 3) were despatched to assist the disabled train. No. 90's fireman, whose name was Finch, was transferred to No. 15 and, as things turned out, it was certainly not his day.

Having gone as far as Tring with the goods train No. 15 returned light towards London in the early afternoon. As she approached Harrow Station a railway policeman signalled the driver, Bradburn, to stop, and instructed him to go cautiously. There had been another accident farther south at a place known as Woodcock Hill, a broken wagon axle having caused the derailment of an up merchandise train. For the next three hours or so, No. 15 was employed to convey messages between Woodcock Hill and Harrow Station, where all up trains were being crossed to the down line.

This form of single line working was arranged under the instructions of John Bedford, superintendent of the company's police, who was also directing the gang of men which had been assembled to clear the up line. About 6 p.m., Bedford sent No. 15 to Harrow on the obstructed line with a message to the effect that no up trains were to pass on the down line until the 6 p.m. from Euston had gone by. He also told Bradburn to order refreshments from the "Queen's Arms", close to the station, to be sent to the men at Woodcock Hill.

Having delivered the message to the Harrow policeman, Bradburn left his engine in charge of Finch, telling him that if an up train should approach he was to move No. 15 forward out of the way. No sooner had he set off towards the inn, than a train was heard approaching in the darkness. Finch started the engine as he had been told but, before he had gone very far, realized he would be overtaken. He shut off steam and jumped clear as a goods train bore down upon his engine.

This train had left Wolverton about 4 p.m. worked by two engines; No. 82 was the train engine, and No. 1, returning to Camden after repairs in the works, was attached in front. The leading driver subsequently described in evidence how he had seen the Harrow policeman holding up a red light. He had shut off steam and "lifted the valve, but did not blow the whistle", which was evidently a recognized signal to attract the attention of the other trainmen, as the escaping steam made "a loud sharp noise". As a collision seemed inevitable, he reversed his engine and jumped clear, but his fireman, who was applying the hand brake, remained on the footplate and was killed.

The driver of No. 82, Simpson by name, did not shut off steam, and his engine was still in forward gear at the time of the collision. He was fatally injured. His fireman described how the train had called at several stations, and some warning of the derailment ahead had been given at Watford. Simpson had become "flurried and angry" with the policeman who stopped him and, approaching Harrow, had ignored the red hand signal. "It is time for us to be jumping off now," his fireman had said on seeing No. 15 ahead, but Simpson had made no reply and remained on the footplate. There was further evidence that he had been in the habit of "running hard", seldom looking ahead, although the brakesman said he had previously seen another train following theirs and had told Simpson of this at Boxmoor.

Among the officers who gave evidence was Edward Bury, Superintendent of the Locomotive Department, who said Simpson had come from the Newcastle & Carlisle Railway with a good character. Bury doubted whether the whistle was a satisfactory signal because of the speed, and the practice of enginemen to "tie their ears up to keep warm". He said London & Birmingham drivers were paid from £2 to £2 15s. a week. Other statements show there were no buffers on the goods wagons, and that an additional guard in the employ of Pickfords was travelling with the train. The driver of an Aylesbury train, which had passed shortly before the collision, explained that he was unable to read, but had "a printed list of instructions which his wife constantly read over to him before going on duty".

Sir Frederick Smith subsequently reported on this collision to the Board of Trade, pointing out that London & Birmingham goods trains did not run to a timetable, so that no check could be made on excessive speed. He blamed the company for its "backwardness in enforcing a strict system of discipline essential to public safety".

In January 1841, deputations from the boards of the principal lines attended a conference in Birmingham under the chairmanship of George Carr Glyn, of the London & Birmingham. Seven resolutions were proposed and seconded by men of the calibre of Hardman Earle, Theodore Rathbone, Charles Russell, and George Hudson (to name only a few). They showed awareness of their responsibility for safety, recognized their opportunity to profit by their combined experience, and stressed the necessity for a uniform system of regulations and signals.

Rules and regulations modelled on those in force on the Liverpool & Manchester were submitted for consideration, and consisted of Orders for Enginemen and Firemen, Rules to be observed during a Fog or in Thick Weather, Orders to Gatemen and Policemen, and Regulations as to Signals and Engine Whistles. The long struggle to prevent railway accidents began in earnest and it is surely a remarkable coincidence that a mishap causing so much concern should have happened at Harrow, where one of the most tragic of all railway disasters was to take place almost 112 years later (October 18, 1952) in circumstances which again brought widespread anxiety.

Before the end of 1841, an accident which may be described as the first major railway disaster befell the 4.30 a.m. train from Paddington on Christmas Eve. In the darkness, it ran into a landslip which had covered the rails in Sonning Cutting following heavy rain. The two third-class "carriages" next to the engine were no more than open trucks, and in the derailment they were badly crushed by the 18 goods vehicles marshalled behind them, killing eight people on the spot and injuring 17 others. The Great Western company established a remarkable record for safety in the closing years of its long career, and it seems to have been particularly unfortunate in this and other early accidents, although perhaps less so than the London & North Western, for it was the lot of that company to be concerned in a number of serious mishaps and, in turn, to pioneer a variety of safeguards.

When *Herapath's Journal* remarked on the crowding together of accidents of a similar kind, the writer might well have gone on to quote an example which must have come to the minds of some of his readers at that time. In November 1840, when an experimental locomotive named *Surprise* was being tried on the Birmingham & Gloucester, her boiler exploded at the foot of the Lickey incline. The driver's grave in Bromsgrove churchyard has become quite well known and photographs have been published from time to time showing the carving on the headstone which depicts, not *Surprise*, but one of Norris's American bogie engines, so familiar on the line in those days. A few months later there was a second, though less well-known, boiler explosion nearby, in which one of the American engines *was* concerned. Her name was *Boston*, and she was employed at Bromsgrove as a bank engine.

The contemporary accounts of these explosions seem a little unreal today, yet the boiler of another American locomotive was to explode in the West Midlands more than 100 years later. The engine was one of the 2-8-os sent over from the United States during the war, and the accident happened near Honeybourne as she was working a Great Western freight train from Banbury to Margam.

Explosions of this kind are so rare that the similarity between two more on the former Caledonian main line is quite extraordinary. On September 10, 1940, a streamline L.M.S.R. Pacific working an up express from Glasgow came to a standstill through shortage of steam some six miles south of Motherwell. Her crew, endeavouring to carry on, allowed the water level in the boiler to fall and this was so affected by a change of gradient that a sudden surge forward caused the crown of the firebox to collapse. On March 7, 1948, the streamline Pacific working a Glasgow—London train came to grief at Lamington, not far from the scene of the accident of seven years before and again the crown of the firebox collapsed.

The first explosion was attributed to lack of experience, and the second was brought about by a defective water gauge which had misled the enginemen. But mishaps which are so similar and concern the same class of locomotive cannot always be treated as coincidences. In 1907, the Midland Railway introduced 0-6-4 tank engines of the "2000" class, which were much used on its suburban and branch-line passenger services. On February 25, 1935, one of these (No. 2023) working a passenger train at Ashton-under-Hill became derailed when the track spread, allowing it to drop between the rails. It was recalled that a sister engine, No. 2024, had met with a similar accident when working the same train some five years before, and the Inspecting Officer tested the riding of one of these engines (No. 2011) on March 15, when he travelled on the footplate from Burton-on-Trent to Leicester. Less than a week later this engine became derailed near Moira, and was buried up to the axles in ash ballast. All the "2000" class were quickly withdrawn, although they appeared to have done their work satisfactorily for close on 30 years.

Several examples may be found where there have been two, or even more, accidents in the same place. On October 26, 1947, the 11.15 a.m. from Edinburgh to King's Cross was derailed at Goswick, when the enginemen overlooked exceptional arrangements for working traffic during engineering work on the line. Six years later, almost to the day, on October 28, 1953, the Glasgow to Colchester train was derailed at Goswick from quite a different cause: a mechanical defect in the locomotive.

The Great Western's immunity from accidents has already been mentioned. After the collision of the "Cape Mail" with a shunted goods train at Norton Fitzwarren on November 10, 1890, the company was not involved in a serious accident for all but 50 years. Then, on November 4, 1940, the night sleeping car train from Paddington to Penzance was derailed and wrecked, and once again the scene of the disaster was Norton Fitzwarren. Yet another example was noticed on the former Cambrian line. On New Year's Day 1883, there was a spectacular derailment on the Friog incline north of Llwyngwril, where the single line runs along a rock shelf on the cliffs overlooking Cardigan Bay. The evening train from Machynlleth struck a mass of soil which had suddenly fallen on to the line and the engine, parting from its tender, fell to the shore below. Fifty years passed and the accident was almost forgotten, but on March 4, 1933, the early morning mail train ran into an obstruction at Friog where part of the coast road had fallen on to the line. Again the engine, an elderly Cambrian 0-6-0, was thrown on to the shore, and again both enginemen were killed.

Another coincidence was noticed in 1933 when the Thames—Forth Express collided with a local goods train at Little Salkeld (between Carlisle and Appleby) on July 10. The engine, a Midland Compound No. 1010, had been involved in another serious accident at the same place on January 19, 1918, when earth had slipped into the cutting during a sudden thaw and caused the derailment of a down express.

The chances of such things happening seem the more remote when one realizes there are a great many places, even extensive areas of country, which are not associated with any notable mishap. Some of the smaller railway companies, the North Staffordshire and the Furness for example, could claim freedom from serious accidents throughout their long lives, although the Furness came near to marring this splendid record when its down mail train was derailed on the Levens Viaduct during a violent storm on February 27, 1903. Another line which has been almost entirely free from catastrophe is that between Lancaster and Carlisle, although it has carried heavy traffic through exposed and hilly country since it was opened in 1846. On the other hand the corresponding Midland line between Settle and Carlisle, opened 30 years later, seems to have had more than its share of misfortune: apart from the two accidents at Little Salkeld already mentioned one recalls Hawes Junction (December 24, 1910), Ais Gill (September 2, 1913), Culgaith (March 6, 1930), Blea Moor (April 18, 1952), and Settle (January 21, 1960).

These accidents, as well as those already mentioned on the Lickey and Friog inclines, had little connection with the gradients at the places concerned. However, instances of trains or vehicles running back and colliding with following trains *have* been the subject of enquiries from time to time, particularly the accidents at Round Oak, Abergele, Stairfoot and Armagh. Otherwise the working of passenger trains on the steepest inclines has been remarkably free from disaster, especially when one considers those where trains were hauled up on ropes by stationary engines. The first passenger trains in and out of Liverpool were all so worked, and locomotives were not used between Lime Street and Edge Hill until 1870. On several other inclines the same methods were employed; for instance east of Manchester Victoria, near Oldham, and at Cowlairs, outside Glasgow, where the stationary engine was at work until 1909.

The incline from Euston up to Camden was also worked in this fashion from a time shortly after the opening in 1837 until 1844. It was here that an accident was narrowly averted one night in October 1840, when the "breaksman" at Euston, on the point of attaching the rope to the departing mail train, thought he saw a light moving on the incline. He waited a few seconds and was amazed to see a locomotive backing down the road on which the mail was about to leave, its ashpan coming into contact with the sheaves which guided the rope. The driver, who was alone on the footplate, said the foreman had sent him to fetch the Yorkshire train. He was found to be drunk and the engine was sent back up to Camden on the rope.

It might have been claimed that passengers travelled up and down these rope-worked inclines in complete safety but for one or two accidents. The most serious was probably that on the Whitby to Pickering line in 1864, when a train ran away on the very steep gradient between Goathland and Beckhole because of the breaking of the rope. The North Eastern Company, which had taken over the line ten years before, was most unfortunate in this, as a deviation line, avoiding the incline, was actually under construction at the time and was opened in the following year. There was a rather similar accident in 1844 at the Bagworth incline on the Leicester & Swannington.

The working of trains over single lines has also been less hazardous than might be imagined. Even in the early days collisions were quite rare, and for a very long time it seemed that the safeguards provided by the electric token system had completely overcome the obvious dangers. Following two shocking disasters at Thorpe, near Norwich, on September 10, 1874, and near Wellow, on the Somerset & Dorset, on August 7, 1876, Edward Tyer produced his electric tablet instrument which was patented in 1878. Although he lived to a ripe old age, dying in 1912, there were no more collisions of this kind in his lifetime. The Cambrian's disaster on the single

The line to Kyle of Lochalsh seen from the footplate of the preserved Highland Railway
"Jones Goods" No. 103

Morning train from Glasgow to Fort William, double-headed by 4-4-0 Glen Loy and Glen Falloch, at Rannoch Station

Southbound "Yorkshire Pullman" at Leeds Central, with 4-6-2 No. 60130, Kestrel

line between Abermule and Newtown happened on January 26, 1921, nearly 45 years after the Wellow collision, and the story is a particularly unhappy one, developing from a succession of almost incredible oversights and misunderstandings. Another 30 years went by in which no passenger train was involved in a collision on a single line, so it is most extraordinary that in 1951 there should have been two such collisions in three weeks. The first happened at Fishguard on July 11, when a pull-and-push train started against a signal without a token, travelled half a mile and came into collision with a goods train, injuring several railwaymen although no passengers were hurt. Then, on August 1, there was a similar mishap on the former Highland line at Dalguise when a passenger train from Perth to Blair Atholl started in the same irregular way. Probably the driver was not expecting to cross another train at that station but a special conveying a party of railway officers from Inverness to Glasgow was approaching in the opposite direction. Eight passengers and six railway staff were injured.

Although passenger trains were not concerned in collisions of this kind between 1921 and 1951, a very unusual accident on January 16, 1931, may be recalled. The early morning newspaper train made its usual trip to Clacton-on-Sea and returned to Thorpe-le-Soken to continue its journey to Walton-on-Naze. The Clacton branch token was received from the driver and he was handed that for the Walton line, after which he started against a signal at danger and took the Clacton line again. Evidently unaware that they were on the wrong line the crew travelled two miles towards Clacton before the train collided head-on with a light engine.

There have also been accidents in which train crews were unaware of the direction in which they were moving. The heavy 6 p.m. train from King's Cross to Leeds on February 4, 1944, hauled by a Gresley Pacific, came to a standstill 40 yd. from the north end of the Gasworks Tunnel, and began to move slowly back down the 1 in 105 gradient unnoticed by the enginemen and guard. In consequence part of the train was derailed outside King's Cross station and two passengers were killed. A "Green Arrow" class locomotive was concerned in the same kind of accident in the old and notoriously foul Woodhead Tunnel which has since been superseded by a modern tunnel, opened when the Manchester—Sheffield electrification was completed. A similar thing happened during 1959 in the Sough Tunnel between Blackburn and Bolton, which a train entered at its normal speed but came to a standstill when the engine began to slip. In this case, the train moved backwards until the rearmost coaches were derailed at catch points outside the tunnel mouth. Then, in 1954, a Pacific, hauling 13 coaches up the steep gradient from Inver-keithing to the Forth Bridge, slipped to a standstill about 300 yd. inside the North Queensferry Tunnel and moved back so that the last three coaches were derailed at low speed on catch points where they were partly over-turned on the edge of a high embankment. A much earlier accident of this sort is recorded on the Midland Railway at Kibworth in 1880. One of Kirtley's 2-4-0s working a down night express to Scotland was halted by signals and, in stopping, the driver reversed the engine. On restarting, he failed to notice this and the train set back into a stationary ironstone train which was behind it.

One is apt to judge the severity of an accident by the number of casualties and the amount of damage done. Little is heard about narrow escapes from accident; they are not easily discussed, as only railwaymen are likely to know when they happen, and there is a possibility that, when they are mentioned at all, the account may be elaborated to make a more exciting story.

A remarkable account of narrowly averted disaster comes from a news-paper report of proceedings in a Salford magistrates court at the end of 1847, when a driver and fireman were charged with drunkenness and gross neglect of their duty. At Christmastime they had been in charge of the engine work-ing the up night mail train from Liverpool which, in the days before Run-corn Bridge, took the old Grand Junction route through Warrington. This involved negotiating the sharp curve off the Liverpool & Manchester line at Earlestown, where the maximum speed permitted was then 5 m.p.h. On this night the pointsman noticed that the train was approaching at about 40 m.p.h., and therefore set his points for the straight line, towards Manchester. Finding the train taking this direction without reducing speed the guard made his way forward to the engine by climbing from carriage to carriage, found the enginemen drunk, and managed to stop the train just before reaching Patricroft Station, where another passenger train was stand-ing.

A newspaper report which came to the notice of Caledonian shareholders led to questions at a general meeting in 1863, and brought to light some extraordinary happenings at Beattock on February 26, 1863. Early that morning, a defective goods engine limped into Beattock Station from the summit, having left its train in a siding. It was crossed to the down line to take water and here the driver, who was the worse for drink and alone on the footplate, set off towards the South on the down line when the down Limited Mail was almost due. The fireman and crew of another engine started in pursuit on the up line and their engine was able to overtake the runaway and continue in the hope of stopping the Mail. They were halted, however, by the guard of another train who had walked back to protect it, so, sending the guard to stop the Mail, they returned to meet the engine on the down line which by this time was short of steam. The fireman managed to board it and stopped it north of Dinwoodie. A vivid account of this incident was published in *The Railway Magazine* in 1950 under the title "A Runaway at Beattock", by David Smith.

In his "Railway Reminiscences", G. P. Neele mentions at least two startling narrow escapes. In the course of Queen Victoria's journey from Aboyne to Windsor in October 1865, the Royal Train was approaching Forfar, when a shunter of the Scottish North Eastern Company took a horse-drawn wagon across the main line just in front of it. In March 1888, three goods vehicles were being lowered on a rope down the incline above Cromford on the High Peak line when the rope broke and a van and wagon ran away, leaping across the Midland's Derby to Manchester line at the bottom and knocking down a wall beyond.

It goes without saying that in making a miscellaneous selection of some unusual accidents which have taken place over a period of 130 years there has been no attempt to show how higher standards of safety have been attained. The block signalling system, the automatic vacuum brake, track circuits, the automatic warning system and a wide range of other safeguards have been brought to perfection as a result of experience in a number of disasters. Rules and regulations have been designed to direct drivers, guards, signalmen and others who may suddenly find themselves faced with an unfamiliar situation. Although British railways are the safest in the world there is still a general impression that serious train accidents occur with some frequency.

It may therefore come as a surprise to the reader to hear that there have been three years since the railways were nationalized in which not a single passenger lost his life in a train accident. These years were 1949, 1954 and 1956. In another year, 1959, only one passenger was killed. This was the result of a most unfortunate accident to a child standing at a carriage window as a train entered Liverpool Street, who was struck by an open door of a train on an adjoining line. Thus in 1959, as in 1830, one passenger died as a result of a train accident, and we are reminded that there can be no end to this struggle for complete safety, for no precautions and safety devices can remain forever proof against mistakes.

Ghosts Underground

ALAN A. JACKSON

A CLOSED RAILWAY STATION attracts little attention nowadays—the sight alas is too common; but there remains a very special fascination in the closed and forgotten stations scattered about London's busy tube railways. Indeed, most passengers are quite unaware of their existence, and it requires some skill to locate them exactly as a train rushes through. Above ground, tucked away in odd and often unfashionable corners of London, their buildings still stand (with one exception), looking sufficiently like an open station to deceive the stranger. Down below, there is an atmosphere of eerie mystery about these lost stations, with their subways and platform tunnels buried deep in the London clay.

From the cosiness of a well-lit train, some may have savoured *Schaden-freude* as they contemplated an unwary passenger alighting by mistake, to be embraced in their forbidding catacombs, not to be released until almost dying of starvation. This has happened at least once (but fortunately without the dramatic sequel) and in the *T.O.T. Magazine* for April 1933, there appeared some amusing verse and sketches by the late F. H. Stingemore inspired by a true incident at South Kentish Town after it had been closed. John Betjeman, the poet of the Underground, has also developed the theme in his short story *South Kentish Town*, and when this was read on the BBC at a late hour some years ago, it sounded disturbingly vivid. Anyone visiting a closed station "on business" must equip himself with a red handlamp, for very obvious reasons.

As his train speeds past, the curious passenger may glimpse a few dim electric bulbs, and perhaps a moving figure, apparently staggering under a heavy load, a sight which will cause him to wonder what might be going on in the gloomy depths of these abandoned stations. Usually the answer is prosaic; the man was probably carrying a pile of old records to a vacant place on some shelving in the subways. London Transport puts most of these stations to good use.

King William Street, the very first electric tube railway station to be closed, did not die for lack of traffic, but rather because it was pitifully inadequate. City terminus of the City & South London Railway for its first nine years, it was sited on the corner of King William Street and Arthur Street East (now Monument Street). Its 25 ft. diameter lift shaft, which contained two hydraulic lifts descending to platform level, was constructed inside the existing building at 46 King William Street. For ease of operation with the cable haulage originally proposed, there was a single terminating track, flanked by a platform on each side in a gas-lit station tunnel, 26 ft. wide by 20 ft. high. The platforms were about 75 ft. beneath King William Street, and at right angles to it.

Leaving the station, the track bifurcated into single line tunnels, at first pointing almost due west and then turning very sharply towards the river under Swan Lane. The southbound line dropped fiercely at 1 in 40, and then 1 in 14, on a wicked curve, to pass under the northbound tunnel. This alarming arrangement, which was apparently required by cable working, caused the Board of Trade to impose a 5 m.p.h. speed limit. Trains entering the terminus had to fight their way up 1 in 40 on an even sharper curve.

This gloomy and monumentally inconvenient little terminus somehow managed to handle an average of 15,000 passengers a day, using manual signalling and electric locomotives. An attempt was made to improve matters in 1895, when the layout was changed to an island platform with a track either side, but this palliative was only obtained at the expense of reducing the platform length to three cars, as room had to be left for a crossover.

It soon became clear that if the railway were to gain more traffic it must extend further into the City, bypassing its twisted end. On February 25, 1900, the new line was opened, from "Borough Junction", just north of Borough Station, to Moorgate, with intermediate stations at London Bridge and Bank. The King William Street section thus became a 1,267-yd. branch, and was not used for passenger trains from that time. Some optimistic schemes were evolved to make use of the abandoned tunnels for a City & Brixton tube railway (later expanded to the City & Surrey). They came to nothing, and would in any case have involved very drastic reconstruction.

On the outbreak of the First World War, G. A. Nokes, the editor of *The Railway & Travel Monthly*, brightly suggested to the police that there might be enemy agents and explosives hidden in the old tunnels. Flashing their bullseye lanterns, the policemen descended, but to everyone's disappointment, nothing was found apart from a few old tickets. After they had left, Underground staff boarded up the tunnels and covered over the lift shaft—the tracks and platforms had previously been removed. The darkness of the musty subways then remained undisturbed until 1930 when the company unsuccessfully offered the premises for sale or lease, attempting to gain a little publicity by luring down a party of journalists to look them over and report back. By the light of acetylene flares, the reporters descended the emergency staircase. Arrived below, they found nothing more exciting than the remains of the manual lever signal box at the end of the platform, a few torn posters and some signals.

Shortly after this, the lift shaft was filled in, and in 1933 an office block, called Regis House, was completed over the site. In 1940, the owners of this block secured a tenancy of the old station and converted the platform tunnel into a two-storey air-raid shelter, sinking an additional 64 ft. shaft in Arthur Street to provide access at the western end. Earlier, the under-river sections had been sealed off with concrete plugs to prevent flooding should the tunnel be breached by a bomb. After the war, the tenancy was continued, and the station was used to store documents.

One Saturday afternoon in February 1959, a party from the Railway Club, resplendent in sou'westers and rubber boots, stood in the entrance hall of Regis House. Feeling rather like explorers about to set off into the unknown, and having duly indemnified the authorities against all loss or damage to their persons, they descended to the basement and were then led down the original white-tiled emergency stairs to the platform tunnel. Here they stood among dusty files and faded wartime posters, trying to imagine top-hatted City men of the 'nineties waiting in the yellow gaslight for the noisy and cramped little train that would return them to their comfortable Clapham villas for dinner. At the far end, the intrepid amateurs entered the under-river tunnels. Stalactites glistened in the light of the handlamp held by the London Transport official who was solemnly counting them in before closing the watertight doors behind them . . . .

Around the City Road Basin of the Regent's Canal is an area of industry and run-down housing. Here, at the junction of City Road and Moreland Street, only 25 chains from Angel and 48 from Old Street, is the former City Road station of the C.S.L.R., opened on November 17, 1901, with the extension from Moorgate to Angel. There was vigorous competition from a busy electric tramcar line, and the station was too near its neighbours to attract much traffic in its own right. When the Underground Company took over the C.S.L.R. in 1913, some trains began to pass it without stopping. An incident of note in its otherwise uneventful career occurred in August 1916, when a guard started a train while some passengers were still getting off and a man was killed. It seems possible that he was so unused to anyone alighting at City Road that they had taken him completely by surprise.

After traffic had ceased on August 8, 1922, the Moorgate-Euston section was temporarily closed to allow reconstruction to standard dimensions in preparation for through running with the Golders Green and Highgate lines *via* new junctions at Camden Town. The poor traffic returns of City Road did not justify the expense of alterations, and when the section re-opened on April 20, 1924, the doors of City Road remained firmly shut. Sixteen years later, the place resounded again to human voices, when it was opened to the public as an air-raid shelter, with bunks installed in its subways and on its platforms. Now all is quiet again under the top station, a building whose architectural style resembles an Edwardian Salvation Army Citadel, incongruously crowned by a huge modern ventilating shaft.

Two years after the closing of City Road came the first casualty on the London Electric Railway network. South Kentish Town, on the Highgate branch of the Charing Cross, Euston & Hampstead tube, was opened with the line on June 22, 1907. Sited at the junction of Kentish Town Road and Royal College Street, it was a mere 650 yd. north of Camden Town, and an equal distance south of Kentish Town. It was originally proposed to name it "Castle Road", and this name appears on the platform tiling. Two Otis electric lifts served the platforms, 60 ft. below the streets, and the small top station was in the standard style of L. W. Green, the Underground Company's architect. Station spacing hereabouts was much too close for the area, an inner suburb and shopping district, well served by the efficient electric tramcars of the London County Council. After 1913, some trains missed the stop, and in 1918 it was one of a number of stations chosen for closing earlier in the evening to save fuel.

An excuse for shutting this Cinderella station came with an unofficial strike of power workers at Lot's Road, which began overnight on June 4-5, 1924. With many other stations, including all on the Highgate branch, South Kentish Town did not open that morning, in order to save current for busier stations. After the strikers had resumed work on June 13, things returned to normal, but the gates of South Kentish Town were never opened again to passengers. Like other closed stations, it played its part in sheltering local citizens from German bombs in the Second World War and, as already mentioned, it has its niche in literature.

Eight years elapsed before any more tube stations were closed, and then two were shut in the same year, as part of the modernization of the Piccadilly Line. A third Piccadilly Line station was closed in 1934. It was the elimination of these three lightly-used stops, together with wider station spacing on the extensions, which permitted the average speed of the line to be increased from 19 to 25 m.p.h.

The first of the trio was in Down Street, behind Piccadilly, barely 550 yd. from its western neighbour, Hyde Park Corner, and little more than 600 yd. from Dover Street (now Green Park). Southwards stretched the empty spaces of the Royal parks, and the station's catchment area was confined to large houses, clubs and luxury hotels, whose occupants would prefer to use private transport or cab rather than venture irksome contacts with the unwashed on the Underground. There were two lifts to the platforms, 73 ft. below Piccadilly, and a substation at street level. After 1909, Down Street was missed by some trains, and it was affected by the economies of 1918, when it was also closed on Sundays.

The end came after traffic had ceased on Saturday, May 21, 1932, and it was "replaced" by the modernized Hyde Park Corner, which was ready the following Monday. Work then began on the construction of an 836-ft. reversing siding between the running roads, connected to the Hyde Park Corner crossover tunnel by a foot subway at its western end. This enabled trains to be turned back at Green Park, to provide a more frequent service on the inner section. On at least one occasion a train full of passengers has been signalled into it in error. Additional ventilation plant was installed in one of the Down Street lift shafts for the siding and running tunnels.

During the Second World War, the remains of Down Street's deep-level works were converted to serve as the headquarters of the Railway Executive Committee, and offices, kitchens and sleeping accommodation were installed. Provision was also made for the War Cabinet, and Churchill often deliberated there with his Ministers, bringing the once quiet little station its hours of glory. A very short length of platform was retained on each road so that users of the accommodation could step on and off trains *via* the driver's cab. A plunger-operated red light on the tunnel wall warned drivers that they were required to stop and pick up.

One of London's less attractive areas is that immediately north of King's Cross station. Optimistically, the Piccadilly Railway provided a station here, on the corner of Bingfield Street and York Road (now York Way). Facing a vast expanse of railway-occupied land, and backed by an area of poor housing, it was half a mile north of King's Cross, and almost three-quarters from Caledonian Road. An altogether bleak prospect from all points of view, its traffic was little better than that of its neighbour, the

North London Railway's Maiden Lane, which was closed completely at the end of 1916.

Two Otis electric lifts descended to the platforms, where a small signal box controlled a crossover. Non-stopping by some trains began in 1909, and early evening and Sunday closure followed in 1918. The last passengers were handled on the evening of September 17, 1932, and the imposing frontage of the top station is now occupied by a firm of printers. After closure, a reversing siding was constructed in the platform tunnels, to enable trains coming from the Northern Line (*via* the 1927 single-line interchange loop at King's Cross) to reverse on to the westbound line and proceed to Acton Works without interfering with normal traffic.

The last victim of the "Piccadilly Purge" was Brompton Road, which was sited just east of the Oratory, only 550 yd. from South Kensington and less than 750 yd. from Knightsbridge. Its proximity to these stations, the lack of a viable catchment area, and good bus services along Brompton Road all served to hasten its demise. Some trains ceased to call after 1910, and it was involved in the early closing list of 1918. Like all other tube stations it was closed on May 4, 1926, as a result of the General Strike, but when normal services were resumed, no effort was made to reopen either Brompton Road or York Road, and they both remained shut all that summer. Eventually, after the matter had been raised in Parliament, the Company was forced to reopen both on October 4, 1926, no doubt much against its will. No Sunday service was provided.

Those passengers who did use Brompton Road tended to be among the more articulate members of the public and the difficulty of reaching the station owing to the complications of "non-stopping" became a subject for correspondence in *The Times* during 1933. Indeed so well known was the call *Passing Brompton Road* that it became the title of a play which starred Marie Tempest. When Knightsbridge was modernized, escalators were provided at the south end of its platforms leading to a new entrance at Hans Crescent. This was sufficiently near Brompton Road station to enable London Transport to close it with a fairly easy conscience after traffic had ceased on July 29, 1934. The lift shafts, which had contained four Otis electric lifts, were sealed with a concrete plug, and the premises were sold for commercial use.

Only two stations have been shut on the Central Line, and both of these were replaced by new ones close by. British Museum Station, in High Holborn, on the corner of Bloomsbury Court, was opened with the line on July 30, 1900. The new street called Kingsway had been proposed, but not yet begun; even so, the siting was not very imaginative, because the route of the Great Northern & Strand tube was also authorized, and this passed

Ghosts Underground

east of the British Museum station. When the Piccadilly tube opened six years later, it passed under the Central London and had a station at this point, at the junction of Kingsway and High Holborn. Passengers wishing to change from one line to the other had to come up to street level and walk 170 yd. across two busy thoroughfares. A low-level subway between the two stations was proposed as early as 1907, and an interchange station at the crossing point of the two lines was authorized in 1914, but nothing was done until 1932. Then platform tunnels were constructed round the Central London tubes at Kingsway while trains continued to run. A new station, with escalators and interchange facilities for both lines, was completed on September 25, 1933. British Museum closed on the previous night. Its top station in the C.L.R. light brown unglazed terra-cotta is converted to shops and offices, while the platforms, after use as an air-raid shelter in the last war, are now demolished.

King Edward VII and President Faillères opened the great Franco-British Exhibition in May 1908. All London flocked out to see the wedding-cake buildings, the gardens, the fountains and the amusements which had transformed the wastelands west of Wood Lane. To carry the crowds, the Central London had extended its line on May 14, 1908, opening on that day a new station at ground level opposite the Exhibition's Wood Lane entrance. The extension was a single-line loop formed by the existing depot access tunnel and a new single-line tunnel, and the two platforms of the new station were at the top of the loop, on either side of the single track.

On August 3, 1920, the line was further extended to Ealing Broadway, and two more platforms were provided at Wood Lane Station for the through Ealing trains. These were in covered ways just below the loop or local platforms, which remained in use for trains reversing at Wood Lane. The southernmost of the loop platforms (No. 1) was too short to take all the doors of a six-car train, and could not be extended as the only space available was blocked by lines to the depot. It was true that passengers could use No. 2, on the other side of the train, but there was a gap and in any case it was desirable to load one side and unload the other. A solution was found in 1928 when a swivelling wooden platform extension was installed at the east end of No. 1. About 35 ft. long, it provided platform space foul of a depot track. Fully interlocked with the signals, it was electro-pneumatically worked from the signal cabin.

To provide accommodation for eight-car trains, an entirely new station, named White City, was eventually built in Wood Lane as part of the extension westwards to West Ruislip. This station was above ground, about 350 yd. further north, almost opposite the stadium, and had three roads. It was opened on November 23, 1947, Wood Lane closing the previous night. In the following February there was a derailment in the new station, and the Ealing platforms at Wood Lane were brought into use again for a few hours. Weed-covered and bereft of their track, the local platforms now sleep precariously beneath the rusting girders of the Exhibition Arcade. Dark and dirty in their subways, the Ealing platforms still display a few tattered 1947 posters, just visible in the weak daylight that enters the portals.

Apart from the closed stations, there are some stations whose original surface buildings have been replaced by other entrances—Dover Street (now Green Park), Hyde Park Corner, King's Cross (Piccadilly Line), Chancery Lane, St. Paul's, Marylebone, and Euston. Stockwell is an unusual case in that it has new platforms, constructed in 1924, about 100 yd. south of the original island platform, while its top station remains in the same position, although rebuilt. Another rearrangement of this kind took place above ground, at Hammersmith. When the Piccadilly tube opened in 1906, it ran into a new two-road, four-face terminus called Hammersmith Broadway, under an all-over roof alongside the District station. This disappeared in 1931–2 when alterations were made to allow through running of Piccadilly trains to Hounslow and South Harrow. The street frontage constructed for both railways in 1906 to the designs of L. W. Green still remains, boldly lettered in *art nouveau* capitals: G. N. PICCADILLY & BROMPTON RAILWAY. HAMMERSMITH STATION. DISTRICT RAILWAY. Both Aldwych and Holborn have an abandoned platform, no longer necessary now that the double-track Aldwych branch is worked as a single line.

Finally there are facilities which were provided, but never used for passengers. Deep below Hampstead Heath, platforms and subways were constructed for a station to be called North End, but the lift shafts were never sunk because it was decided that a station here would not attract sufficient traffic. In later years, the platforms were replaced by wooden stages, used to store records and supplies.

The District Deep Level Railway was planned to relieve the parent line, running beneath it from Earls Court to Mansion House, with a single intermediate station at Charing Cross. Later it was arranged that the section between Earls Court and South Kensington should be built as part of the Piccadilly tube (the District retained running powers) and South Kensington tube station was constructed as a junction between the Piccadilly and the District Deep Level. Thus it included a separate westbound station tunnel for the Deep Level alongside the westbound Piccadilly platform. Successful electrification and resignalling of the District so increased its capacity that the parallel tube was not required, and the partly-tiled platform tunnel at South Kensington remains as its only tangible asset. This platform was used in the

First World War to harbour the crown jewels and precious books and manuscripts. It became the Underground Signal School in 1927, and since 1939 it has again been used for storage purposes.

Other tube stations have been threatened with closure, notably Covent Garden and Mornington Crescent. The first is only 280 yd. from Leicester Square, and closure was considered in 1935 when that station was modernized. It seems unlikely that it will survive the removal of the market to its new site. Mornington Crescent, which has been missed by Edgware Line trains ever since December 1, 1924, has a sparse traffic, and its situation is comparable to that of South Kentish Town. It was proposed for closure in 1958, but the decision was deferred on the advice of the Central Transport Users' Consultative Committee.

Both are fossilized examples of the early tube station, and can readily convey the atmosphere of the Edwardian tube to the sensitive explorer. Covent Garden has the distinction of being haunted by the unhappy spirit of a tall man, dressed in the grey suit and white gloves he was wearing when he committed suicide there some years ago. He has been seen many times and favours particularly the cross passage at the signal box end of the platforms and also the staff mess room. The only authenticated ghost on the Underground, he walks with his arms outstretched before him. Soon he may have the place to himself.

It is a strange and shivery experience to visit these half forgotten and forgotten tube stations, oases of calm set in the feverish bustle of London. Disturbed only by the brief rumble of passing trains, their silence is so intense that the ticking of a wrist-watch can be heard fifty yards away.

A PERIPATETIC WATCH

A remarkable story of a wrist-watch, which travelled many miles on a locomotive after it had been dropped by its owner, was reported in the Great Eastern Line Edition of the "Eastern Region News". Early one morning, a railwayman at March lost his watch in the locomotive department, and after a thorough search, gave it up as lost. Four hours later, the watch was found at Lincoln, 60 miles away; it had travelled all the way on the 4 in.-wide step of a tender. When the watch was returned to its owner, it was none the worse for its hazardous journey, and still indicated the correct time. The tender must have ridden with remarkable steadiness for the watch to have remained for so long in such a precarious position.

Exposure!

THE REV. A. W. V. MACE

THE STEAM LOCOMOTIVE produces some of the most satisfying sights, sounds and even smells, associated with any form of machinery. The smell of hot oil, the hiss of steam, and the feathery plume from a safety-valve, seen against the background of blue sky: each of these is strongly evocative, and helps to explain the regard, the affection even, in which the steam engine is held.

It is surprising that artists have not often attempted to record the railway scene, when this has so much to offer to the eye. Railway subjects are rare on the canvases of professional painters. One of the earliest and best known is Turner's "Rain, Steam and Speed", with its sub-title "The Great Western Railway", which was shown at the Royal Academy in 1844. It portrays a train approaching along a viaduct in stormy weather, and conveys the atmosphere of the scene, without much attention to detail. At the opposite extreme is W. P. Frith's picture of Paddington, entitled "The Railway Station", and painted in 1862. Here the pre-Raphaelite tradition is evident, and while the artist's chief interest is in the passengers and other figures portrayed, the background detail is precise enough to give a good impression of a broad-gauge train of those days.

Claud Monet, working in France and in England some ten or more years later, is the most notable artist to have been attracted by railway subjects, and his imagination certainly was captured by the sight of steam and smoke. "La Gare St. Lazare" (1877) is perhaps his best-known railway picture: it shows the Normandy express about to depart from the Paris station. But

"Le Chemin de Fer", painted in the previous year, is equally attractive—there is a side view of a moving train, with a long trail of steam seen against a hilly background. No great detail is to be found in his paintings (he was a leader of the Impressionist school) but they are full of railway atmosphere.

However, if painters in general have failed to respond to the railway scene, the opposite is true of photographers. To the passenger gazing out of the carriage window, the figure of a man bending over his camera and photographing the train has become a familiar sight, and since the war this practice has been so common that some of the more famous expresses can rarely have arrived at their destination on a summer's day without having been photographed somewhere or other *en route*.

There are certain similarities between the development of railways, and of photography. Both have roots which go back into the past, to the sixteenth century at least; but it was not until the first half of the nineteenth century that either took the pattern which is now familiar. The railway age is generally considered to have been inaugurated by the opening of the Stockton & Darlington Railway in 1825, while in 1835 Fox Talbot made the first photograph using the now characteristic process of separate negative and positive, with development of a latent image in each.

This new art of photography progressed rapidly, and its importance was accepted by the 1850s, so that when the Crimean War broke out in 1854 photographers as well as journalists were sent out as press correspondents. By this time, the first railway photograph had been taken. The earliest that can be dated with certainty is that of the South Eastern Railway locomotive *Folkstone*, on show at the Great Exhibition of 1851. This was presumably taken by a professional photographer; a picture of some broad-gauge locomotives outside a running shed—probably at either Swindon or Chippenham—may be even earlier, and is likely to have been the work of an amateur.

These early photographs were tedious to produce. The glass plates used for the negative had to be sensitized immediately before being used, and had to be developed immediately after the exposure, which was lengthy. Thus the photographer had to take with him a portable darkroom, as well as his camera. Consequently, railway photographs taken in the 1850s and 1860s are not common, but the results obtained were quite permanent. The writer possesses a print, made in 1961, from a negative made in 1856. It was taken for Beyer, Peacock, and shows one of the 2-2-2 locomotives which the firm had built in that year for the Edinburgh & Glasgow Railway.

Things became simpler for the photographer from 1874 onwards when the so-called dry plates were first put on the market. As with their successors today, they were loaded into their holders in the darkroom before the photographer set out, and could be developed at leisure, after the day's photography had been done. Lenses were being improved too, so that it was less necessary to use a small stop to secure good definition. This improvement, together with the increased sensitivity of plates after the "ripening" process had been added to their manufacture (from about 1878) enabled so-called "instantaneous" photographs to be made at last—pictures could now be taken in a small fraction of a second, instead of requiring seconds or even minutes for the exposure.

For those who were interested in railways this meant that photographs could now be taken of trains in motion. The broad gauge was still in operation, and many of the earliest pictures of moving trains are of Great Western broad-gauge expresses. The last such train—the "Cornishman" of May 20, 1892—must have been recorded at numerous points on its journey from Paddington to Penzance, to judge from the number of photographs purporting to show this melancholy occasion, but it has to be admitted that not all of them show the same train!

The next significant advance in photography took place from 1885, when the American firm of Eastman (Kodak) began to supply negative material on a flexible base, at first paper, then nitrocellulose. This quickly led to the production of the familiar roll-film, permitting daylight loading of the camera. This invention, which dates from the 1890s, at once increased the popularity of photography. There was a phenomenal growth of amateur photography at about this period; in 1897 a Birmingham firm of opticians was advertising the fact that in the previous 12 years it had sold 180,000 cameras and 250,000 lenses.

At about the same time, public interest in railways was also rapidly increasing, having no doubt been stimulated by the Railway Races of 1888 and 1895. (These took place between London and Edinburgh, and London and Aberdeen, and were a result of the rivalry between the East Coast and West Coast groups of companies.) Naturally, some of those who were interested in railways turned their hand to photographing railway scenes. Particularly popular were the photography of trains in motion, already mentioned, and the portraiture of locomotives, taken at rest in stations or outside running sheds. These two aspects of railway photography have ever since remained particularly the province of amateur photographers.

The enthusiasts taking these pictures have for the most part had no professional connection with railways. Thus in the period just described, Dr. Tice Budden made one of the most valuable collections of photographs of British trains during the 1890s, mostly taken while he was a student. During the first quarter of this century, there were several notable railway photographers, of whom Mr. F. E. Mackay must be mentioned. His career was in law, but his spare time must have been largely devoted to photographing express trains, more than 500 of his pictures appearing in *The Railway Magazine* during this period.

At the present time, so many names are well known that mention of individuals is almost invidious. But Mr. M. W. Earley would certainly figure in any list, as his work has been prominent for nearly 40 years: until his recent retirement he was in banking. Some amateurs have a particular flair for obtaining pictures which are works of art, as well as being faithful records of the railway scene. Notable amongst them is the Bishop of Pontefract (the Rt. Rev. Eric Treacy), while among the post-war generation, a young Scottish business man, Mr. W. J. V. Anderson, has an extraordinary gift in this direction.

Linking almost all these generations is Mr. Gordon Tidey, who for over 60 years has devoted his annual week's holiday to photographing trains in various parts of the country, and whose collection must be unique in its span of time.

But to return to the development of photography during this period: the first decade of this century saw the increasing use of the reflex camera with a focal-plane shutter. Using it, exposures of as little as one-thousandth of a second could be made, and fast-moving expresses portrayed as sharply as if they had been standing still. This, however, destroyed the sense of motion, unless steam and smoke were being emitted by the locomotive. Steam was difficult to render, since the plates and films of those days were partly colour-blind, and rendered blues and whites in much the same tone.

This problem began to be resolved with the invention of the so-called panchromatic emulsion, sensitive to all colours. With this the blue of the sky could be held back by use of a yellow filter, without undue loss of sensitivity. The first panchromatic plates were marketed about 1906, but general use of this new emulsion did not begin to take place until after the First World War. The year 1927 is generally regarded as marking the effective beginning of the "panchromatic era". However, it is only since the 1939–45 war that panchromatic film has become really popular with the amateur, and the older colour-blind emulsions have almost disappeared.

Once the panchromatic emulsions had been marketed, the way lay open for colour photography, and the development of this, and of ciné-photography, have been the other great features of the twentieth-century photographic scene. It is a pity that colour photography has come too late to be used on the varied and often magnificent liveries of the pre-grouping companies, but the recent practice of preserving a few old locomotives and coaches, and restoring these to their original colours, has given an opportunity to photographers not yet born when these liveries had disappeared.

South Eastern Retrospect: a suburban train from Holborn Viaduct, headed by a Stirling 0-4-4 tank with a domeless boiler, on the connecting loop between Bickley and Orpington, shortly before the line was electrified in 1925

Old-time "Flying Scotsman" coaches and Stirling eight-footer No. 1 on a special excursion at Cambridge in August 1938

The "Irish Mail" picking up water from the troughs at Aber, North Wales, in July 1956

Exposure!

It is worth recalling that railways had a formative influence on the development of the cinema. The earliest moving pictures to be shown to the public were brief shots of scenes with plenty of movement, and railway trains were a natural subject. Then short playlets were attempted, and it was the success of one of these, which happened to have a railway theme, which persuaded the producers that full-length cinema plays might prove a rival to the traditional stage. The decisive play was entitled "The Great Train Robbery": what a modern ring this has!

Since the Second World War one of the most interesting advances has been the use of "synchronized" flash equipment, which makes it possible to take photographs of moving trains at night. The earliest attempts at this kind of photography go back to the beginning of the century. As these involved producing a long gigantic flash by igniting a pound or so of flash powder, and hoping for a successful snap of the passing train during the flash, such efforts were infrequent—they were far too expensive and chancy. The present method of firing a flash-bulb by aid of the shutter movement has eliminated the uncertainty and most of the extra cost of night photography, but this still calls for considerable skill if good results are to be obtained.

Of course, flash photography can still be expensive if practised in a big way. The classic example of this comes from America, where a Pennsylvania Rail Road train traversing the famous horse-shoe curve in the Allegheny Mountains was photographed by the light from 6,000 flash-bulbs, fired simultaneously. This was in 1954, and marked the centenary of the opening of the curve.

America can also claim what is almost certainly the largest railway photograph ever taken. This was made in 1901, to advertise the Chicago & Alton Rail Road's new daylight service between Chicago and St. Louis. The train operating this run was photographed using a specially-made camera which employed a plate 8 ft. by $4\frac{1}{2}$ ft. in size. In its holder it weighed 4 cwt. It is presumed that contact prints were considered adequate!

Mention of this giant camera prompts the always vexed question: "What is the best kind and size of camera for railway photography?" Everyone has his own opinion, and what follows is but one particular point of view. In one sense, any camera will do, provided that the user of it knows what it is capable of doing, and does not expect impossibilities. The writer began, like so many of us, with a box Brownie, and soon learnt that it was not suitable for photographing express trains in motion, but could cope adequately with pictures of trains and locomotives that were not moving. What he did not learn until much later was that a tripod is really necessary, if crisp negatives full of detail are to be obtained. Camera shake accounts for the great majority of unsatisfactory negatives, and it can happen even during the shortest of exposures, unless the camera is held rock steady—and a rigid tripod is the only certain way to be sure of this.

If the photographer has the ambition to produce a large print—say 10 in. by 8 in.—with crisp detail, then he will need a good lens, and a fairly large size of negative. The popularity of colour photography has led to the 35 mm. camera becoming by far the most common size today. This is a pity, because even with a first-class camera of this small size the slightest fault of technique becomes apparent when a large print is attempted. The great majority of 35 mm. negatives fail to provide satisfactory prints of size larger than post-card, where technical subjects are concerned, if the photographer is not a competent professional.

The leading railway photographers normally use a negative size of $3\frac{1}{2}$ in. by $2\frac{1}{2}$ in., or larger. To arrest the motion of a fast-moving train an exposure of 1–500th of a second or less is necessary, although a skilful use of "panning" (following the motion of the train by swinging the camera) will hold the front part of the train sharp, but with increasing blur towards the back of the train. Modern plates and films are fast enough for a lens of maximum aperture about f/4.5 to be sufficient. It should be a four- or six-element anastigmatic lens, and it is desirable that it should be surface-coated, as definition is undoubtedly improved when there is minimum scatter of light by internal reflection between the surfaces.

The writer's own choice is to use a quarter-plate ($4\frac{1}{4}$ in. by $3\frac{1}{4}$ in.) for the best work; he uses a Sinclair Una Camera which has stood him in good stead for over 30 years. It has a four-element f/4.7 lens, and a Compur shutter going down to 1–500th second as minimum exposure. Unfortunately, it is expensive to use—plates cost just over a shilling each—and so for more casual work he uses an Ensign Selfix camera ($3\frac{1}{4}$ in. by $2\frac{1}{4}$ in.) with a Ross Xpres lens and an Epsilon shutter giving a nominal 1–250th second minimum exposure. It has the advantage of being also equipped to take negatives $2\frac{1}{4}$ in. square, and so can be used for colour transparencies of this convenient size. It is also an entirely British camera, and loses nothing by comparison with Continental rivals.

It is well to get used to one particular make of film, and to employ one particular developer for it. (The writer's preference is for Ilford FP3 film and Microphen developer.) So also with the printing paper—his selection here being Kodak or Agfa Bromide, and Johnson's Contrast developer. Standardizing procedure like this results in minimum deviation from normal working, and enables the photographer to give all his attention to the individual treatment that each print will normally require—for example, the sky area usually needs extra exposure to bring out the clouds and steam.

Good results are the reward of taking care in these and other ways. Before a photograph is taken, care should have gone into the selecting of a good site where the surroundings are harmonious and do not distract from the main subject, which is the train. Mr. Anderson, whose outstanding pictorial work has been mentioned, will move up and down a section of line till he has found the best spot, and even carries a pair of garden shears with him, to deal with any foreground grass which may be in the way of his picture! The actual photograph may indeed have had days of thought and planning beforehand—and the result, as has been said, is usually outstanding.

What are the particular attractions about this hobby of railway photography? For many it is the recording of the railway scene in all its variety, trains, locomotives, signals, stations and the like. For others it is the pleasure of making a picture which is a work of art, and which has a train as its subject.

To the writer, there are a whole series of contributory pleasures. He prefers to photograph his trains in country surroundings. Unless the line is exceptionally busy, there are long periods of waiting for the next train to appear. The photographer is then free to sit or lie at his ease in the lineside grass, the sights and sounds of nature as the background to his thoughts. Insects are busy about the stones and blades of grass; butterflies flutter by; birds perch on the telegraph wires. And there is always the slow-moving panorama of the sky and its clouds to watch.

Then a signal goes to clear, and the train is heard in the distance. At once the photographer is on his feet and checking the focusing and the shutter settings of his camera which—it is hoped—is already in position on its tripod. As the train approaches the feeling of excitement mounts; if the train is something special, there may be a feeling of tense anxiety lest anything should fail, for perhaps the shot is one which cannot be repeated on another occasion.

As the buffer beam of the locomotive passes over the predetermined spot, the shutter is fired, and the photographer has a split second in which to note the number of the locomotive as it roars past him and is gone. The film is wound on, and details of the photograph recorded. Then he settles down again to his siesta, and the contemplation of nature; or maybe moves on to another site.

Some locations are particularly pleasant at the time, and in recollection afterwards. The south end of Sevenoaks Tunnel has agreeable memories for the writer. The grass-clothed cutting swept steeply up to the tree-covered hillside, and the relative silence would be broken from time to time by the cry of the woodpecker. Down trains could be heard when still some distance inside the tunnel, and the front of the locomotive seen a moment or so before the train burst into full view amidst a scurry of steam and smoke. It was a very satisfying spot. Another was the Warren near Folkestone. It was a solitary visit, but memorable for the fact that 13 consecutive trains had each a different class of locomotive at the head, so that the memory of that sunny day amidst the Kentish chalk remains a cherished one.

Photography of trains has a certain element of chance which gives it a sporting flavour. One cannot wait for the sun to shine, and if it goes in just before the train arrives, that is bad luck, but all part of the game. Even worse, it may be shining on one half of the train, and not on the rest, an almost impossible situation.

Another sporting risk, if the train to be photographed is on the further track, is that it may be obscured at the critical moment. Recently the writer was travelling in a special from Paddington to Ruabon, hauled by the restored L.N.E.R. Pacific *Flying Scotsman*. It was a royal progress; stations were packed with spectators, and lineside photographers were legion. One of these, as the train passed, was seen writhing in agony. It was not a sudden attack of appendicitis—a passing goods train had eclipsed the express just as he was about to photograph it.

Then, if the photographer does his own processing, there are the particular pleasures of the darkroom—in developing, the impatient wait until the film or plates are sufficiently fixed to take a cautious look at what they are like. Later there is the excitement of a detailed examination, to see whether the definition is really sharp, and so forth.

Lastly, there are the pleasures of looking over the collection of pictures that in time the photographer will have amassed. The railway scene never stands still, any more than the trains that constantly move across it. Even if the photographs cover a period as brief as five or ten years, there will be many pictures recording locomotives that by then will have been scrapped, or branch lines that have been closed, but the vanished scenes remain in the pictures of the collection.

Then there will be some photographs that represent a special triumph—some unusual train, or perhaps an old-fashioned signal that was a relic from an almost vanished past, even when the picture was taken. Maybe these triumphs will prompt the memory of the "ones that got away"—every photographer, like every fisherman, has his recollections of these. Or again, he will be prompted to think of photographs which he has always meant to take, but which have not yet been added to the bag. So he begins to plan some future expedition which will help him to fill some of the gaps, and in so doing he will realize once more that railway photography is an interest which has about it a perennial fascination.

By Train to Bantry

C. L. MOWAT

MY FIRST SIGHT of Ireland from the boat at Rosslare, early on a July morning, was of a low green coastline and a single-track railway, marked by trim white signal posts, slanting down from the sandhills to the pier. The station, with the attractive C.I.E. (Coras Iompair Eireann) colours of green and yellow, and the train to Cork, with its old-fashioned carriages in two shades of green, confirmed my good impressions. Inside, the train was roomy, thanks to the broad Irish gauge of 5 ft. 3 in.; it seemed solid, with its heavy, dark woodwork and the large glass bowls of its gas lamps.

The Cork express ran non-stop to Waterford, and made the journey at a good clip. Crossing stations on this and other major single-line routes are laid out to give a straight run in both directions on one line, both loops being signalled for use in either direction; the distant signals are worked, though on other single lines I noticed that they had been disconnected. Smart working with electric staff or miniature staff is typical: on the line to Waterford automatic exchangers were in use. It is pleasant to see lower quadrant signals everywhere, and to find distant signals painted red—an unusual, brick red, the fish-tail stripe being in a pale yellow ochre. Ground signals are of the revolving disc variety, and signal boxes are usually without name boards. Other things which impress the visitor are the green, empty countryside, the long distances between stations, the bare walled platforms and neat whitewashed station buildings, and the good volume of local and long-distance passenger traffic. C.I.E. has a monopoly of passenger transport, and its buses complement rather than compete with the trains (though several branch lines have been closed to passengers).

At Waterford the station is roomy and well built, and like others I saw later (Dun Laoghaire, Wexford, and the famous Limerick Junction) has only one through platform serving trains in both directions. The connecting trains here were typical also: a sleek diesel railcar, two other trains of old carriages, no two of the same height, several six-wheelers, brake vans with birdcage roofs and side look-outs. The prevalence of six-wheelers was surprising. Even the Dublin-Cork expresses, including some of the latest C.I.E. compartment stock—quite as good as the latest on British Railways —frequently ended with a six-wheel brake van. Among tender engines, the 4-4-0, 2-6-0 and 0-6-0 predominated; and 2-4-2 tank engines handled many branch-line and suburban workings. All were satisfyingly solid, with tall chimneys, large steam domes, high splashers, sturdy smokeboxes.

Soon we were on our way to Cork again, first crossing the River Suir and running alongside it for several miles. Then we began a long, slow climb through hilly, heathy country, our speed dropping to $7\frac{1}{2}$ m.p.h. until we made an unscheduled stop at Carroll's Cross, while the fire was made up. There were many more miles across high, bare, empty country before descending to Dungarvan, set beside a wide, calm estuary; many people left the train here. On to Fermoy, where the train halts beneath a handsome all-over roof, beside a long range of station offices. At Mallow, I noticed the unusual junction of the Killarney line, a mile or so south of the station. It connects only with the up main line, the points being power-worked from Mallow South box; down Killarney trains thus follow wrong-line working over the up main line from the station to the junction.

We were further delayed by engine trouble on the last lap to Cork; after a very slow climb to Mourne Abbey, we made a long, unscheduled halt. The journey ended with the steep descent into Cork, the final stretch in the tunnel which ends right at Glanmire Road Station. This is another roomy station ("open", like several others), with two through platforms under an all-over roof on a sharp curve, and three bays at the east end for the Cobh and Youghal trains.

Later journeys were to confirm rather than change first impressions. I went out to Cobh and back in a well-filled train of six-wheel carriages hauled by a small 2-4-2 tank. The train follows the estuary, close to the shore and the mudflats, and calls at several neat little stations before reaching Cobh, which has been rebuilt (for the Atlantic steamer traffic) with two long platforms and large, modern buildings.

Later (after visiting Bantry), I journeyed from Killarney to Dublin. Killarney is another curiosity among stations: it is a terminus, into which there is a straight run from the Mallow line, but trains from Tralee must run into a siding and back into the station. The train to Mallow was headed by a o-6-o tender engine, No. 175. At Headford Junction there was much activity; the Kenmare branch train, two coaches followed by a long string of goods wagons, was waiting at its platform. Then we climbed through hilly, rocky, bracken-covered country to a summit, and ran downhill to Rathmore, a typical crossing station with a solid station house of stone.

At Millstreet we were passed by an up express and took the loop, drawing up at a curious, low, narrow platform. A nun was joining the train here, and there was a crowd of nuns at the station, and more on the bridge, and many more on the bank of the cutting, beyond the station, all waving their handkerchiefs as we passed, while the engine whistled continuously in response. At Banteer (junction of the Newmarket branch, still in use for goods) we took the down platform in order to give a down express the straight run through the up loop.

At Mallow, I joined the Dublin express from Cork, headed by the powerful 4-6-0 *Maeve*. We had a fast run to Dublin, stopping only at Limerick Junction. The main stations we passed—Thurles, Ballybrophy, Portlaoise, Portarlington, and Kildare—all have solid, handsome Victorian buildings, well maintained. The country stations, with tall station houses and commodious goods sheds in stone or stucco, are equally impressive.

In Dublin, I visited all the termini. With the exception of Westland Row, they have fine stone buildings which are now rightly much admired by students of Victorian architecture, but inside all are very small, by English standards. All except the Great Northern side of Amiens Street have, as an incongruous touch, colour-light signalling—even tiny Harcourt Street, with its one platform and two sidings under an ample all-over roof. A trip to Howth gave me a taste of the Great Northern's roomy and well-filled railcars, with their wide views on all sides; and the enjoyment of the journey round the Hill of Howth on that company's electric tram route, the only one remaining in Ireland.

A journey to Dalkey on a Saturday afternoon showed me the intensive suburban service to Bray. The trains, though running every 15 min., were absolutely packed. I had taken the precaution to book first class, and the door was locked after I got in. But at Sidney Street a man (with a third-class ticket) got the door unlocked for him and his little boy, and the flood poured in. The guard's van was full; and people were jammed, seated or standing, in all the compartments, with as many as 24 people in one. Between Booterstown and Dun Laoghaire, where the line runs alongside the shore, not only were the sands dense with people, but the walls and ledges on the lineside were crowded with sunbathers, many of them dangerously close to the railway.

The final journey by the boat train from Harcourt Street to Rosslare showed me the old Dublin & South Eastern main line, with its combination of superb coastal and mountain scenery. Its signals still remind one of its separate identity; they are on lattice posts, and suggest the North British Railway; the old Great Southern & Western signals are more suggestive of the Great Central. The signal box at several D.S.E.R. crossing stations is a curious corrugated iron building, high up on one end of the station foot-bridge (the supplier, according to a plate on the box at Gorey, was the old firm of McKenzie & Holland). This journey was memorable for its crowded station scenes. Whole families had come down to speed the parting son or sister on the way to England, and to give the fond farewells which have long been all too familiar for Irish people. At Wexford, where the train proceeds slowly along the quay, beside the street, there were shouts and cheers from large crowds throughout our progress.

But what of Bantry? For my objective was this terminus of the old 5 ft. 3 in.-gauge Cork, Bandon & South Coast Railway. The line starts at Albert Quay station in Cork, across the river from the main line, but connected with the latter by a siding which crosses the river on one of the road lift-bridges. There is only one down train in the day, the 5.30 p.m. It was a substantial train of five bogie carriages, headed by a 4-6-0 tank, No. 468. I was in a semi-open carriage of former first-class stock, which was most comfortable. As befitted its importance, the train was very well filled, and its arrival at each station was clearly the event of the day.

Albert Quay Station has two platforms, a short all-over roof, plain but attractive stone buildings at the platform end, and a large goods yard and crowded engine shed. On starting the train plunges under a large iron signal box which straddles the main track and into a deep rock cutting. A long climb follows, with views northwards over the placid valley of the Lee, to Waterfall, the first stop and a crossing station. The line is worked by electric staff; and nearly every station is a crossing place, manned, apparently, by one man who serves as signalman, porter and clerk. At first, the country is hilly and well farmed, reminiscent of Devon.

Rock cuttings and a tunnel lead to Ballinhassig Station, and a wide, shallow valley in which is Crossbarry Station, formerly Kinsale Junction; the Kinsale branch, served by the outer face of the down platform, has had its rails taken up, though its grass-grown course is visible. The country continues to be high and open, but becomes more hilly and closed-in beyond Upton; rock cuttings, a viaduct, a view of a ruined castle down a wooded valley, romantic in a golden evening light, intervene before the line sweeps

By Train to Bantry

down to the valley of the Bandon, and reaches the town and station of that name. This, the largest station on the line, has an island platform, and was a scene of much activity. We crossed an up goods and cattle train, so long that its tail was standing on the loop points.

Another long run brought us to Clonakilty Junction, where the one-coach branch train and small tank engine were waiting on the other side of the down island platform; the layout here, as at other country junctions, is generous and complete. As we continued farther west, the country grew wilder, with rough pasture, hillsides covered with gorse and bracken or outcroppings of rock, and stacks of peat beside the fields. In the distance were the large, bare outlines of the Kerry mountains. At Drimoleague, where the 2-4-2 tank for our rear coaches, bound for Baltimore, was waiting just beyond the junction points, the train was divided, and we proceeded forward with three coaches only. Only when we neared Bantry did we see the sea—the broad expanse of Bantry Bay, 23 miles long between the mountains. The railway comes out high up above the bay and the town, but does not stop there; it makes a broad horseshoe sweep, round the town and round a hill, descending as it curves until it brought us down to the tiny station at the water's edge, with its yard and stone-built engine shed and, in former days, a line extending to a short pier. The sun was still warm and high, at 8.8 p.m.; and, indeed, it was still above the mountains at ten o'clock, when I returned to the station. The gate was locked: the coaches were parked at the platform, the engine standing silent outside the shed, and awaiting the return journey at eight next morning.

AUTHOR'S NOTE: *These impressions of railways in the Republic of Ireland were written in July 1952. Dieselization was then still far from complete, and the Great Northern Railway (Ireland) was an independent company. Some of the lines visited have since been closed. These include the whole of the Cork, Bandon & South Coast Railway, the Kenmare branch, Harcourt Street Station, Dublin, and the Hill of Howth tramway. The suburban services between Dublin (Westland Row) and Bray have been severely reduced.*

"The L.M.S. is running 33 special trains from Scotland. The first of these football expresses will bring to London over 11,500 Scottish supporters." The train must have been at least double-headed, and the carriages fitted with seats on the roof!

From the *"Evening News,"* April 1932

Private Stations

J. HORSLEY DENTON

ON FEBRUARY 26, 1963, in the bitterest winter in living memory, Parliament was working its way through a British Railways Bill. Plodding through dreary technicalities, the majority of Members might have been dozing in the warm security from the biting cold outside. But then they came to Clause 34 and the House awoke. They had reached that part of the Bill which dealt with "contractual obligations", and in no time at all, tempers rose and the two sides of the House of Commons found themselves once again poles apart in having to deal with deeply rooted legacies from the past.

It is either a lack of understanding of these roots or possibly an inability to convert them into modern terms that causes such political difficulty today. Modern thought decrees that the only way to undertake a new project, providing it is legal, is to find enough money to pay for it, and when something protrudes from the past that did not evolve from that method, it is labelled with such phrases as "Feudal System" and demands for its immediate abolition follow.

Private stations are frequently a striking example of this. Inevitably many have ceased to exist, but because the survival of some causes more controversy today than it did previously, they will be considered in the present tense. They are numerous; far too many in fact to catalogue here, and a look at a cross-section will show that the private station cannot even be accurately defined. Their origins vary considerably; they serve all kinds of people; they differ in their status; they are found all over the country, and in other countries too. Some date back to the early days of railways; some are of quite recent origin. Some were an embarrassment to the railway company from the day they opened; others are even tolerated in the vastly changed conditions of today.

What is a private station? It is easier to say what it is not. It is not necessarily a station from which the general public are excluded. There are stations which are privately owned which can be used by anyone. It is not necessarily a station which is in private ownership, for British Railways themselves own some from which the public are excluded. Perhaps we can get no nearer to a definition than to say that it is a station in which some degree of restriction or special privilege is always present. And therein lies their charm and interest.

Railways were promoted by all sorts of people. Some were rather like a local bus service to the nearest main line, the product of local enterprise and financed by the traders and small landowners of a town which the railway had passed by. Others were the result of skilful persuasion by professional promoters to acquire the necessary powers, land and finance by convincing all concerned that the proposed line was fully desirable and likely to be an excellent investment. In neither of these types of railway would one expect to find many private stations.

But the railways came to other places, wild areas of meagre population where their termini presented stark contrast with the busy industrial towns which grew busier and more prosperous as the railway network assisted their prosperity. Here the line was often a desperate social necessity and the promoters had no illusions of high dividends. Landowners in remoter parts found their workers leaving for the brighter lights and higher wages of the towns. They saw, too, the productive capacity of their estates wasted through lack of cheap transport.

Building a railway through such terrain did not attract the railway financier and the capital required was never raised with ease. Hard cash was only one form of currency. On a more promising railway project, the contractors often accepted shares in the line in lieu of part payment. On one with less prospects they wanted their money. But if cash had to be found for the works, the track, and the rolling stock (the buildings, perhaps, could wait), the line had at least an ally in the local landowners whom they served and in these areas where a single man might own many thousands of acres, special relationship between landlord and railway company was necessary to both parties. A private station was often the child of this relationship.

Without this alliance there was, on the one hand, the railway company, faced with a long detour round a big estate or a difficult Parliamentary battle against an influential adversary to fight for a right of way across it.

On the other hand was the landlord. To his vast estate a railway could be useful but the initial proposal merely threatened to cut his estate into two unworkable halves by a man-made eyesore; an intrusion, and possibly a dangerous one at that. To charge a high price for the land required would be unsatisfactory compensation for the inconvenience. The rich landowner would scarcely notice the money and the poor railway would scarcely— if at all—be able to pay it. Compensation must take a more practical form. The railway must be of use to him, and it was no use at all if it only traversed his land *en route* between towns miles away and did not enable him or his friends or possibly his servants and estate workers to use the trains that passed through. With the nearest public road often some miles distant, there was clearly no question of the public having access to a station that was primarily sited for the convenience of the "Big House", and so there came about that strange institution known as the private station.

But it must not be suggested that such a facility was the price the railway paid the landlord for the land they required. The privileges of a private station were sometimes but a tiny recompense for a wealth of assistance given to a line by sympathetic landowners, and the circumstances which gave rise to the creation of one of the most famous private stations, Dunrobin, provide an excellent illustration of this.

North of Inverness, the long and tortuous line to Wick and Thurso was an ambitious undertaking. The section between Bonar Bridge and Brora was authorized in 1865 as the Sutherland Railway. Construction reached no farther north, however, than Golspie, some two miles short of Dunrobin Castle, seat of the Duke of Sutherland. At this point, the Duke stepped in and not only financed the completion of the authorized part but promoted a private railway which took the line 17 miles farther to Helmsdale. Although the new line was properly authorized by an Act of 1870 (which also covered the transfer to the Duke of Sutherland's Railway of the previously in-completed six miles of the Sutherland Railway), construction was begun before powers were obtained. From Dunrobin to Gartymore, a mile or so short of Helmsdale, the line was opened in isolation and two daily trains ran for seven months before the through workings were possible, beginning in June 1871. With the completion of the through route, Dunrobin became a private station serving the castle. The station buildings were reconstructed in 1902 in ornamental half-timbered style designed by the estate architect. The Duke's private saloon was housed in a shed nearby. His private loco-motive did not, however, mar the sylvan landscape surrounding the station; it was shedded at Brora, and later at Golspie. Some years after the railway was opened, the Duke generously transferred his line to the Highland Rail-way, and the capital, believed to be about £300,000, was extinguished.

It is difficult to believe that even the most socialistic of critics would begrudge the Duke of Sutherland his private station. It was but small return for his oustanding generosity to the people of the Highlands. Without it, there would have been little hope of the railway reaching those remote parts; indeed, in the continuation northwards from Helmsdale, the Duke subscribed a further £60,000 to the Sutherland & Caithness Railway, which was £10,000 more than that subscribed by the "parent" Highland Railway. Eventually the public were permitted to use Dunrobin Station, although it remained technically a private one and carried that description in parentheses in timetable entries and elsewhere. This was unusual and in something like 8,000 entries in a railway pre-grouping gazetteer, Dunrobin appears to be the only entry carrying the "private" label. For the most part, private stations seem to have been very much "ex-directory", and even maps tended to pretend they did not exist.

This is particularly curious at places like Westmoor, on the Midland Railway line between Hereford and Three Cocks Junction, where there was a private station which was substantially built, and was, in fact, the only brick-built station on the whole line, the public stations being built of wood. Yet the one-inch Ordnance Survey map, perhaps rightly, gives not the smallest indication that a station existed there. The platform was extremely short but the buildings incorporated a main house block, a three-arched porch with slated roof and a further tower block topped by a curious half-hip. The station, built by agreement for Mr. G. H. Davenport, a local land-owner, had been out of use some time before the line closed at the end of 1962.

The possession of a private engine and coach in addition to private station is, of course, exceptional, but there were other concessions. The Marquess of Lansdowne, for instance, had a private halt at Black Dog on the Calne branch from Chippenham, and his rights did not stop there. The rail motor which worked the branch had a specially reserved compartment which could not be used by anyone else, unless the Marquess was not travelling on the line, and then only if all other accommodation was taken. By September 1952, the halt was appearing without restriction or special designation in the public timetables.

Appearances can be deceptive. Reverting to the Highland Railway, a platform was opened in 1878 to serve Borrobol shooting lodge, and at one time trains called only during certain periods of the year and by request. A similar platform was opened in 1908 to serve Salzcraggie Lodge which was also a "request stop", but neither of these were in any way private stations. On the other hand, there are cases of normal public stations being affected by certain private concessions. In 1899, the Duke of Beaufort made a covenant with the G.W.R. which required four trains each way to stop on each weekday at Badminton, and even after the local service between Bristol and Swindon had ceased, five express passenger trains continued to call. Hinton Admiral, on the Bournemouth line, was similarly endowed with the right to cause five-minute delays to expresses. It is probably these concessions that have caused more controversy in recent years than the existence of the purely private station. Particular anger was expressed in certain circles recently at the report that one conditional stop was for first-class passengers only. Yet it can be argued that it is better to delay a train for a more expensive fare than to risk pulling up for a price that does not even pay for the wear on the brake linings.

The actual ownership of a station is not necessarily indicative of its psychological status. Something akin to a private station seems to be implied by the *Aberystwyth Observer* in its issue dated May 22, 1904, when it reported that the Vale of Rheidol Railway had just opened Glanrafon Halt "partly as a compliment to Mr. Powell, Nant Eos, in return for his kindness to the contractor during the construction of the line". It suggests, perhaps, the railway equivalent of conferring the freedom of a city on one of its benefactors.

But mention of the Vale of Rheidol Railway is a reminder that while some stations are privately owned and yet permit the public to use them, others are owned by the railway company although created for private use. Military purposes sometimes give rise to the latter, and the Vale of Rheidol increased its revenue greatly from this source. Within the first ten years of opening, an annual summer camp was established some two miles from Devil's Bridge for several battalions of "regulars" which kept the railway busy. Later on, when territorials were encamped also at Lovegrove, the railway built a temporary halt there to cope with the traffic.

Many military establishments have their own station to which public access varies from normal to non-existent. In some cases, the railway itself is also a private one. The Admiralty purchased the whole of the Cleobury Mortimer & Ditton Priors Light Railway for £40,000 in recent years, but a line of this kind is mainly for the conveyance of goods, and seldom involves private stations in the accepted sense. Some are built, however, and the military occupation of the Shropshire & Montgomeryshire Railway saw the creation not only of several halts, most of them near to and replacing former civilian stations, but also a large four-road terminus at Nesscliff Camp. Although connecting with the normal public railways, such a line under war-time control was inevitably something of a law unto itself, and it is possibly deceptive to consider their stations in the same light as ordinary private ones. The workers' trains and the evening leave trains slithering down the 1 in 50 gradient into Shrewsbury Abbey Station must have brought many a wince from the professional railwaymen observing from the nearby Coleham yard who doubtless disowned the "Potts" (as it will always be known), especially on the odd occasion when the grade proved too much for the brakes and vehicles demolished buffers and wall, and finished up in the main road by the abbey.

There were other examples, such as the single-platform terminus of the private branch to R.A.F. Cranwell, but there were also interesting instances of partly private stations. In certain cases, the railway put in a station at a camp or aerodrome on the condition that some capital and running costs were borne by the customer. Cosford Aerodrome Station, also in Shropshire, was opened in 1938, and renamed "Cosford" in 1940, having normal public access from the road between the camp and the aerodrome. But even to this day certain connections with the R.A.F. there remain, one of which is the special production of a local timetable sheet for use in various parts of the camp. Surplus copies of this sheet have the heading "Trains from Cosford" cut off the top and minor stations between Wolverhampton and Wellington are able to display an excellent local sheet which would otherwise be absent on grounds of economy.

Change from private to public status sometimes has peculiar repercussions. The lover of legal battles would delight in the story of Crathes Castle private platform on the Deeside Railway. This was replaced in 1863 by the public station of Crathes on the site of the private platform and the necessary land was provided by the estate on the condition that all trains stopped there except privately chartered specials.

At the time, this would have been no great difficulty, as nearly all trains in the North of Scotland stopped at most stations anyway, but circumstances change. When the Royal Family was at Balmoral, the branch ran, in addition to the Royal Trains, a daily special for the couriers with their confidential despatches *en route* to and from London. But the trains were soon advertised in the timetables and ordinary passengers were carried, so that they ceased to be special in the strict sense of the term. In 1883, Sir Robert Burnett, who had recently succeeded to the Crathes Estate, pointed out that neither the "specials" nor the afternoon down Sunday train were calling at Crathes, and demanded that the agreement should be enforced. Getting no satisfaction from the railway company, he went to the Court of Session, and there the railway successfully claimed that both the couriers' trains and the Sunday ones were subsidized services and not therefore fully under its control. Sir Robert was not satisfied with this and took the matter to the Lords, who reversed the judgment and thereafter both types of train had to call at Crathes, although there was no mention of the fact in the time-tables.

The conversion of a private station into a public one is inevitably rare. For the most part, private stations are inaccessible to large numbers of the public, and many of them must have proved a great deal more advantageous to the estates they served than to the railway who stopped its trains for an economically inadequate number of fares. The right to stop any train became an increasingly severe penalty upon a company as services developed, and this was particularly so at Boreham, on the Eastern Counties Railway, about three miles east of Chelmsford. The opposition of Sir John Tyssen Tyrell, Bart., was only bought off by legal agreement to provide a station to serve Boreham House and by giving him the right to stop any train there for the duration of his life. This was in 1843. As the years passed, Sir John's rights became more and more of an embarrassment to the railway and repeated efforts were made to terminate or at least modify them. But he stuck to his guns and all attempts failed. He died on September 19, 1877. Nothing was done until after the funeral on the 21st; but the very next day a gang of men was despatched to Boreham Private Station, and in no time at all it was demolished and every vestige obliterated.

Although it would appear that the majority of private stations were built to placate large landowners in the line of a proposed railway, there are many others of a vastly different nature serving factories, holiday camps, hospitals, and even cemeteries. Of the last mentioned, there was the special London Necropolis Company station at Brookwood Cemetery among others, and the railway funeral business even had its own London termini near King's Cross and Waterloo. Factories are served by private stations, and in a few cases there are works train services over lines closed to ordinary passenger service. Near Birmingham, the line from Old Hill through Halesowen to Northfield Junction had four daily trains conveying workers to and from the Austin Motor Company's works at Longbridge until 1958, even though the regular passenger service ceased in the 1920s. One works service was run, free of charge, by the C.W.S. Soap Works over the metals of the Manchester Ship Canal Company from the works to its private halt adjoining the former Cheshire Lines Committee station at Irlam. This ceased in 1959.

Even the Church makes use of private stations. At Bishop's Court, some 8½ miles from St. John's on the Manx Northern Railway, a private halt serves the residence of the Bishop of Sodor and Man, while in Italy is perhaps the most elaborate private station of them all. Entered through seldom-opened huge bronze doors in the city wall is the station of the Vatican, used only infrequently for the special train of some high Church dignitary.

The variety is endless. Every one reveals some oddity in the fascinating panorama of railways. Leave them by climbing the Festiniog Railway round tortuous curves to Tan-y-Bwlch. On the tightest of them all, originally only 116 ft. in radius, is the site of Plas Private Halt. Here the Oakley family had the right to stop all passenger trains. In 1875, this was extended to goods trains, for some were more convenient if less comfortable. Nearby was a tank, into which the railway delivered sea water for the Oakley family's swimming pool. All this was probably an operating nuisance—but it satisfied the landowner. It brought some business too. And railway business is hard to come by today.

OPENING DAY AT SOUTHWOLD

As with all else change came to the "White Hart" and its inmates, quietly, imperceptibly, and by reason of a toy railway that was to have gone to China, but settled down to spin a way from Halesworth to Southwold instead; passing the old house en route. All kinds of jokes were made about this little bit of mechanical civilization, particularly about the speed, or lack of it. It was said that passengers could get off, collect mushrooms and eggs, and then catch up with the train again. It ran hard by the inn, and one wonderful day the first train with roses round the engine was due to pass. They were all there, gathered on the bridge, for it was a rare occasion, perchance the turning point in their history. For the mayor and corporation of Southwold were on board! They all stood there, tensely expectant, gazing in the direction of their fine old church. Presently Mrs. Pasque addressed the missus thus in a solemn voice.

"Dew yew know, maa'm, I must gew hoom!"

"Go home, Mrs. Pasque, whatever for? It'll soon be along, and you have been waiting some time. It's a pity to miss it!"

"Yis, maa'm, I must gew. Dew yew know I ha' bin a-washin' this marnin', an' all my linen's a-blowing' about on my line. I'm feared as how that'll frighten the poor thing when thet come past!"

From Allan Jobson, *"Under a Suffolk Sky"*, Robert Hale Ltd., 1964

NOTE: *The 3 ft.-gauge Southwold Railway connected the holiday resort of Southwold with the East Suffolk line of the Great Eastern Railway at Halesworth, nine miles distant. It was opened in 1879, with locomotives and rolling stock said to have been intended for use in the Far East. Handicapped by a severe speed restriction and the break of gauge at Halesworth, the railway succumbed to road competition, and was closed in 1929.*

Railways of the Cordillera

ROBERT SALVAGE

ONE NIGHT in the 1850s, a prominent citizen of San Francisco boarded a ship in the harbour, taking care not to attract attention, and was soon being carried southward, away from a host of angry creditors. Although he himself was unaware of it at the time, the fleeing man, Henry Meiggs, who had made a fortune out of the rush to the newly-discovered goldfields of California and lost it again, was heading for a new career as one of the world's greatest, but least-known, railway engineers.

In the 1840s, another American, William Wheelwright, had started a steamship service down the Pacific coast to Chile, following it up by building a railway from the coast at Caldera to the mining town of Copiapó, 50 miles away. Meiggs may have travelled south in a Wheelwright ship—we do not know—but in 1855 he landed in Chile and looked round for something on which to exercise his undoubted talents. It was not long before he turned to railways and bridges, and by 1863 he was established and had completed the Wheelwright railway as far as Valparaiso. Thirteen years of railway building brought him back to fame and fortune again.

Still looking for fresh fields to till, Meiggs moved to Peru in 1868. Making friends with President José Balta, he obtained contracts for as many new lines as he could handle. In the south he built a line from Mollendo on the coast to Arequipa, 7,550 ft. above sea-level, and on to the junction at Juliaca and to Puno on Lake Titicaca, 12,541 ft. above sea-level. To the north, in central Peru, he built a line into the mountains from Callao towards Oroya and

94

Huancayo. Of these more later. Meiggs's friend Balta was assassinated in 1872, and Meiggs himself died, reduced again to poor circumstances, four years later. Colourful adventurer as he was, he has left much brilliant work behind him, and he seems to have been adept at dealing with politicians and handling the railway labourers. He was also in great demand among the ladies of Lima.

Meiggs was only one of the engineer-adventurers who brought the railways to the Andes. The Clark brothers, surveying a path for the telegraph over the mountains between Argentina and Chile in the late 1860s, came to the conclusion that their proposed route would equally well serve for a railway. In 1872 they put a scheme, with a request for a concession, to the two governments. Argentina responded almost at once, granting the concession in 1873, and Chile followed suit the next year.

From concession to building was a long step. The surveyors had to raise the money—and this was not easy. It was not until 1887 that work started on the eastern side of the divide in Argentina, and another two years were to pass before work could begin in Chile. The first section to open, 17 miles of line on the Chilean side, marked the temporary exhaustion of the funds. Work stopped in 1893, with 140 miles of line still to be built. Travellers were still bound to the coaches and mules which made the four-day journey over the Cumbre Pass between Mendoza and Valparaiso, and bulk goods still had to make the stormy trip round Cape Horn.

This was a time when the British were specially interested in South America, and the railway across the Andes, saving so much time and so many miles, was seen from London as a good business proposition. In 1896 the Transandine Construction Company was formed in London, to buy the section of railway already completed and to finish building over the rest of the route. Now the metre-gauge line was pushed ahead rapidly, climbing from Los Andes to Juncal by 1906, and to Portillo in 1908. At Caracoles the line enters the international tunnel through the ridge, with the boundary between the two countries running through its centre, at 10,515 ft. above sea-level. High above the tunnel—2,500 ft. higher—the great bronze figure of Christ stands on its pedestal at the head of the pass. On the easier Argentinian side the railway runs down to the wine centre of Mendoza in a fertile valley fed by the snow-waters of the Mendoza river. The through route was opened in 1910, when the tunnel was completed.

This international journey is still complicated, as we can see if we travel back from Mendoza to Chile. At Mendoza the traveller must change from the broad-gauge train, which has brought him across the Pampas from Buenos Aires, to a metre-gauge train. Hauled by a rack-and-adhesion steam locomotive, the train runs through the Mendoza River valley for some miles, and then climbs through a gorge towards Cacheata, 23 miles from Mendoza and 1,600 ft. higher. The train continues to rise through the valley for another 33 miles, when it emerges on to a high plateau. Still climbing, it crosses the plateau and enters rocky country beyond. In all, the railway climbs 5,300 ft. in the 90 miles from Mendoza to Punta Vacas. From here on the rack rail is frequently in use, and near Puente del Inca, named after a natural stone arch, 70 ft. long and 90 ft. wide, which spans the river, the passenger can catch his first glimpse of Aconcagua, at 22,834 ft. the highest mountain of the Americas.

The panorama of high peaks, towering under their blankets of snow, is lost as Puente del Inca is reached, 8,915 ft. above the sea, for the railway is now approaching the ridge itself, and only nine miles on, at Las Cuervas, 10,338 ft. above sea-level, the Argentine metals meet those of Chile, and steam gives way to electricity. A Swiss-built 2-6-6-2 locomotive takes the train over the next section, electrified between 1927 and 1942 at 3,000 V d.c.

From Las Cuervas the train plunges into La Cumbre tunnel, all but two miles long, and out into the open again at Caracoles. The line falls away with gradients as steep as 1 in 12 and here, as on the Argentine side, the track is protected by snow sheds in many places. In 25 miles the train descends 5,600 ft., leaving the rack section behind at Rio Blanco. Easier gradients take the line on to Los Andes, where the traveller changes once more to broad gauge for the run to Las Vegas and Valparaiso.

Six 1,100-h.p. three-car diesel-electric trains are being delivered to Argentina to take over the through Mendoza-Los Andes run from the existing steam and electric locomotive-hauled trains. Built in Hungary with British electrical transmissions and traction control equipment, the new trains are capable of climbing gradients of nearly 1 in 12 without using the rack rails. Every axle is motored and there is provision for automatic wheel-slip correction, ensuring that the available adhesion is used to the full.

Rheostatic braking, as well as air brakes and a special brake operating on the rack rail, is provided for use on the long, steep descents. A maximum speed of 50 m.p.h. can be reached, but on the descents speeds will be only 10 m.p.h. or so, and the air brakes will be applied automatically if speed rises above 15 m.p.h. The outer cars of the 150-ton trains will each have a 550-h.p. diesel engine supercharged for high-altitude work, and the centre car will incorporate a buffet.

This is a classic example of a railway climbing one side of a range, tunnelling through the ridge, and then descending the other side, but some of the railways of the Andes climb up and stay up, sometimes at fantastic heights. Such are the Meiggs railways in Peru, now run by the Peruvian Corporation.

The standard-gauge Central Railway was begun in 1870, leaving Callao, port of Lima, and climbing up through the valley of the Rimac, following a

The zigzag by which the Callao-Oraya line of the Central Railway of Peru climbs through the Rimac Gorge, at an altitude of nearly 9,000 ft.

A heavy freight train, headed by a Beyer-Garratt 2-8-2+ 2-8-2, crossing the Sumbay Bridge, 13,600 ft. above sea level, on the Arequipa-Puna line, in southern Peru

route originally planned by a Polish engineer, Ernest Malinowski, who was Engineer-in-Chief of the railway. (Meiggs was officially the contractor.) Meiggs used the same reversing station technique of gaining height that had been used on the Bombay Ghats some years before by British engineers, but he did it on a much grander scale. There were 21 of these zigzag inclines with reversing stations to get from one to the other, as well as 66 tunnels and 59 bridges. The cold, the rarefied air, and fevers carried off many men, and others had to be brought in from Chile. Chinese labourers were brought in from the coast, and proved themselves first-class workers. Henry Meiggs was an adept at handling a mixed labour force of this kind and work pressed ahead. In 1876, as his railway approached Chicla, 88 miles from Callao and 12,251 ft. above sea-level, Meiggs, then out of political favour, died.

In 1879 came war between Peru and Chile, and work on the railway had to stop. The four-year War of the Pacific, as it was called, coupled with several months of civil war, left Peru exhausted and miserable in defeat, and with some of her most valuable land lost. There was also a huge external debt. Some of the troubles were solved by the incorporation of the Peruvian Corporation in London in 1890. The Corporation took over the entire external debt of Peru in return for being handed the country's railways, and steamships on Lake Titicaca, for a period of 66 years. The agreement also included certain guano rights, free use of ports, and an annual subsidy. At first, subsidiary companies were formed to run each of the seven railways concerned, but the Corporation itself now runs them direct, having become the owner of the railways as a result of a later agreement. The whole of the Corporation's capital is now held by a Canadian company, and the head office is in New York.

With the Corporation's capital behind it, the work on the Central Railway continued, and it reached Oroya (12,225 ft.) in 1893, and Huancayo, a market town in the chief wheat-producing area of Peru, in 1908. The highest altitude is 15,692 ft., the summit being in the Galera tunnel, on the watershed between the Pacific and Atlantic oceans. From Ticlio, near the mouth of the tunnel, a branch built in 1901-2 to Morococha runs even higher into the mountains, reaching a height of 15,806 ft. at La Cima. A branch from La Cima to the Volcan mine reaches 15,848 ft., the highest altitude reached by any standard-gauge railway in the world and well above the 15,782 ft. of Mont Blanc, the highest mountain in Europe. Morococha is a large mining centre for lead, silver and copper, which is smelted at Oroya.

High as this central section of the line is, there is relatively little perpetual snow to obstruct the working of the railway, the Equator being so close to this part of the Andean Cordillera. There are, however, other natural obstacles to contend with, one being landslides in the rainy season. The builders, as we have seen, had to build many tunnels and bridges. These sometimes follow one another in quick succession. One which caused great trouble to the builders was the Infiernillo bridge, which spans a gorge from the mouth of one tunnel into another, so that a train bursts from blackness to give the traveller a glimpse of a deep canyon with a river below, bare rock walls towering above, and a road bridge on each side, before plunging into darkness again. This bridge is between San Mateo and Rio Blanco on the climb to the summit, but nearer the coast, between San Bartolome and Surco, is a bridge with an even more famous name, the Carrión Bridge.

The Carrión Bridge, which spans the Verrugas Canyon just over 50 miles from Callao, is 717 ft. long and is 264 ft. above the canyon floor. It is the third bridge on the site, the first having been swept away by a landslide in 1889, and the second having been dismantled as inadequate for the growing weight of traffic. The bridge takes its name from a young Peruvian doctor, Daniel A. Carrión, who sacrificed his own life during experiments to discover the cause of the Verrugas fever which was killing many of the railway builders. The doctor injected himself with the disease and died from it. His heroism is commemorated in many ways, of which this bridge is one of the best-known.

An unusual feature of passenger trains on this line is that they carry supplies of oxygen to administer to passengers who may suffer from *soroche*, or mountain sickness, because of the rarefied air at high altitudes. Today there is a good motor road between Lima and Huancayo, so that some traffic has inevitably been lost. There is still a good freight traffic, especially in ores and metals, and a place for the railway in the economy of the country.

Meiggs's (and the Peruvian Corporation's) other main railway, the Southern, has no parallel motor road and is therefore even more essential than its brother. It connects Matarani and Mollendo, on the coast, with Arequipa, in the shadow of the great volcano, El Misti, and then climbs on through the Western Cordillera to the 15,666 ft. summit at Crucero Alto. The line runs on from there to Juliaca, a junction station 296 miles from the coast, and at an altitude of 12,551 ft. From here one line turns northwards along the ridges to reach Cuzco, 210 miles away and the capital of the old Inca empire. With its host of well-preserved Inca buildings, Cuzco is a tourists' paradise. The railway runs at high altitude all the way to Cuzco, crossing the Eastern Cordillera summit at La Raya (14,153 ft.) and then falling to Cuzco itself at 11,008 ft.

The other line from Juliaca turns southwards to Puno, 30 miles on, and the main port at the northern end of Lake Titicaca. Here passengers change to a railway steamer, a remarkable thing to find on a lake at 12,500 ft. above sea-level. This is almost certainly the highest body of water in the world to be navigated by ships of any size. The first steamer of the lake fleet, the *Yavari*, was built in 1861, and was working up to a few years ago. It was carried up in sections into the mountains by mule, for the railway was not completed to Puno until 1876. There are more modern steamers on Titicaca now, and the passenger is carried the 120-mile length of the lake in about 10 hours and landed at Guaqui, some 60 miles from La Paz, capital of Bolivia.

Guaqui is in Bolivia, but the Guaqui-La Paz railway, built by the Bolivian Government in 1904, was purchased in 1910 by the Peruvian Corporation. This line is metre gauge, to conform with Bolivian regulations. A connecting railway along the lakeside from Guaqui to Puno has long been planned, but if it is ever built there will still be the difficulty of different gauges to overcome.

The Guaqui—La Paz line runs at over 12,000 ft. all the way, and at Viacha, just over 40 miles from Guaqui, it comes to the junction with the Arica–La Paz and the Antofagasta (Chili) & Bolivia railways. From El Alto, six miles from La Paz, the train is taken over by electric traction for the 1,500 ft. drop down to La Paz, in a deep valley nestling below the 21,200-ft. Illimani. The electric locomotives, built in Britain, tackle 1 in 14 gradients entirely by adhesion. They are 0-4-4-0 machines picking up current from an overhead line at 550 V d.c.

Until quite recently the Peruvian Corporation lines were worked almost entirely by steam, although there were some railcars for shorter runs. While steam is still the most important source of power, diesel locomotives and railcars are becoming more general, and the days of steam are probably numbered. The Southern Railway made the decision to start converting to diesel traction in 1956. It bought six 1,800 h.p. diesel locomotives, and found that though they had to be derated to as little as 1,320 h.p. because of loss of power at high altitudes they still compared very favourably with the steam locomotives.

The modernization programme, of which the diesels formed only a part, had to be restricted from 1958 to 1961, during a recession in the Peruvian economy, but things improved from then on, and the World Bank agreed, in 1962, to lend nearly £5 million to be used for railway improvements. The Export-Import Bank added nearly £3 million to this sum, and the Corporation ordered diesel locomotives, wagons and track materials to bring the railways up to modern standards. Enough has been said, perhaps, to show what remarkable lines these are, but their very daring in construction, and the terrain through which they pass, with its snow and other hazards, mean that maintenance is necessarily expensive.

It is the fashion for the visitor to South America to fly from place to place in these days, but such is the attraction of the high railways that many still ride them for pleasure. For one who knows the history of the railways it must be strange to sit back in the dining car as a train rumbles through the Cumbre tunnel and watch fellow diners eating calmly, all unaware of the near-miracle of the steel tracks on which they are moving through the roof of the Western world on their 36-hr. trip from coast to coast.

Far above stands the great bronze figure, looking down at the pass over which struggled men on foot, men with mules and horses, men with carts and coaches, and now—no longer a struggle—men in cars and lorries. Far down is the steel link which first brought swift communication between the two countries, a tie of which the Argentinians must have been thinking when they drew up the inscription at the statue's base: "Sooner shall these mountains crumble into dust than the people of Argentina and Chile break the peace which they have sworn to maintain at the feet of Christ the Redeemer".

The following letter was received by the Suggestions & Inventions Committee of the New Zealand Railways Department from a Chinese resident in the North Island:—"Seeing that the Railway is a plaid out thing and every Little good to the Public as a carrying Concern, I am sure it would be better to scrap the whole turn out, sell the land to Chinan for a Market garden. Let them have the Engines and trucks to cart their cabbage to Market with hoping this will meet your favour."
From "The New Zealand Railways & Harbours Magazine," 1931

HIGH SPEED VETO IN 1899

The forthcoming extension of the Southern Region electrification to South-ampton and Bournemouth recalls a fascinating story of the way in which the first attempt to run a high-speed express on this route was nipped in the bud. In the spring of 1899, Sam Fay (afterwards Sir Sam) rejoined the London & South Western Railway, after an absence of some years, and was appointed Superintendent of the Line. Full of enthusiasm for his new post, Fay ran a non-stop train from London to Bournemouth one Sunday in 1 hr. 50 min. He then prepared a schedule for new weekday expresses covering the 108-mile journey in 1 hr. 55 min. in the down direction, and 2 hr. in the up. The service was to have begun on July 1, but when details of the timetables were made known, Sir Charles Scotter, who had recently retired as General Manager, and had become Deputy Chairman, summoned Fay and told him not to do it again. He is alleged to have said, most emphatically, "Not in my time, Fay, not in my time." The new expresses made their first journeys on July 1, but with the schedule slightly eased to 2 hr. 5 min. in each direction.

Three Faces of Independence

R. K. KIRKLAND, B.A., A.K.C.

FOR THE OLDER GENERATION of railway enthusiasts the darkness fell in 1923. Learned editors of railway periodicals were then faced with the need to convince otherwise sane and well-informed people that there was no longer a London & North Western Railway, and therefore it was no longer proper to print that name as a heading to current news from Crewe. For those who grew up after that awful day, the transition in 1948 from four groups to a unified system came as less of a traumatic experience.

Four groups . . . and what else? A round-up of independent railways, joint lines and other anomalies that survived until 1948 makes a surprisingly long list, even though modest by comparison with the schedule to the Railways Act 1921. Such is the foreshortening of time past that some of these independents are now all but forgotten while the pre-1923 names live on. Only the other day a walk down Aldersgate revealed window cards in business houses requesting calls from the road carters of the S.E.C.R. and the G.N.R., an eloquent testimony to the quality of pre-grouping cardboard!

Most of the railways that escaped the net in 1923 did so for reasons of penury and local interest. They were, to borrow the French legal phrase, *lignes d'intérêt local*, often built or operated under the provisions of the Light Railways Act 1896, a last pathetic fling of the railway building age when the motor vehicle was ceasing to be a curiosity. Since they lived out solitary, starving lives, nobody, even at Government behest, was anxious to swallow them up. The classic examples that so survived to blazon their own odd initials throughout the grouping era were the members of the family of light railways sired by Colonel Stephens, a man who combined competent engineering with a child-like love of his wayward stud of engines and could never bring himself to scrap one. Even the oldest might have some bits that would come in useful, so was put out to grass against the day when *Hesperus* might need a new cab, or *Pyramus* a new buffer beam.

For some reason, the Kent & East Sussex and the Shropshire & Montgomeryshire Railways seem to have captured the imagination of the enthusiast. Fewer people ventured on to the farthest east of the Stephens domains, the East Kent Railway. Perhaps this is no wonder, for the passenger train service was more than usually eccentric. Did the nearness to France account for the fact that one of the two daily services involved a London departure at 3.13 a.m.? Yet the East Kent Railway served a useful purpose during its short life and developed a personality of its own, for it was a coal-carrying line set oddly in the bleaker, chalkier end of the Garden of England.

The history of the Kent coalfield is complex and in some respects Byzantine. Few of the pits that were sunk justified the Klondike-like superlatives used to describe their prospects. Some took other turnings and produced bricks or supplied water to Margate; some just decayed into early dereliction. Only four survive today, of which only one was served by the E.K.R. and still accounts for the few miles that survive for coal traffic. Though the East Kent Light Railways Company, to give it its full official title, dated from 1911, actual construction was slow to start and was handicapped by the First World War, which shattered the ambitious schemes of Anglo-French mining development interests.

On paper, the E.K.R. could look heroic, with authorized lines filling up many blanks on the railway map of the Canterbury-Dover-Thanet triangle. The reality was somewhat less heroic. Only a line from Shepherds Well (otherwise Shepherdswell, or, in Saxon, Sibertswold), on the old Chatham & Dover main line, running north-east to a muddy "port" on the River Stour at Richborough, and a long branch from Eastry to Wingham were actually constructed, together with a few short branches to collieries, only one of which, that to Tilmanstone, was to be significant in later years. Though the word "branch" has been used to describe the Eastry–Wingham section, that became in later years the main line, leaving the Richborough route in grass-grown slumber.

The roseate dreams of its promoters were shattered by war and slump, so that the memory that lives on is of the line in the 1930s, when the guard of the twice-daily mixed train would all too often enter "nil" on his loading sheet for passenger traffic, and a few baskets of soft fruits in season would suddenly double the line's earnings compared with a month before. At its

best, the afternoon train from Shepherdswell would drowse along in the
sun with one railway enthusiast in its old L.C.D.R. six-wheeler. Should
the odd *ami du chemin de fer* venture over from Calais, he would find himself
threatened with *une amende de 40 shillings* if through fright or boredom he
should venture to play with the *signal d'alarme* that the Chatham had bequeathed as part of the furniture and fittings, along with the monogrammed
carpet. At each little station or halt, the ritual slowing down was followed
by a wave of the guard's hand to avoid any unnecessary wear of the brake
blocks. Only occasionally would a stop be made (and then not always at an
official place) for a farm worker and bicycle to come aboard for a few miles.

So over the bare chalk downs and then to the flood plain of the Stour,
until in a jungle of bushes the line petered out at Canterbury Road, Wingham—which was where the money had run out. The neat little town of
Wingham rejoiced in no fewer than three stations, but since the line was a
late comer and skirted the buildings, even Wingham Town was a good walk
to where the pubs are (and there are plenty for the size of place). Besides,
who would go boxing the compass on the E.K.R. when the latest thing
in elegant Tilling-Stevens petrol-electric buses would drop you in the
centre of Canterbury in under the hour?

But on went the E.K.R. by sheer inertia, waiting for the Kent coal
industry to wake up. The colourful personalities faded from the scene. In
coal, Mr. Arthur Burr gave place to Pearson, Dorman Long, and thence to
the anonymity of the National Coal Board. Col. Stephens's successor, Mr.
W. A. E. Austen, went about the practical business of being Receiver and
Manager, with no inclination to call the engines by their pet names, until
British Railways inherited the lot, dreamed up five-digit numbers for them
and then scrapped them before their new numbers were painted on. (The
E.K.R. itself produced the statistical oddity of engine No. 100 in a stock of
nine.)

The locomotive shed at Shepherdswell was more substantial than most
Col. Stephens sheds; moreover, it housed only steam, for the eccentric
back-to-back pairs of buses never graced this line, whose goods and coal
traffic needed more substantial motive power. If nobody important was
about (for E.K.R. public relations were not exactly Madison Avenue), a look
inside the shed was always a prelude to a journey. A mixed bag, though
Stirling six-coupled tender engines were the mainstays of traffic. Years
before, an archaic Beattie "Ilfracombe Goods" had lived there, but in later
years the L.S.W.R. was represented by an Adams 4-4-2 tank that Stephens
picked up as a bit of First World War army surplus stores. (Did he know a
brother officer who knew a man who . . . ?) This engine even outlived the
E.K.R., to rejoin its two fellows on the Lyme Regis branch and then to go

to the Bluebell Railway, having served five civilian railway administrations, as well as its war service.

Another Nine Elms veteran, although somewhat modified with bits of a Whitland & Cardigan engine, was a Beattie-period saddle-tank (whose counterpart on the K.E.S.R. was called "the big engine"), which had for saddle-tank company a contractor's style import from another Stephens domain, the Weston, Clevedon & Portishead Railway, where she had picked up the name *Walton Park*. Apart from this rather unimaginative flourish, the E.K.R. did not follow the Stephens-group habit of decking engines with names like *Pyramus* and *Thisbe* (or his other favourite, *Hesperus* —a nice name for a wreck?).

Modern times were represented by a solid-looking side-tank built in 1917 for government service, of a class of 0-6-0s which also found their way into the Kent collieries and survived to become N.C.B. property. Though the engines were officially green, years of penury had brought most of them to wear the "invisible" variety of that colour. Coaches might be a faded red or bottle-green, equally faded, but when after the Second World War the few remaining passengers were treated to the luxury of a L.S.W.R. corridor bogie coach, this emerged smartly painted in very S.R. green, with the company's title in full.

One could go on about the variegated tickets, with a separate colour for each station, or about that macabrely named halt Poison Cross, or reminiscent detail of fly-shunting with passengers still aboard. But in the autumn of 1948 the passenger service vanished, to be followed shortly by all but the Tilman-stone coal trains. Never a substantially engineered line, the E.K.R. has all but disappeared from the face of the landscape, though its course can be traced through the weeds and shows still like a scar from the air.

One day, when we enter the Channel Tunnel in a futuristic electric train, we shall spare a thought of what might have been, and see in dreams a Beattie saddle-tank trundling uncertainly with a six-wheel coach towards the tunnel terminal, whose walls bear a timetable showing but two trips a day and exhorting the reader to "Support the local line", with much more about using British steel and coal rather than imported rubber and petrol. Colonel Stephens would not have *liked* a Channel Tunnel, but he would have tripped over its very portal if he had built all he intended the E.K.R. to be.

Coal in rural Kent was a very different thing from coal in County Durham, but where there is coal there are railways and they are usually railways of character. None were more so than the many colliery lines of that area where British railways began. These were no mere sidings but lengthy cross-country lines in their own right and sizeable studs of locomotives served

A Sylvan Scene in South Devon: the up "Torbay Express", with No. 5011, Tintagel Castle, *leaving Greenway Tunnel, between Kingswear and Churston*

Train from Whitehaven to Penrith headed by former London & North Western Railway 0-6-0 running beside Bassenthwaite Lake

An Adams 4-4-2 tank on the steeply-graded Lyme Regis branch

them. One that shall serve as example for them all was the South Shields, Marsden & Whitburn Colliery Railway, for this had a personality all its own. Indeed, it was a split personality, for closely linked together under the banner of the Harton Coal Company were a group of mineral lines and the multi-purpose railway to which the ponderous title quoted above truly applied. This latter boasted a passenger service open to the world at large and, in its later years at least, the sanction of a Light Railway Order to confirm its respectability.

This was the railway that the casual traveller or visiting enthusiast saw, but tucked away from public view was what amounted almost to an urban freight network, electrically operated in highly un-English fashion. Was, we have said, but happily the whole lot still *is*, though now a domain of the National Coal Board, only the public passenger trains having vanished from a line that otherwise remains busy enough.

Though the authorities of South Shields bravely advertise the claims of the town as a seaside place and do their best to present a brave front to the sea, the workaday world hangs rather much about it. Though new buildings abound, past privations still show over-much in sooty brick walls and the kind of paint which, having been chosen not to show the dirt, has given up the struggle by becoming dirt itself. Yet the sands are genuine enough for bucket and spade work (weather and circumstances permitting) and if at the end of the day you can take home some lumps of coal from the beach, that is a better reward than the tarry mess left on your clothes by the beaches of some give-themselves-airs resorts on the genteel South Coast. Nowadays the posters in the Co-op offer 14 days on the Costa Brava, but it was not always so; a sunny day spent at Marsden Rocks was remembered all the more for the fact that in truth the day was about all there was to spend.

So it came to pass that some of the busiest traffic on the line from South Shields to Marsden was not the coal for which it was built but parties of pleasure-seekers, taking their fun economically but not usually sadly, however they might look when they used the same trains on the other days of the fortnight (for in those days the pay did not always come weekly). On working days the trains ran at the odd times of day and night that are even now one of the many things that set even the urban coal miner apart from his fellow men.

Since home-going men in their pit dirt could be no respecters of cushions, the coaching stock was rugged, even by the not very exacting standards of paddy trains. The motley collection of four- and six-wheelers came not from the polite neighbouring North Eastern, but from spartan Scottish lines like the Great North or the North British, that even knew what a fourth-class coach should look like. Good enough, they seemed, in the eyes of colliery companies that had not yet seen the need for pit-head baths. A few compartments had a sort of "front parlour" status and were unlocked only for non-pitman passengers of outward respectability, but as bus services lured away such travellers, even this distinction faded and one might easily find that the only concession to comfort was a few surviving springs that had long since lost their attendant upholstery.

In pre-bus days, however, people took things like that more philosophically, and the Marsden Railway saw many a school treat, club beano or family day out, with the compensation that, however rough the going, it didn't break the bank, and there was therefore something to spare for tea and buns, or a drop of ale, according to taste, when you got there. That this might sometimes lead to indelicate happenings on the return trip mattered less than it might have done in the Super Pullman Luxury Coaches that took such trade when better times came.

By contrast with the Hogarthian aspect of the passenger stock, the locomotives had an air of normality, born of the fact that most of them were six-coupled tender engines purchased from the N.E.R. or its successors, and thus similar in aspect to many that passed through the area on main-line metals. In earlier times, there were some eccentric oddments, such as a 2-2-2 well-tank of Furness Railway origin. Wagons, too, were native in character, and most were of the high sloping-sided type popular in the North-East; many of them did not circulate beyond the confines of the Marsden Railway and Harton Coal Co. lines.

Anonymity is an odd characteristic to find in a station, but Westoe Lane, the terminus of the passenger service in the town of South Shields, did its best to conceal its location and its functions. The diligent can still find it, in a side street, but even in passenger service days no nameboards or notices adorned its grimy brick, there being a strong presumption that those who penetrated so far had such a good knowledge of geography that they knew where they were already. At the Whitburn Colliery end, matters were little better, since what looked like an exit footbridge led into the output end of the pithead bath installation. There is no record of any unwary passenger being processed in reverse through the baths to emerge grimy at the other end.

Even more "secret" and shy was the associated Harton Coal system of electrified freight lines, for the traveller by passenger train scarcely saw them, except for the overhead wires that came into Westoe Lane station, where the occasionally observed electric locomotive suggested by its number that it was no isolated phenomenon. British coal mining is largely a rural industry, but exceptionally, South Shields had pits among the houses right in the town. These pits were connected one with another, and with staithes on the riverside, by an intricate network of private railways, most of which still survive to wind their way past the cemetery and between the backyard walls of the terrace houses. To their lasting credit, the civic fathers of South Shields saved washday from being a completely hopeless struggle by requiring the colliery company to electrify these urban routes, on which the existence of steep gradients would have otherwise occasioned a high level of cinder fall-out had the Gateshead goods engines been left to serve them.

In 1906, there was little British experience of electric traction for freight work (though the N.E.R. was early in the field on the nearby Newcastle Quayside branch), so German technical assistance and equipment filled the bill. The original overhead smacked strongly of so many German tramways and light railways, with double contact wires very close together, supported from lattice girder standards. The steeple-cab electric locomotives looked as though they had come out of early catalogues of a prominent German model railway supplier, as well they might, since all but two came from that country. Though their handling of trains on the gradients was altogether smog-free, it was not without fireworks as their bow collectors bounced on and off the wires. Though this was largely unseen by the passer-by, the groan of motors from behind a wall as a coal train rumbled along one of the narrow cuts between the houses suggested that something a bit unusual was afoot.

In its final form, the railway system associated with the Harton group of collieries was well developed and efficient, the ultimate development of the "Mark 1" type of railway, namely, a line from a colliery to a port of shipment. As an integral part of mining activity, it passed in 1947 to the newly-formed National Coal Board, which, we may surmise, expressed collective surprise that its many inherited ancillary activities included the operation of a public passenger railway service—a year before the nationalization of railways as such! For a while, the casual passenger could continue to use the trains, receiving a pre-nationalization ticket overprinted with a N.C.B. rubber stamp, but the new owners were not long in withdrawing (in 1953) this facility from the general public without any formalities, the relevant Act of Parliament not having included among its many clauses any protection for the officially recognized paddy train rider.

Otherwise the lines continue to flourish though the old Gateshead-built tender engines have given place to the workmanlike, though hardly handsome, "Austerity" saddle-tanks which the N.C.B. has favoured to the extent of commissioning further examples to this design to supplement the war-time specimens bought in the "Government surplus" market. On the electric division, five new locomotives from English Electric have reinforced the ageing Germans, without really altering the unique character of the network, which even captivated the new owners sufficiently for the electric lines to form part of a "newsreel" type of film on the Board's activities. There is plenty more coal to come out yet, so long may the sparks fly as the wagons rumble down to the Tyne whence the coal still follows the route of centuries past, coastwise to London.

Though Britain made a substantial contribution to the early history of electrical engineering, this was not too apparent when electricity was applied to railway working in the first few years of the present century. We have seen how German techniques were used by the Harton coal lines, as a rare manifestation of electric traction for freight haulage: in urban passenger service the influence of the United States was more evident. Nowhere was this more striking to the eye than on the Mersey Railway, which in 1903 changed itself from a sooty and woe-begone steam underground (and under-water) railway into a rapid transit system which ranked in efficiency and usefulness with anything that American cities could show. The early history of the Mersey Railway includes a "near miss" at being a pneumatic tube, through which passengers would have shot like the change in a department store, and some very fine civil engineering in the construction of the tunnel under the river between Liverpool and Birkenhead.

Steam traction, provided by the gallant efforts of 0-6-4 and 2-6-2 tank engines, was obviously far from suitable for such closely enclosed conditions, and not calculated to draw passengers away from the fresh air of the ferry decks, except when fog reproduced on the river the habitual conditions of the Mersey Railway's tunnels. The services from the low-level station at Liverpool Central to Rock Ferry and Birkenhead Park cried out for electric trains, to such an extent that the company boldly decided in 1900 that electrification was the only alternative to bankruptcy. The then British Westinghouse Co. was given the complete job, which included the provision of a power station and, not least important, a complete "spring clean" of the tunnels.

If we now say that the electrification followed conventional lines, we merely emphasize how much the success of rugged direct-current, low-voltage equipment on the Mersey and other early lines influenced subsequent British policy in suburban electric traction, for there was then little British experience of its use under such exacting conditions of service. To the ordinary traveller, the electric trains that took over the Mersey service in May 1903 bore no resemblance to orthodox British practice. Gone were the undersized compartment coaches, and in their places came saloon stock with end doors, massive hooded clerestory roofs, lattice guards between the

Restored Highland Railway 4-6-0 No. 103 and Great North of Scotland Railway 4-4-0 No. 49, Gordon Highlander, *running light through Barrhill, Ayrshire, on their way to work a railway enthusiast's special from Stranraer on April 13, 1963*

No. 53807, the last-surviving Somerset & Dorset 2-8-0, at Bath shed after its final day in service, September 6, 1964

Pacific No. 60156, Great Central, on the now-demolished turntable at King's Cross

vehicles which one had never thought necessary in steam days when the
space between coaches was wider, and even a new terminology in which
these magnificent saloons had to be referred to as "cars".

As might be expected, traffic grew and much of it was exchanged with
the L.N.W.R. and G.W.R. joint line at Rock Ferry, while even more
passengers used the end-on junction with the Wirral Railway at Birkenhead
Park, where the two companies indulged in the luxury of a joint station,
with special staff cap badges. Grouping in 1923 left the Mersey independent
and still flourishing, with its smart maroon livery and distinctive crest
contrasting more and more with the degenerating appearance of the main-
line trains with which the Mersey connected, especially at Birkenhead Park.
Belatedly, the L.M.S.R. decided to electrify the services in the Wirral
peninsula and came to terms with the Mersey Railway whereby L.M.S.R.
electric trains of tube-like steel stock ran to Liverpool Central, and the stately
Mersey antiques, as they appeared by 1938, provided the service to New
Brighton.

A journey on the Mersey had many distinctive features, apart from the
distinctive rolling stock, which was always beautifully maintained, even in
its old age, and ran more smoothly than much more recent electric trains
in the South are wont to do. The crypt of Liverpool Central Station con-
cealed some technical achievements, such as the early automatic operation of
points so that reversal of trains could take place without the intervention of
signalmen. One of the most notable features, however, was the neat three-
colour bull's-eye light installation in the long subway, to indicate the
destination of the next departing train. As the appropriate colour lit up, so
the Rock Ferry passengers would break into a trot and sweep out of the way
the unhurried New Brightonians whose train was not yet signalled. The
intermediate stations at James Street, Liverpool and Hamilton Square,
Birkenhead also boasted similar aids to navigation.

At platform level, these stations are still distinguished by their cavernous
size, which seems the more enormous to passengers used to the tight dimensions of London tubes. The effect was heightened by the Mersey Railway's
use of enamel bull's-eye station name signs which towered above the passenger and were lost in the darkness. The cult of vastness also extended to
Mersey Railway lifts, for those at Hamilton Square in particular were
enormous, and in early days worked to a timetable in connection with
trains. Unlike the London tube lines, the Mersey favoured hydraulic lifts,
which were bequeathed from steam days; Hamilton Square Station still
boasts a fancy campanile whose purpose was to get a good head of water for
lift operation. Preoccupation with water was inevitable in a submarine
railway, and pumping the tunnel dry was a constant problem whose costs

were slightly offset by selling the water to Birkenhead Corporation for use in the municipal swimming baths.

The Mersey Railway was important enough to come under the control of the Railway Executive Committee at the outbreak of war in 1939, though the distinctive features remained largely unchanged and the very unlike Mersey and L.M.S.R. rolling stock kept mostly to their traditional services. Occasionally, however, the modern L.M.S.R. trains would turn up at Rock Ferry or the vintage Mersey cars would essay a coast-to-coast trip across Wirral to West Kirby. As the "Blitz" prompted more people to move out of the cities, travelling conditions at peak hours became more London-like, and the spacious, club-lounge atmosphere of Mersey first-class cars was compromised by strap-hangers.

Unlike its near neighbour, the Liverpool Overhead Railway, the Mersey was included in the scope of nationalization, which was inevitable in view of its close relationship with the L.M.S.R. Wirral services. At first, the old autonomy seemed to remain, for posters and other official documents acknowledged the existence of "London Midland Region, Mersey Section", into which the Wirral lines were thrown, for all the world as though it were the Mersey Railway that had done the absorbing, and not vice versa.

Lovers of the picturesque feared for the future of the ageing but still well-kept Mersey stock, so it came as no surprise when new stock, to the 1938 L.M.S.R. design, came to replace it. In the process, the fourth rail vanished from the Mersey line, and with it the intriguing arrangements at Birkenhead Park for switching from three-rail to four-rail working and vice versa. In 1938 these complexities had seemed fearsome, though they pale beside the sophisticated voltage-changing devices of modern alternating current traction. The original American-style cars, together with some very noble later variants on the design, were quite unceremoniously scrapped, for the present concern with preservation of historic rolling stock was not then officially acknowledged. It is a thousand pities that one of the Mersey motor cars was not retained, for examples of that early period of American-influenced rolling stock would have filled an unfortunate gap in our museums. Not even the normally enlightened London Transport and Underground administrations have contrived to keep a complete and typical car from that important formative period.

If the rolling stock of the Mersey services is now more commonplace, the distinctive architecture and atmosphere of its stations survive as something quite unlike the rest of the London Midland Region. By contrast with either the East Kent or the South Shields, Marsden & Whitburn Colliery Railways, the Mersey remains an important passenger line whose significance grows as suburban development in Wirral proceeds and road tunnel congestion becomes daily more impossible. If ever the local authorities of the Merseyside area can agree on a common traffic and transport policy (and one is bound to admit, on the evidence of history, that agreeing one with another is not the strongest feature of Merseyside authorities), the rail link beneath the river is bound to be developed further as part of a wider suburban electric system. It is an asset of immense value that should be carefully guarded and not allowed to become a football in local politics merely because it is in an area where there are also politics in local football. Even now the old independence might assert itself, and the Mersey Railway, with its Wirral dependencies might hive off from the British Railways network to become the core of a Merseyside urban rail network.

Such independence would add to the gaiety of the contemporary transport scene, which is too often afflicted with excessive uniformity for its own unattractive sake. Perhaps we can be forgiven the nostalgia with which we look back to the former independent survivals, and wish that the legislators of 1947 had been less completely briefed so that one or two minor lines might have been forgotten. Ironically, Britain, above all the country of what the French describe as *la libre concurrence* in matters of railway construction, now has fewer independent lines than countries such as Germany and Switzerland which were early practitioners of nationalization. It is food for thought indeed that Switzerland, which has in practice one of the best integrated systems of transport of all, in which diverse kinds of service make perfect connections one with another, has more independent railway operators than one would believe possible in such a compact area. Perhaps second thoughts may yet suggest that the local railway, operated under local auspices, may have a place in our transport scene on a more utilitarian basis than the laudable, but primarily entertaining, activities of the preservation societies.

"WE'RE POOR LITTLE LAMBS"

Scene: Fenchurch Street Station in the morning rush hour, with only one barrier open and City workers forced to crawl in single file past a very conscientious ticket collector.
Voice from the back of the large crowd: "Any more for the sheep dip?"
"Peterborough", in "The Daily Telegraph"

"There's a Lot of Old Stuff!"

L. C. JOHNSON

THE WORDS "old stuff", often spoken in a rather contemptuous tone, have sometimes heralded the discovery of hidden treasure. In some dark vault, or back room to an office, in dusty attic, or dilapidated store-room, long forgotten, except perhaps by some aged servant or caretaker, have lain papers, books and documents which have proved to be veritable mines of historical information. Exciting discoveries of this sort have frequently rewarded the diligent probing of archive-minded folk, pursuing a mere hint or positive clue as to the whereabouts of historical records.

In the world of transport, a great deal of such material was stored in many places, having escaped the devastating salvage drives of the war years, and the demands for more storage space for current papers. To their everlasting credit, too, many of the transport undertakings had followed a deliberate policy of preserving and recording valuable archives relating to the inception and subsequent development of their companies, and had on occasions made such papers available to researchers and students.

When the National Coal Board was formed under the Coal Industry Act 1946, the records of the various undertakings were made "public records", with control vested in the Public Record Office. Although similar provision was excluded from the Transport Act of 1947, the Government was fully aware of the historical importance of the records of these nationalized undertakings, and soon urged their preservation on the same principles as the archives at the Public Record Office. The British Transport Commission embraced railways, docks, harbours, river and canal navigations, and organizations such as the Railway Clearing House, together covering 250 years of transport enterprise, a period unparalleled for the vital expansion of our national economy.

In November 1947, the then newly-formed Commission invited the chairmen of the main-line railway companies and the London Transport Board to consider the best means of preserving the records which would pass to the Commission a few weeks later, when nationalization became effective. The Commission had already formed its "Executives", and these, together with the long-established road and transport undertakings and independent canal companies, discussed the whole question of preservation. Lord Greene, then Master of the Rolls, proposed that advice should also be sought from the Public Record Office. It was inevitable that, in the general reorganization and upheaval of nationalization, there would be a grave danger that records might be dispersed, or even destroyed, and the concerted effort of all concerned to ensure the safe keeping of the valuable documents was a most commendable action.

A special committee was formed to examine the situation, and its report, submitted in August 1950, recommended the establishment of two new departments within the Commission—the Historical Relics Department, under a Curator, and the Historical Records Department, in the charge of an Archivist. The two departments were established in July 1951. The present writer was appointed Archivist to the Commission, and gained invaluable insight into the principles governing archive administration by a period of study at the Public Record office through the kind offices of Sir Hilary Jenkinson, then Deputy Keeper.

It is not easy in some cases clearly to define the difference between a relic and a record, but for working purposes it was agreed that if the main interest and importance of any item lay in its physical form it should be treated as a "relic", and that written or printed matter should be classed as a "record". Borderline cases must occur, and the Curator and the Archivist arrange between themselves as to the custody of such items. Cross-references are made in their respective catalogues.

A large steel and reinforced concrete building, at 66 Porchester Road, Bayswater, London, W.2, was available for the headquarters of the Archivist's department. This building dates from the early years of the present century, and is of some historical interest because it was one of the first of its kind. Its storage capacity is considerable, but it required some internal rearrangement. Existing equipment had to be adapted to some extent, but new fittings were gradually installed, and the repository made serviceable for the staff and for researchers. The lighting and ventilation are good, and the fire risk is low. The launching of this new enterprise was quite an exciting adventure. It was an asset to have the assistance of the great transport system, for furnishings, as well as records, required transport on a large scale. Everyone was exceptionally helpful, and researchers, to whom the whole project was of considerable interest, were early marshalling themselves for invasion.

The Great Western Railway Company, always a pioneer in the preservation of valuable records, passed over with the building in Porchester Road a large number of archives, including its own valuable minute books. This was fortunate, for when staff had been appointed, there was already in the repository a nucleus of archive material upon which to test the efficiency of the new system of record keeping which had been devised. This had been planned with great care, and on a scale that would accommodate documents in vast quantity, not to be estimated by number. Things were shaping splendidly; the system worked smoothly and well, but there were administrative preliminaries still to be worked out.

One curious feature of human nature so often asserts itself when the question of acquiring archives arises. Although those in whose custody the "old stuff" had lain for so many years may have cared little for it, and may even have been unaware of its existence, there was a complete change of outlook when someone desired to take it over. "You can't possibly take that; we refer to it almost every day!", or "We might require to make urgent reference to that, and where should we be if you took it?" Inches of dust (and this is no fable) frequently belie that "every day" story. As for "where should we be if you took it?", the fact is that they would almost certainly be in a much better position, for if it was retained, it would often be of little use to them because of its disarray or lack of adequate means of reference.

If taken and dealt with properly, the "old stuff" immediately becomes readily accessible, and of real value to the staff who previously owned it, as well as to the research worker. Departments which pass over archives always have prior right to immediate reference, and, if necessary, to return for business purposes. But that quite natural possessiveness has to be reckoned with as something calling for tactful negotiation. This was realized at the outset, that confidence in the archives department must be created to secure the co-operation essential to its success, and plans were drawn up for adequate liaison with all divisions of the Commission. Not only was it essential that confidence in the passing over of important documents should be created, but it was equally necessary for all staff to recognize from the beginning that the new department was not a convenient dump for worthless books and papers.

The Commission was embarking on a scheme for the preservation of its priceless heritage of records. Pride was to be fostered in the splendid pedigree of transport operation over the centuries, and the enthusiastic co-operation of all staff throughout the country was to be sought. They were to be partners in the scheme for the permanent preservation of, and ease of reference to, the story of the generation of courageous, shrewd and far-seeing men who built the great British system of transport with such skill, flexibility and permanency. A great serial story was to be gathered, arranged and exhibited in the form of archives. The staff of the new department looked upon their work in this fashion. They were not merely doing a job; they were recording an epic.

Early in July 1951, the Chief Secretary and the Chief Publicity Officer of the Commission met the Curator and the Archivist to discuss the best means for liaison. Officers were to be appointed through whom the Archivist would negotiate for the examination and transfer of records to his department. This was a most important step; for the liaison officers were high-ranking men in their own divisions, interested in the preservation of archives, and able to negotiate with unquestionable authority. Their assistance and advice has been a marked feature in the establishment and progress of the department.

In order that so large and varied a collection of records should be properly catalogued and made readily available, it was of the utmost importance to devise a system of record keeping which was capable of almost unlimited expansion. The first essential seemed to be some register from which the researcher could quickly ascertain in broad outline what the repository contained. He must be able to discover readily whether the repository holds the type of record likely to reward the amount of time he has available for research. A card index would not fulfil this need. Flipping through vast numbers of cards is a task tiresome to eyes and patience.

The solution to the problem was a loose-leaf register arranged in two sections, one for company groups, in which each company appeared in strict alphabetical order, and one for miscellaneous groups. The former is divided into railway, canal, and other companies, and the latter takes records which are chiefly of a subject nature, and not related specifically to one particular company. Acquisitions of additional items are readily inserted in strict alphabetical sequence, so that the register is capable of infinite expansion while always maintaining strict order. The first page of the records of each undertaking contains a short history of the company, tracing its progress from its first Act of Incorporation until its dissolution or amalgamation with some other body. Items of major significance are included in these histories. The same principle is followed for the miscellaneous groups, a description of the subject nature of the group being given for each entry.

When the researcher has found that the repository holds the records and an outline of the history of a particular company, or that papers dealing with a particular subject are available, he can ascertain details of the records— minutes of the meetings of the governing body, reports of engineers and other officers, accountancy records, registers of shareholders, agreements, contracts, locomotive and rolling stock records, petitions and memorials to directors, correspondence and relevant papers, miscellaneous documents, and so on. The varying types of record take distinguishing class numbers. For instance, minutes are always Class 1 items. In this register (termed the Inventory Summary) the items are shown in total together with their date-range, number, and nature. Therefore, when the question is asked "What have you got?" there is a ready and concise outline answer. A synopsis of the summary has been prepared which gives only salient details. This is invaluable for desk use, so that a ready answer can be given to telephone and other urgent enquiries.

Another loose-leaf register has been compiled, this time arranged in the strict alphabetical order of what are termed the "group letters"—*i.e.* L.N.W. for London & North Western Railway Company—which are shown in the summary. This register records each individual item within the group, its date-range, description and filing location, hence the name "Location Register". A third and very important aid in tracing information is the comprehensive card index. This, unlike the Inventory Summary, is for specific and detailed referencing. Here each item is indexed under the name of the company and also the subject, and for subject referencing as many cards are created for each item as seem necessary to provide adequate references. This is probably the most used of the finding aids, though its use is restricted to the staff dealing with the enquiries of the research workers. For obvious reasons, a card index is not suited to general use. This comprehensive index, like the other registers, is capable of almost unlimited expansion, and is so subdivided by guide cards as to make reference speedy and without tedium.

By the end of 1951, the system of classifying archives had been proved capable of carrying not only the large number of records of the transport system already in existence, but also the almost limitless records yet to be produced by so large and continuing an industry. All was now ready for casting the gathering net throughout the country, and records began to flow in steadily. Their intake was carefully regulated, so that the staff should not be submerged in a flood of paper, but could begin and fully complete the classification, recording, and filing of each collection as they progressed. It was a golden rule of the department that there should be no partly finished tasks waiting for a convenient time to complete; that would have been fatal to good work. The maxim was: "Complete the job, put it away, and leave the referencing system to find it when required. There must be no loose ends to tie up later."

By this time, numerous research workers were making regular visits for study of a wide variety of subjects, and this early test of the methods of recording and production gave confidence to the staff and much stimulus for expansion of the work. The department was fulfilling itself.

London was not to be the only centre either for custody or research of the records. A notable transport museum had existed for some years in York, and a quite natural concern was expressed that this collection should not be broken up. York not only housed locomotives and other large exhibits, but a quantity of purely archive material had been assembled and placed on exhibition there. The possibility of opening a branch of the archives department at York was considered at an early date, and this was established in July 1955. Another branch office was opened in Edinburgh in November of the same year. These two branches, which are essentially part of the one archive organization, have been greatly appreciated by students, and their work continues to grow.

As the department has expanded, it has become increasingly clear that the records of the transport industry have a very wide interest for many types of researcher. Apart from the study of the development of transport as a subject in itself, the records display a richness of material arising from the intimate manner in which transport has so vitally affected the way of life of the whole community. Over many centuries, the sea had a profound influence upon the character of this island people, and so far from placing a limitation on their activities and interests, had provoked in them a boundless outlook, setting them roaming the oceans in search of new worlds for adventure and trade. The sea was itself the medium of great transport enterprise—of merchandise richly exciting in romance and beauty as well as prosaic and utilitarian. It also carried those dynamic items of exchange—ideas.

All the characteristics implanted in a seafaring adventurous people received a new orientation in this revolution of inland transport, and are vividly reflected in the live records created by these bold enterprising men of transport. When delving into their original papers, one receives a stimulus from the forthright recital of their projects, their refusal to be frustrated by difficulties, their immense courage and astonishing foresight. This new industry of transport was touching the life of the whole community, uprooting customs, methods and people in a manner never before experienced.

The large collection of original letters now made available for study is a vivid illustration of the character of these pioneers and a revealing narration of facts. The reports of eminent engineers and other officers managing these rapidly growing transport undertakings reveal these men not only as masters of their own crafts but as having a wide range of knowledge and skill in fields not specifically their own. One sees a secretary, or a manager, or a director, performing for his own satisfaction and instruction at first hand, the task of surveying a route with fundamental knowledge and no little insight, and then making his own report with clarity, vision and professional correctness. One is filled with admiration for this generation of giants.

The repository also contains many items about which surprise was at first expressed by some who viewed the new department with constructive interest, but wondered whether the task of handling archives was not sufficient in itself. Early published works and periodicals relating directly or indirectly to transport matters were to be included, and this decision has proved of incalculable benefit to the office. A most useful library of about 7,000 books, including some of the most rare and earliest of published works, together with a large collection of varying types of periodical have been acquired.

Current works on transport are also acquired from time to time, some of them as presentations by authors who have benefited by study at the repositories. Though relatively small, the library embraces a wide range of subjects bearing upon the varied aspects of transport. These often supply information supplementing the archives, and, particularly in the earliest works, furnish clues for further research in the records themselves. Students are allowed access to these volumes, and many have expressed appreciation of the opportunity of having them available, side by side with original documents. Generous donations of books and records have also been received from lifelong students of transport who wished to ensure the preservation of their collections.

Two notable periodicals call for special mention—*The Railway Magazine*, and *The Illustrated London News*. The former is a complete collection, and a comprehensive index to it has been produced in the office. *The Illustrated London News* is remarkable for its record of transport matters, and for the detailed engravings it contains of various types of transport vehicles and machines, and of buildings and engineering works connected with transport. The small paragraphs recording transport events, such as the opening of lines and stations, and many other items of interest topical at the time, are frequently the only known records of such events. Transport was vital news in the early days of this periodical; and the department has an excellent collection from the first issue to modern times. These, too, have been indexed from the commencement well into this century. Other periodicals, such as *The Engineer, Engineering, Tramway & Railway World*, and the famous *Herapath's Journal* are available for reference.

The records now included in the repository relate to over 1,000 railway undertakings and their joint committees. The latter present a somewhat complicated, though fascinating, picture of rivalries and flirtations for the capture of trade, and reveal a certain shrewdness, not to say cunning, and sometimes a degree of ruthlessness in negotiation. The records handed over by the London Transport Board relate to over 100 companies—steam and electric railways, omnibus and tramway undertakings, and property-owning bodies.

River, canal, dock and harbour companies number about 100, and the records of these undertakings are among the oldest and most interesting. Minute books of the Aire & Calder River Navigation Company are a noteworthy collection almost complete from 1699 to 1947. Reports by Rennie, Telford, and other famous engineers are found in these records. There are records, too, of about 300 miscellaneous companies, such as those relating to roads and hotels, together with a large and most valuable collection from the Railway Clearing House, including the well-known railway maps, junction diagrams, distance tables, station handbooks and coaching arrangements.

Mention must be made of a few of the records which have been placed in the non-company group, such as details of law cases, reports of Royal Commissions and select committees, rules and regulations, staff records and negotiations with trade unions. There is also an extensive collection of maps, plans, and surveys. Another group includes timetables and traffic notices. The advertisements and illustrations in many of these are a social study in themselves.

The collection of annual and half-yearly reports and accounts is a valuable source of information, frequently covering the whole life of a company, and recording major events, decisions and prospects, and presenting an historical picture of the life and activities of the undertaking.

Although the archives department was established primarily to assist other departments of the transport organization, students and research workers are always welcome, and the repositories are open to the public every weekday (except Saturdays) from 9.30 in the morning until 4.30 in the afternoon. The London office also remains open until 7.30 on Tuesday evenings. There are, of course, some reservations. For instance, minute books are not made available until they are more than 50 years old, and certain papers are still regarded as confidential. No fees are charged for research.

The work of the department has aroused considerable interest, both at home and overseas. Visits have been arranged for a special study of the methods of classifying and recording archives, and these have led to the establishment of cordial relations and exchange of information and ideas.

" There's a Lot of Old Stuff! "

The expert repair of books and papers is a special feature of the department's work that has been very highly praised.

The task of assembling and arranging the archives has been most rewarding, for the collection has now taken its place among the historical records of the nation. However, the work is still far from complete, and a large number of documents have yet to be received. A greater sense of security has been given by the Transport Act of 1962, which has placed the department on a statutory basis. Redistribution of the records, which some had feared might occur, has been avoided, and research workers will continue to enjoy opportunities for delving among the "old stuff" that is "the very stuff of history".

A railway conveyance is a locomotive prison. At a certain period you are compelled to place your person and property in the custody of a set of men exceedingly independent, and who have little regard for your accommodation. Till your journey is accomplished, you are completely subservient to their commands. You pass through the country without much opportunity of contemplating its beauties; you are subjected to the monotonous clatter of its machinery, and every now and then to the unpleasant grating sensation of the brake. To all these things must be added the horribly offensive smells of rancid oil and smoky coal. "Phoenix," 1838

NEW LOOK FOR WINTER!

The following conversation was overheard in a bus travelling from Berkhamsted to Hemel Hempstead, one day in late autumn. The main line from Euston is visible from the road for most of the way, and the down " Royal Scot" happened to be passing.

First lady passenger: Oh, look! the carriages of that train are all painted red.

Second lady passenger: Yes, they always do that for the winter months.

From a letter to the Editor in *" The Railway Magazine"*

The earth has a thousand noble things that loud for praises call,
But the grimy engine black with smoke is as noble as them all.

The Great Locomotive Row

HAMILTON ELLIS

OUR EARLIEST RAILWAYS began with locomotives purchased from manufacturers, originally to the makers' own designs, and then to those prepared in railway drawing offices under the officer generally known in Victorian days as the Locomotive Superintendent. There were indeed exceptions to that last title. Francis W. Webb came to style himself Chief Mechanical Engineer of the London & North Western Railway, and fully lived up to the title. Not only the design and building of locomotives at Crewe were his. So were rail-rolling mills and the manufacture of steel itself. Under him Crewe was a principality and his word was absolute law. His brother Canon Webb was vicar of the parish, and those in the works who were not impeccable Conservatives and members of the Church of England could not expect much when it came to promotion.

Successive general managers, such as Sir William Cawkwell and Sir George Findlay, formidable though they were, nevertheless knew better than to interfere with Francis Webb, and even the terrifying Sir Richard Moon, Chairman of the London & North Western for 30 years, seemed to regard Crewe as an entirely self-governing dominion, which Euston might offend at its peril.

Crewe had built its first locomotive, *Columbine*, early in 1845, under Francis Trevithick. Now Trevithick was an easygoing character, too kindly and too lenient with his people, so he had to go. Between him and Francis Webb came John Ramsbottom, as stern a martinet as any eighteenth-century admiral, and a brilliant engineer, who made the establishment what it was when Webb succeeded at the beginning of the 'seventies.

There the London & North Western built all its locomotives, all its machinery in fact, not to mention making its own rails and bridge girders. Then it started making locomotives for other people, and had Webb known it, the fat was in the fire. Preliminary splutters, however, may have been drowned by the roar of the works machines. The great locomotive-building firms, of course, were much annoyed at a statutory company incorporated by Act of Parliament for the purpose of furnishing transport, setting up a rival business. That the company should think fit to build its own equipment might have been a pity from the manufacturers' point of view, but they could not stop it. But when a company, furnishing transport for profit, took upon itself to build locomotives for profit, and not for its own convenience, the locomotive-building firms believed they had a case. The confederacy they formed was the beginning of the Locomotive Manufacturers' Association.

On the London & North Western side, the position was this: the company worked in close alliance with the Lancashire & Yorkshire Railway. While it owned actual track in Ireland, at North Wall, Dublin, it also acquired practically all the stock of an Irish local railway, the Dundalk, Newry & Greenore, though this remained a separate company. Locomotives and vehicles were built at Crewe for the D.N.G.R. Had that been all, the London & North Western might have got away with it.

But there was also the Lancashire & Yorkshire, an entirely separate undertaking which had been allowed, by mismanagement and misfortune, to get into a parlous state. Its traffic had long been worked by an extraordinary collection of old-fashioned, worn-out locomotives. Early in 1873, its locomotive works at Miles Platting, Manchester, was gutted by a spectacular fire. There were 26 locomotives and more than 100 carriages in the shops at the time.

Now an inefficient Lancashire & Yorkshire Railway was as embarrassing to the London & North Western as an exhausted ally was to a stronger nation at war, and the London & North Western was always at war with its neighbours. *Aid*, that magical word with which we are now so familiar, was clearly needed, and if the L.N.W.R. could get some money for its aid, out of the L.Y.R., so much the better. As the locomotive position was the worst of several uncomfortable ones in which the L.Y.R. found itself, it seemed a good thing for the L.N.W.R. to rectify this, building new L.Y.R. engines, to existing London & North Western designs, at Crewe.

In 1875, the indignation of the manufacturers took stately legal form, and the application for an Injunction against the London & North Western

Railway took place in the Chancery Division, before the Master of the Rolls. Counsel for the Plaintiffs were the Attorney-General and Mr. Macnaghten, instructed by Messrs. Hargrove, Fowler & Blunt, of 3, Victoria Street, acting for Ephraim Hutchings, Secretary of the Locomotive Manufacturers' Association. Mr. Southgate, Q.C., and Mr. Speed appeared as Counsel for the Defendants, instructed by Mr. Roberts, Solicitor of the London & North Western Railway Company.

The Attorney-General said that he was instructed to move on the Answer to the Information filed in this case, for an Injunction "to restrain the Defendants from manufacturing locomotive engines or other rolling stock, for sale or hire, and from manufacturing or repairing any locomotive engines or other rolling stock not required for the purposes of the undertaking of the London & North Western Railway Company". That the Defendants— "may be restrained by the Order and Injunction of this Honourable Court from employing any of the funds of the company in the manufacture of locomotive engines—" and so on; the Motion was somewhat repetitive. The Attorney-General, having quoted Act, Order and Paragraph, concluded: "Now, my Lord, the Information is very short, and it simply alleges that the London & North Western Railway Company have been manufacturing engines for sale."

His Lordship: "I am afraid I am a stockholder in the London & North Western Railway Company. Who appears for them?"

Mr. Southgate rose. The Judge asked him if he objected. He said no; it was rather for the Attorney-General to object. He did not. There were exchanges on technicalities, then his Lordship said: "What I suppose you want would be to restrain them from manufacturing or repairing engines, except with the view to their being hereafter used on their railway. That is what you mean?"

The Attorney-General: "That would satisfy us, I think. I do not know that I can have it more general than that. But I must finish this clause: 'and I now add that they will not manufacture locomotive engines or rolling stock, for the purpose of letting them out on hire; these provisions are not to apply to any of their engines or carriages in stock.'"

It thus applied to new construction only, not to what had been done already.

The Attorney-General then said that the L.N.W.R. had made a contract with the L.Y.R. for the manufacture by the former of ten engines for the latter. Since the Information was filed, they had not gone on with those engines, and did not intend to do so if the Court restrained them, and granted the Injunction. But according to a letter of July 19, from Mr. Roberts, the London & North Western Solicitor, if the Injunction agreed to in that letter were granted, the L.N.W.R. could still sell those ten. Twenty-five engines were to have been constructed for the L.Y.R.

His Lordship said that Mr. Hutchings had made the application in the interests of the Locomotive Manufacturers' Association. That was quite immaterial. "You," he said to the Attorney-General, "appear on behalf of the Crown, and say that a corporation incorporated for a limited purpose shall not go beyond that purpose."

The Attorney-General agreed. It was sometimes difficult to define going beyond the purpose, but making a locomotive for sale was so. Quoting the Answer, in this it was stated that Crewe Works had been used solely for making equipment for the L.N.W.R. or lines leased to, worked by, or used in connection with its own system. For some time prior to 1871, the two companies had carried much traffic over each others' lines, and they were joint owners of various lines. In November 1871, amalgamation had been agreed. Since then the L.N.W.R. had made engines and vehicles for the L.Y.R., but amalgamation had been thrown out by Parliament, therefore the sales in question ought not to have been made. In April 1875, the L.N.W.R., at the request of the L.Y.R., agreed to make ten more engines. They were nearly complete when the Information was filed against them. They would be completed but not sold unless the Court sanctioned this.

His Lordship remarked testily that he had read all that. Would Mr. Attorney-General look at Paragraph 18 of the Answer?

This referred to the sale of old surplus, obsolete and "worn-out" engines. With one exception they had never sold a new engine intended for the L.N.W.R. (It went, the present writer believes, to Sweden, a "DX" goods; and met with a sad end there.) The Attorney-General said he had no objection to the *bona fide* sale of old stocks. Many companies did this. "Of course," he added, "we shall have to rely upon the railway company not making the engines ostensibly for their own purpose but practically for other purposes."

His Lordship observed grimly: "If they do, they will be liable to sequestration."

The Attorney-General: "No doubt, my Lord! As your Lordship says, the question is simply as to the form of the Injunction."

They argued this over, including the use of the word "undertaking" to define all railways owned, worked or used. The Attorney-General kindly suggested that when a foreign engine broke down on the L.N.W.R., the latter should be entitled to repair it.

Was this, one wonders, done often? One can imagine neither the L.N.W.R. caring for a Midland engine, except as to its removal, nor the Midland entrusting one of its own engines to Crewe!

Sunshine and Shadow under the Roof: Gresley Pacific No. 60037, Hyperion, *with the northbound "Flying Scotsman" at Newcastle*

Contrast in Specials: (above) L.N.E.R. Pacific No. 4472, Flying Scotsman, *leaving Paddington on April 20, 1963, with the Festiniog Railway Society's special train;* (below) *two S.R. class "Q1" 0-6-0 at Baynards, between Horsham and Guildford, on June 13, 1965, on a tour arranged by the Locomotive Club of Great Britain*

There was more discussion, on the position in respect of working over colliery lines, also the provision of rolling stock for other railways in an emergency, then a rather interesting passage:

His Lordship: "You will see what the Injunction is—let me repeat it to you: You are restrained from manufacturing engines except for the purpose of being used on your line; that is, used on any part of your line. I suppose the Attorney-General will not object to the words: 'or some part thereof', therefore, if you wish your engines *bona fide* to be used on every part of the London & North Western Railway Company's system, you are not in danger as regards manufacturing. Then you do not want to manufacture engines except for this purpose, or you ought not."

Mr. Southgate, for the L.N.W.R.: "I am told that all (*sic*) the colliery proprietors in the North of England work their traffic with engines which are not good enough for the London & North Western Railway Company —old stock which they hire of the London & North Western Railway Company."

His Lordship: "That is on the question of hiring. Will you keep the two things distinct! We will first of all dispose of the question of manufacturing. Let me in each case know how you submit that this Injunction, as regards manufacturing, will improperly affect you or injure you. . . . I should like you to tell me for what purposes you say you ought to manufacture an engine, except for the purpose of being used by the London & North Western Railway Company or any railway worked or used by them, or some part of it."

Mr. Southgate: "I will just mention one case—the Dundalk, Newry & Greenore Railway, which is in Ireland. It has a capital of a considerable amount, £533,200, of which £503,200 is the capital of the London & North Western Railway Company. But it is a corporation, and £30,000 is all the capital that belongs to it. That railway is a valuable feeder to this railway. They take passengers out of Holyhead; they take them over in steamers belonging to this company, which they have power to do; they land them at Greenore, and take them on from there. The London & North Western Railway Company may manufacture engines and rolling stock for that line."

His Lordship, severely: "What legal right have they to do that? Because they hold shares in a foreign line, what legal right have they to manufacture engines? As I understand, the Attorney-General says you have no legal right. If you say that you have, I will hear you on the legal point."

Arguing this point, he ruled that the L.N.W.R. was not a corporation for the purpose of working the traffic on the Dundalk, Newry & Greenore Railway. Mr. Southgate objected that the Irish line brought traffic to the railway, to which the Judge countered that he might just as well say that the establishment of ironworks, or collieries, or the building of a town in the neighbourhood of the L.N.W.R. would bring traffic upon it. He "could not imagine" that the L.N.W.R. had any power to supply engines to the Dundalk, Newry & Greenore Railway.

Under the date of December 16, 1875, the Master of the Rolls ordered "that a perpetual Injunction be awarded against the Defendants the London & North Western Railway Company to restrain them their Directors Servants and Agents from manufacturing locomotive engines or other rolling stock for sale or hire or any other purpose except for the purpose of being used by the London & North Western Railway Company upon any railway worked or used by them or some part thereof also from letting for hire any locomotives or other rolling stock except for the purposes of the traffic on another railway in extraordinary emergencies also from repairing any locomotive engines or other rolling stock not belonging to the London & North Western Railway Company except when required by the exigencies of their traffic But this Injunction is not to extend to prevent the London & North Western Railway Company from occasionally letting for hire locomotive engines or other rolling stock manufactured or purchased or otherwise acquired by them for their own use to contractors working on the Company's line of railway or on any line of railway worked by the London & North Western Railway Company or to the proprietors of collieries and works adjoining their railway or any railway worked by them Nor shall this Injunction extend to prevent the London & North Western Railway Company from building locomotive engines and other rolling stock for and selling them to the Manchester South Junction & Altrincham Railway Company for use on the line of railway of the last-mentioned Company And it is ordered that the Defendants the London & North Western Railway Company pay to the Informant the costs of the suit to be taxed by the taxing-master and any of the parties are to be at liberty to apply as they may be advised."

The Injunction had no more loopholes than it had punctuation; less, indeed, for it had some capital letters and a final full-stop. The L.N.W.R. at once submitted.

The reference to the Manchester South Junction & Altrincham Railway was made in view of the fact that this was a joint undertaking in which the London & North Western Railway was interested, whereas the Dundalk, Newry & Greenore, though almost entirely London & North Western property as far as stock was concerned, was technically an independent company. The disallowance in its respect had curious consequences. No new locomotives or vehicles were built for it thereafter. Ultimately, before its closure, the Great Northern Railway (Ireland) provided equipment for working its rather run-down train service, but for more than half a century the Greenore trains consisted of ancient London & North Western saddle-tank engines stemming from Ramsbottom's designs, and harmoniously mid-Victorian carriages, which, furthermore, continued to be painted in London & North Western style for as long as they lasted, which was long after the demise of the L.N.W.R. as a separate company. The only important difference was in rail gauge: 5 ft. 3 in. instead of 4 ft. 8½ in.

The reasons why the London & North Western had moved into the locomotive market, and thus got itself into legal hot water, have been mentioned in part, but other ones were that it was a time of falling traffics and consequent receipts. From the Lancashire & Yorkshire point of view, not only could it thus get newer and better engines, which it badly needed, but also it could get them more cheaply from Mr. Webb at Crewe than it could from such great manufacturers in the North-West as Beyer, Peacock & Company of Gorton Foundry, Sharp, Stewart & Company of Atlas Works, or Vulcan Foundry at Newton-le-Willows. Richard Peacock, of the first-named firm, was the first chairman of the Locomotive Manufacturers' Association.

Encouraged by their success before the Master of the Rolls, 14 manufacturers went out for new conquests, and in 1877 petitioned against the Arbroath & Montrose Railway Bill with a strong objection to the proposed provision of engines and carriages by the North British Railway. The Chairman of the appropriate Commons Committee ruled that the Petitioners had no *locus standi*. Had it been so, there would have been complications all over the country. Many small local railways were worked by larger ones as parts of their own systems.

But before the decade was out, there was another victory for the manufacturers, and this time the Great Eastern Railway was the target. In and out of Fenchurch Street in London ran the old London & Blackwall Railway. Over part of its line, the London, Tilbury & Southend Railway had running powers to the same terminus. Neither company had any locomotives or vehicles of their own. The Great Eastern was the operating company, and this was already in ill-favour with the British manufacturers because, during the 'sixties, it had purchased locomotives from the French firm of Schneider, at Le Creusot. The incensed head of the firm of Sharp, Stewart & Company, then still at Manchester, threatened to move his works to Russia or Belgium, where labour was cheap, "if we are precluded by the action of railway companies who have large premises and a large amount of money at their disposal from getting orders in this country".

The idea of Sharp, Stewart & Company moving to Seraing or Riga was an engaging one. In 1877, it was about that new engines were needed for the

London, Tilbury & Southend Railway. It may have been, even, that William Adams, Locomotive Superintendent of the Great Eastern Railway, was already scheming them in his drawing office at Stratford. Anyway, on a writ of June 25, 1877, Ephraim Hutchings was again on to the Attorney-General to restrain the Great Eastern from building and supplying engines to the Tilbury Company. That supply was presently under an Agreement made on June 1, 1876, but as yet the critical engines were still not only of Great Eastern type but were numbered in Great Eastern stock.

A long and complicated case ensued. It ended against the Great Eastern, but that company was allowed to continue until expiry of the current agreement. The new engines were certainly designed by Adams—they were the original version of the famous and very handsome Tilbury type 4-4-2 tank engine—but they were not built at Stratford. Sharp, Stewart & Company got the order, the engines were taken into London, Tilbury & Southend, and not Great Eastern, stock, in 1880, and everybody was happy. The drawings, which had in every respect the hand of Adams in them, were probably finished or in a fairly finished state in 1878, for in that year the designer quitted the Great Eastern for the London & South Western Railway, which could not be said to have the remotest connection with the Tilbury.

Thus ended, in its concrete consequences, the Great Locomotive Row of the middle 1870s. Ephraim Hutchings had scored a major diplomatic victory by successfully attacking, of all companies, the London & North Western, for at that time it was one of the largest, richest and most powerful railway corporations in the world.

MISLAID, ONE BULL

A bull was sent last Tuesday to the Eckington Station and placed on the train which passes there at eleven o'clock to be conveyed to the Wolverton Station. He had a direction on parchment tied round his neck to Mr. Anderson at H. C. Hoare Esq., Wovendon House, Nr. Newport Pagnell, Bucks, and it was written legibly thereon that he was to be left at the Wolverton Station. He has I am sorry to say not been heard of there. Will you be so good as to forward him as directed if he is remaining at Euston Square. I am very much surprised how any mistake can have arisen.

From a letter to the London & Birmingham Railway, July, 1842

Modern Monorails

JOHN R. DAY

THE MONORAIL is not much younger than the orthodox railway in Britain, but the right of primogeniture has always weighed heavily against it. Had Henry Robinson Palmer built his horse-drawn monorail lines in the London Docks and the Cheshunt Marshes in 1794-5 instead of 1824-5, we might now have seen monorails where today the normal railway, or "duorail" as it is beginning to be called in the U.S.A., now holds undisputed sway.

The idea of monorails has never died, however, and periodically new versions come into prominence for a greater or lesser period. Few of these have been true monorails, which require some form of balancing mechanism, but the origin of most of the main systems put forward can be traced clearly to Palmer's original patents of 1821. Palmer put his single rail on a timber structure which raised it some feet from the ground, the line being kept level by varying the height of the massive oak supporting posts. The cars were divided and hung down on each side of the structure, supported by two deeply-flanged wheels, in tandem, running on the rail above. Pulled at low speeds by a horse at the end of a tow-rope, the cars were self-balancing.

This principle worked well, but with higher speeds in mind later inventors had to think of controlling sway, so that the Hadden version of the system (1869), worked by steam, had horizontal rollers running on guide rails mounted on the sides of the supporting posts. The Lartigue system was very similar but more sophisticated in that it used metal trestles, or "A"-frame supports for the rails. The first railway on this system was built in

Algeria for use in harvesting esparto grass and had to be portable because the tracts from which the grass is taken have to be changed several times a year. Some 60 miles of this light railway came into use in time in Algeria, and a similar length in Tunisia.

An electrified version of the Lartigue line was used in France in the Ria mines, in the Pyrenees. After a trial track, about 4,000 ft. long, had been built over the worst of the local terrain and thoroughly tested, a 6¾-mile line was built to carry the iron ore. This railway surmounted inclines of 1 in 10 and included curves of 10 ft. radius. An electric line was shown at the General Agricultural Exhibition in Paris in February 1884, at the Rouen Exhibition in July—November 1884 (with a very ornate and elaborate car) and at the Work Exhibition in Paris in July—November 1885. Also in 1885, at the Antwerp exhibition a 1/10th-scale model was shown of a line, to be steam worked, surveyed for the French Government to link Senegal with the Niger, serving a line of forts. Experiments in animal-hauled lines were carried out in Russia for the Russian Government, which seems to have been impressed with the potential military uses of the line. A version with seats on each car for six soldiers, and another with two stretchers on each side of the car, were demonstrated and well received.

An elaborate steam-worked exhibition line was built in Westminster in 1886, with a locomotive designed by Mallet. The best-known Lartigue line was the 9½-mile Listowel & Ballybunion Railway on the west coast of Ireland. This line, with its three Hunslet steam locomotives, was one of the few public passenger-carrying monorails to run successfully for any length of time. Opened in March 1888, it ceased to run in October 1924, killed by rising costs and the convenience of road transport. The story of the Listowel & Ballybunion is too well known to repeat here, but, rural novelty as it may have been, it was of sufficient interest for the delegates to the International Railway Congress held in London in 1895 to make the journey to see it.

The delegates had as guide Fritz Bernhard Behr, Managing Director of the Lartigue Railway Construction Company. Behr deserves a high place in monorail history—a much higher one than he is usually accorded: he came near to triumph many times, only to see his efforts frustrated.

Behr added two more side rails to his monorail tracks, so that there was one rail proper at the top of the "A"-piece and two on each side. After some experiments he showed, in July 1896, in Ham Yard, Great Windmill Street, Piccadilly, a working model of a high-speed railway he had obtained permission to erect near the forthcoming Brussels Exhibition. In 1897 the real thing, a three-mile closed circuit, was ready at Tervueren near Brussels, and on it sat a 55-ton car, 59 ft. long, with seats for 100, and four 150-h.p.

motors. Built by the Gloucester Railway Carriage & Wagon Co. Ltd., this car, with its two-wheel bogies, was described by *The Engineer* as "a very beautiful piece of work". It ran at speeds of up to 83 m.p.h.—some say faster —and Behr was vindicated. Now he was ready to press again his ideas for a high-speed electric railway between Manchester and Liverpool.

The story of the way Behr fought through his proposal against opposition and against the slow and testing procedure of Parliamentary committees and opposing expert witnesses has to be read to be believed. But Behr did not lack supporters, and the Manchester & Liverpool Electric Express Railway was authorized by an Act of 1901. The fruits of victory were bitter-sweet, for it proved impossible to raise the money for a line which would have given a 20-minute run between the centres of the two cities—a timing unapproached by anything, except perhaps a helicopter, today. Behr's five rails can be seen in one of the most successful monorail systems of today, the Alweg, which has but a single massive concrete running beam, which the cars straddle, but uses five bearing surfaces on the one beam.

The second line of development of Palmer's ideas was the raising of the rail and the lowering of the vehicle to make the cars inherently more stable. This was developed by various inventors until the cars were running under the rail. The most important, historically, of these systems is that of Eugen Langen, whose system was accepted for use between Barmen and Elberfeld in Germany. The 8.2-mile line built along the Wupper Valley between the two towns is now known as the Wuppertal Schwebebahn, and since the first section opened on March 1, 1901, it has had a proud record of safe operation. With modern cars, running at up to 25 m.p.h., this suspended railway is usually pointed out as the prime example of a long-lived, quite successful monorail.

A high-speed monorail car was proposed by George Bennie, who built a quarter of a mile of demonstration track over L.N.E.R. tracks near Milngavie, near Glasgow, and gave demonstrations in the 1930s. His cylindrical suspended car was driven by airscrews at each end and ran on a single overhead main rail. A lighter rail under the car took care of problems of swaying. The track was too short for high speeds, but it was claimed that on a full-scale run the car would be capable of 200 m.p.h. Incidentally, systems like the Tunis and the Kearney employed a similar principle but turned the track upside down, the ground-level single main rail bearing the weight and overhead rails keeping the car upright.

The full history of the development of the monorail, supported or suspended, is too long and complicated to detail here, but perhaps enough has been said to show that common ancestry can be traced, even though parts of it may have been independently re-invented from time to time. Standing apart are the three true monorails of Brennan, Scherl, and Schilovsky, all of which depended on gyroscopes for balance, and the type of monorail, largely industrial, which depends on a road wheel on an outrigger for balance. Most so-called monorails are not monorails at all, in that they have either several rails or several bearing surfaces combined in a single rail.

In the last few years traffic congestion has brought monorails to the fore again, and two main types have emerged as contenders for serious use. One is the Alweg, already mentioned, a direct descendant of Behr's high-speed five-rail system in that it uses five bearing surfaces on a massive concrete beam, which the cars straddle. The other is the S.A.F.E.G.E. system, which is called a monorail by courtesy but uses rubber-tyred wheels on two separate bearing strips, and is akin to the pneumatic tyred system used on the Paris Metro, but turned upside down so that the car hangs beneath the track.

At the time of writing the greater amount of operating experience had been gained with the Alweg system and several lines of the "joy-ride" type had been built in connection with pleasure-grounds and exhibitions. In 1964, however, a line was completed which should do much towards solving the problem of providing quick connections between city centres and airports—an 8¼-mile line between Tokyo International Airport (Haneda) and Hamamatsu-cho Station (Japanese National Railways) in the central Tokyo area.

The original Alweg line was built on a reduced scale of 1:2.5 at Fühlingen, near Cologne, in Germany, and was demonstrated in public for the first time on October 8, 1952. It was the idea of the late Dr. Axel Wenner-Gren, and in its original conception formed part of a highly-developed transport system for freight as well as passengers. Methods had been evolved for marshalling freight cars, delivery by road from terminal to consignees' premises, waybill processing, ticket issuing, and so on. It was not conceived as a purely urban system and one of the first proposals for its use was in North-West Canada—in much the same way as Behr had offered to build a monorail in Africa from the East Coast to Uganda some 60 years before.

The small-scale one-mile oval track established many principles, and was used for research into the problems of monorail operation. It used a concrete beam as the running track, and was heavily banked for high speeds. The performance of the scale version led to hopes of up to 200 m.p.h. with a full-scale version, and a full-scale Alweg line was built on the same site in 1956–7.

The new line was slightly shorter than the original but had some 500 ft. of double track, so that experience could be gained in operating the necessarily cumbersome points. The beam track is 31½ in. wide and 55 in. deep, so it can be seen that the pointwork, which must give a track of the same

Stirling "8-ft. single" No. 1, restored to its Great Northern livery and preserved in the Railway Museum at York

Alweg monorail train crossing West Boulevard, Anaheim, California

Monorail train of the Alweg–Hitachi type, at Inuyama, Japan

profile and dimensions, is necessarily massive, heavy, and somewhat slow in operation. The line, which has two-car trains capable of 50 m.p.h., has been visited by transport men from all over the world, and has formed the design basis for several projected urban transport systems.

The next line, however, was to be another reduced-scale version, five-eighths of full size. This was the 3,600-ft. continuous loop track at Disneyland, near Anaheim in California, some 22 miles south-east of Los Angeles. The Disneyland monorail, a joint Disneyland Alweg conception, was intended to be a serious demonstration of the possibilities of the system as well as a fairground attraction. In 1961 it was extended another 12,700 ft. and four-car trains were introduced to supplement the three-car ones already in service.

Next came a 3,800-ft. line for the "Italia 61" exhibition in Turin. This was built to run from the main entrance to the centre of the exhibition site and is laid out for considerable extension as part of the city's transport system in due course. One three-car train was operated during the exhibition and carried an estimated 1,500,000 people.

In March 1962 came two more Alweg lines, one 4,600 ft. long in Japan and the other, some 5,250 ft. long, in Seattle, U.S.A. The Japanese line is in Inuyama, and runs from the Inuyama Yuen Station of the Nagoya Railway Co. to a zoological garden forming part of the large park area round Inuyama. This was the first line in which the well-known Japanese engineering firm of Hitachi collaborated with Alweg. It is frankly a tourist line, with two three-car trains in operation.

The Seattle line was much more important. It was double-track throughout, much of it ran on pillars down the centre of a main road in Seattle, and it was expected that its two four-car trains would run to nearly full capacity carrying passengers to and from the Seattle World's Fair, or "Century 21 Exposition". In fact, it carried more than seven million people during the six months the fair was in operation, and its life was extended another six months for experiments with automatic operation.

After some doubt as to its future, the line was handed over to Century 21 Center Incorporated in 1963 and a four-year street-use permit was granted by the City Council. On the Seattle line, each train runs on its own track, so that there is no "up" and "down". In effect, there are two independent monorail lines side by side. There are, of course, points which enable the trains to reach a maintenance area. The top speed is about 53 m.p.h. but on such a short line it is not often reached.

In 1964, there followed another line in Japan—at the Yomiuri Recreational Park. This is a single-track $\frac{3}{4}$-scale line some 6,250 ft. long connecting the Nishi-Ikuta railway station, just outside Tokyo, with a golf course and other recreational facilities. It was opened on January 1, 1964 with two three-car trains. The top speed is 25 m.p.h. All the Alweg monorails so far described are electrically worked, but there is no intrinsic reason why diesel power, for example, should not be used.

The Tokyo airport line was begun in May 1963 and completed by September 1964 for the use of visitors to the Olympic Games. It runs between the Tokyo-Osaka line of the Japanese National Railways and the north shore of Tokyo Bay. As the area is densely built-up, much of the monorail line has been built with the supporting pillars in open water on the edge of the bay and it has to bridge channels used by shipping.

The whole line is elevated or at ground level except for two tunnel stretches, one of the cut-and-cover type at Ebitorigawa, not far from the airport, and the other a shield-driven tunnel at the airport itself. To reduce costs, only one track runs in the airport tunnel, and there is only one platform at Hamamatsu-cho at the other end of the line.

The timetable calls for 290 trains a day on the line, needing two six-car and five three-car trains. Trains run at six-minute intervals during peak hours. Three-car trains, weighing 41 tons, have seats for 104 passengers and room for 136 to stand, making the total capacity 240. The 81-ton six-car sets will carry 498 passengers. The run is made in 15 minutes, and the top designed speed is 62.5 m.p.h. The power supply is at 750 V d.c. and is carried by conductor rails on each side of the main track beam. As well as the standard electric trains, there is a two-car diesel set used for inspection purposes.

Cab-signalling is provided and there is an automatic train-stop device which comes into operation if signals are not obeyed. An unusual safety device earths the bodies of cars as they enter a station. The positive conductor rail is guarded wherever there is even a remote possibility that it might be touched. The Alweg monorail is thus making considerable strides.

The S.A.F.E.G.E. system has less to show in the way of progress, but is being taken up by groups in many parts of the world. The only line actually built by S.A.F.E.G.E. (Société Anonyme Française d'Études, de Gestion et d'Entreprises), a consortium of 18 leading French companies, is at Chateau-neuf-sur-Loire, some 90 miles south of Paris. Here a test track about a mile long has been built, and has had many visitors.

The main feature of the S.A.F.E.G.E. system is its "rail" which consists of a box girder with a slit along the centre of the bottom. The four-wheel bogies run inside the girder, protected from the weather, with their pneumatic tyres running on bearing surfaces on each side of the slit. They are kept to their proper path by rubber-tyred guide wheels bearing against the sides of the girder. The cars, each supported by two bogies, hang below the box girder, the hanging supports passing through the centre slit. The principle can be readily seen from the drawing. As in the Alweg system, switching is made possible by swivelling complete sections of track.

The demonstration car has a designed maximum speed of 66 m.p.h. and weighs nearly 20 tons. It is powered by two 100-h.p. electric motors in the bogies, taking 750 V d.c. The car is 56 ft. 1¼ in. long., 10 ft. 1¼ in. wide, and 9 ft. 8½ in. high. It has 32 fixed and 24 folding seats and can carry 91 standing. A very comprehensive system is associated with the S.A.F.E.G.E. track, and there are many safety devices as well as cab-signalling and train stops. Much more will be heard of S.A.F.E.G.E.

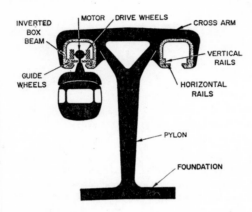

The U.S.A. licence for S.A.F.E.G.E. is held by the American Machine & Foundry Company, but that company's initial plunge into monorail construction came with the New York World's Fair of 1964 and with a monorail system of its own. The A.M.F. track consists of a steel "I" beam, with the car bogies hanging below it, supported by four rubber-tyred wheels running on the bottom flange of the girder with two wheels on each side of the web. There are also horizontally mounted guide wheels bearing on the web of the girder. The principle is well known and is often used for factory monorail conveyors.

The World's Fair monorail has two parallel closed 4,000-ft. loops, with three two-car trains travelling one way on one loop and four trains on the other loop travelling in the opposite direction. Each air-conditioned train carries 80 passengers who face the sides of the car. All trains are automatically controlled, including the opening and closing of the doors, but a train attendant is carried on each train to take over manual control in an emergency. This line is primarily a pleasure ride, and no great speeds are required, as visitors need time to look at the various features of the Fair described en route. The 4,000-ft. ride takes seven minutes giving a speed of about 6 m.p.h.

Modern Monorails

Monorails of similar type have been operated at Santa's Village, Lake Arrowhead, California, and at the Los Angeles County Fair.

One of the crying needs of modern monorail advocates and of those who, without being prejudiced in favour of monorails, are anxious that they should have a fair trial under proper working conditions instead of in the artificial surroundings of pleasure gardens or fairs, has been for a working line to be built to do a real transport job. The Tokyo airport line seems to be the answer to this. From its results, particularly in the years after the end of the Tokyo Olympic Games, it should be possible to draw many conclusions. It is without doubt the most important monorail line so far built.

ELEPHANT versus DIESEL

Soon after they were placed in service, one of the English Electric main-line diesel-electric locomotives of the Malayan Railway was involved in a collision with a bull elephant, while working the night mail train from Kuala Lumpur to Singapore. The $3\frac{1}{2}$-ton elephant was thrown about 25 ft. into a small ravine, and probably was killed instantly. The front of the locomotive was dented and the brake connection was damaged. The elephant, about $11\frac{1}{2}$ ft. tall, and estimated to be about 35 years old, had wandered on to the railway from a nearby rubber plantation.

The house magazine "English Electric and Its People" recalled a similar incident some seventy years ago, in which a train was derailed. The scene of the mishap was marked by a monument bearing the inscription: "There is buried here a wild elephant who, in defence of his herd, charged and derailed a train on the 17th day of September, 1894."

From "*The Railway Magazine*"

LET THEM STAND!

We do not feel disposed to attach much weight to the argument in favour of third-class carriages with seats. On a short line, little physical inconvenience can result from their absence.

"*The Railway Times,*" 1844

Backward Look

M. D. GREVILLE

I AM NOW an old man of 79, and as my attraction to railways really started when my father brought home the first number of *The Railway Magazine*, in July 1897, they have been my principal interest and subject of study for 68 years.

Now, whatever my many faults may be, I think I can claim to be free from one—too prevalent among the elderly—the conviction that everything was better when one was young. My considered view, derived from all these years of experience, is that, although there are, of course, some things regarding which one can say "it was better then", in many respects there have been considerable improvements, and this applies particularly to railways.

Of course, when I was young—in pre-grouping days—railways were very fascinating with all the infinite variety of the great lines and the multitude of smaller companies, ranging from the brave and efficient little North Staffordshire to the comic and semi-derelict Bishop's Castle.

But the position is different from the point of view of the traveller. Now, I have always been a great railway traveller. During most of my adult life (apart from war-time) I have covered every year many thousands of miles and, though I cannot equal the record of my old friend, the late T. R. Perkins, who travelled over every possible line in Great Britain and Ireland, I can claim that, except for about 30 miles (mostly short and little-used curves), I have been over all passenger lines still open in England, Wales and Scotland, as well as many now closed.

Speaking, then, as a passenger, it seems to me that, by and large, there has been a considerable improvement. Exceptions, there are, of course. I look back with regret, and a feeling that something good has gone for ever, on some things; the old Great North of Scotland Railway, the Clyde steamer services, the North Staffordshire Railway, station dining rooms (especially on the Lancashire & Yorkshire Railway), and the wonderful Midland catering in the days of William Towle, to mention just a few. But, in general, as regards cost, train services and speeds, rolling stock, heating, lighting, general comfort and riding, there can be, I consider, no doubt as to the progress that has been made.

To take the last point first, I must insist that anyone whose experience does not go back 50 years just does not know what really rough riding is. I sometimes hear complaints that such-and-such stock rides badly or that some section of track is not in good condition. These may be justified, but I am sure that it is rarely as bad as it could be, all too frequently, in the old days. On some railways it was good—notably on the superb London & North Western Railway track (though, curiously enough, one of the worst tossings I ever had was in a six-wheeler on a stopping train from Wolverhampton to Stafford). The Great Northern Railway and the Great Western Railway also were generally good, but on most lines the riding usually varied from the unpleasant to the definitely terrifying.

On the Caledonian, for instance, the permanent way was appalling (its neighbours were much better), and on one occasion, when I was travelling north from Glasgow, it was so extra bad that I felt constrained to write to the General Manager. As I had mentioned that I was in the Inverness coach he, seeing a good get-out, blamed the Highland, whose vehicle it was. I am afraid I took some pleasure in writing back to assure him that, north of Stanley Junction, on the Highland line, the riding was considerably better. On the whole, I must admit that the Caledonian was not one of my favourite lines; I always thought it, especially in pre-1914 days, a rather second-rate affair, trading somewhat ineffectively on its West Coast connection and its admittedly handsome blue engines.

To return to rough riding, on one occasion I was in the dining car on an up Great Central Railway express, and while we were running down from Annesley summit, everything ceased. The staff stopped trying to serve, and the diners gave up all attempts to eat; it was literally impossible to convey food, even less drink, to one's mouth.

On the Midland Railway the riding was not too bad in places, but owing to the practice of using small engines, time was lost uphill, and this resulted in very high speeds downhill, with a light-hearted non-observance of speed restrictions on curves. On the serpentine line through the Peak district, I believe the ton-mile statistics of broken crockery were a world record.

Then there was the Brighton Line, on which I lived and travelled regularly in pre-1914 days. Stroudley may have been a great locomotive engineer—I think he was—but he should never have been allowed to build carriages. The effects of travelling in his four-wheel suburban stock, combined with the way the points and crossings were laid in, are really indescribable. This stock had its points; it was fairly roomy, at any rate in the second class (one *had* to travel second, there being no third-class seasons then), but the riding! I often heard them described as having oval wheels; and Ahrons once accused the stock of another line of being hexagonal-wheeled. The Brighton stock might not have been so bad if it had had either, but *I* suspect it had both!

Generally speaking, when I was young (that is to say, before 1914), one had to be prepared to put up with rolling stock, even on main-line trains, which, looking back, seems staggering. Corridor, or even non-corridor lavatory, stock was the exception, and so was adequate heating and lighting, while the seats, at any rate in the third class, were generally very hard and uncomfortable. Some of those who complain of overcrowding and delays on suburban trains might be less critical if they had known the early days when I travelled to the City from Croydon. When we had the real old pea-soup fogs it was by no means unusual to take three hours for the ten-mile journey—five-a-side in the aforementioned Brighton stock, or the very short, very narrow, and very light South Eastern block trains (commonly known as egg-boxes), with no heating of any kind.

Then there is the cost of rail travel. How constantly people will describe this as dear, and how wrong they are. Taking into consideration the altered value of money, it is cheaper even than in 1939, and considerably cheaper than in 1914. There were admittedly, in the old days, tourist tickets which gave a considerable reduction on the return fares. But, for example, take the famous Inverness Tourist, the best value of all of them. The cost of this from London was £3, equivalent to about £15 today, when the ordinary return fare is £11 6s. Of course, this ticket, when taken by the West Coast route, provided a remarkable opportunity for the railway enthusiast. It could be used for a journey each way on every Caledonian Railway branch off the route (and this was a considerable number, especially if the ticket was routed *via* Aberdeen), and even here, I would point out that, for £13, a return ticket to Carlisle and a Freedom of Scotland ticket now gives even greater facilities.

There were, of course, phenomenally cheap excursions—notably the famous Great Northern 3s. trip from London to Skegness. I don't suppose one can get equivalent value to this now; but consider that, on a similar excursion today, one would get decent corridor stock, possibly with a buffet car, while on that trip one was quite likely to be conveyed in a Great Northern close-coupled four-wheeled suburban set; and if anyone can conceive anything much grimmer, *I* can't.

Certain very cheap journeys could be made in pre-grouping days, in consequence of competition, by absurdly long routes. For instance, one could travel from Euston to Swansea, *via* Stafford, or from St. Pancras to Gloucester, *via* Birmingham, both at the Paddington fare, or from King's Cross to Stafford *via* Grantham, at the Euston fare. But these were really freaks, and of little interest to anyone other than the railway enthusiast; *he* could get a lot of fun and profit from them.

Later on, when interavailability and break of journey facilities became general, marvellous journeys could be made. It is my lasting regret that I never carried out the best of these—to travel, with the return half of a Paddington to Swansea ticket, back from Swansea *via* Stafford, Uttoxeter and Peterborough, finishing up at Liverpool Street. This is not a joke; it was quite possible and admissible.

As regards train services, it should hardly be necessary to point out the tremendous improvements that have been made in many services, in the way of acceleration or frequency of service, or both, especially perhaps in the Eastern and Southern Regions, and in parts of Scotland. There *are* cases where the reverse applies, but they are not many or important. I realize, of course, that there is a considerable restriction as to *where* we can travel, and I fear there will be more, but that is another question.

Consider, for example, how Portsmouth and Bournemouth fared before 1914, and (perhaps the most striking of all) take the revolution in the Anglo-Scottish services. For all practical purposes there were then only two day trains from London to Scotland by each route, and none on Sundays; and as for the night trains, you either travelled first class or travelled in discomfort. I often wonder what would be the thoughts of the old railway officers who continually reiterated the impossibility of anything but first-class sleeping cars, if they could now be taken any night to Euston or King's Cross.

I think that our sleeping cars are a feature of which we can be justly proud, both as regards accommodation and cost. The two-berth second-class sleepers provide a "first-class" night's lodging at no more than the cost of a room in a decent hotel, and the first class are probably the cheapest in Europe. The only complaint is that perhaps there are not enough routes covered by them compared with some countries. In Sweden, for instance, a country with about one-eighth of our population, there are sleeping-car services between Stockholm and practically everywhere, and also between a number of provincial towns, none of which is bigger than Nottingham and most much smaller.

It should not be thought, from all I have written above, that I did not enjoy

Backward Look

railway travel in the early days; I most certainly did. I was young and keen, and took the discomforts and difficulties in my stride in my enthusiasm for exploring the railway system and studying its working. Up to 1903, my journeyings were largely confined to the Home Counties, apart from holiday journeys to North Wales, to Bournemouth on the so-called expresses (only four of which achieved the journey in under three hours), and to South Devon on the old "Flying Dutchman" (11.45 from Paddington). This train managed to get us to Teignmouth in just five hours, but provided a thrill, when we first used it, as the first complete corridor train in which I had travelled.

In 1903, however, I spread my wings and travelled north, and my journey, by night excursion from King's Cross, provides a good example of what one then had to put up with. We started at 6 p.m., seated five-a-side, in a train of non-corridor (and non-lavatory) six-wheelers, and reached Edinburgh at 4 a.m. Here, those of us going on to Aberdeen were turned out, and the North British, evidently thinking that we had enough luxury, loaded us into aged four-wheelers which were then attached to the rear of the night express (8.15 from King's Cross), an exciting journey in such stock. However, I eventually reached my destination—Elgin—and made my first acquaintance with the Great North of Scotland Railway, with which I was so delighted that, two years later, I returned to Elgin. Having little sense and less money, I took a fortnight's season ticket between there and Aberdeen, and worked it *hard*.

I am very glad now that I did, as the Great North in those days was very well worth knowing—a most inspiring example of what could be done by a small and enterprising line, with clean and comfortable carriages and, on the main line, all corridor (though not vestibuled). The working was outstandingly efficient, and punctuality highly commendable. As an example of the smart working—the 10.22 a.m. from Elgin, on which I travelled many times, ran the 87 miles to Aberdeen (about half of which was single track), *via* the coast, in 153 min., with eight regular and six conditional stops, over a road about which *The Railway Magazine* gradient book has the note "speed restrictions are too numerous to warrant their inclusion". I don't remember all the conditional stops ever being called; I doubt if time could have been kept if they had; but there were always several.

Then there were the highly creditable Aberdeen suburban services. The stock, though four-wheeled, was quite seemly, and the trains were allowed 20 min. for the 6¾ miles to Dyce with nine stops, and 21 min. for the 7½ miles to Culter with eight stops. To attain this station work had to be very brisk; and indeed it was. I cannot refrain from pointing out that, on the Great Western, for the 7¼ miles from Paddington to Hanwell, with four stops, the allowance was just about the same—and, what's more, still is!

Scotland, apart from its natural attractions, was, from a railway point of view, very fascinating, and having started, I visited it regularly up to the First World War, and have continued to do so frequently ever since. Very early, I explored the scenically beautiful Highland Railway, in many ways a slightly comic but rather lovable concern, faced with the almost impossible task of conveying—in the summer—a heavy traffic over long stretches of single line with the severe handicap of frequent late connections at Perth. One feature which sticks in my memory was the ten-minute stop at Bonar Bridge for refreshments, where the wild rush to get and consume something in the time was reminiscent of what one reads of Swindon in early days. It was needed, as the journey between Inverness and Wick took six or seven hours, as compared with four or five now, with refreshment cars.

Perhaps the highlight of Scottish railways, in pre-1914 days, was the Clyde steamer services. The beautiful and graceful steamers, the ultra-smart working, and the excitement of the extreme (and probably *very* wasteful) competition made travelling on the Clyde an unforgettable experience, apart from its scenic attraction. Looking back nostalgically to my trips 50 to 60 years ago, it seems to me that the weather was always fine, and the band always playing "Nights of Gladness", thought neither *can* be actually correct. The races for the piers were frequently really exciting. We all had our pet fleets—mine was the Glasgow & South Western (after the Great North my favourite Scottish line) and here again I liked the Caledonian the least. But I must admit that I think it showed up better here than elsewhere; the train services to the "Coast" were good and fast, with better stock than the average, and their two coast stations, Gourock and Wemyss Bay, quite seemly and well kept. Certainly the working of the boats was a revelation. It was quite usual at Gourock, in business hours (and there was a heavy residential traffic) for three well-filled boats to be got away in less than five minutes after the arrival of the train.

In 1904, I joined the Railway Club (then five years old, and still going strong) to which I owe so much. I am very grateful that I had the opportunity of meeting and knowing most of the leading early railway enthusiasts, whose names will be familiar to those who have read the earlier volumes of *The Railway Magazine*. Among others, G. W. J. Potter, a very sound and well-informed man, who became a great friend, and whose history of the Whitby & Pickering Railway, published in 1906, was one of the earliest histories of small lines (now so numerous) and, in view of the restricted sources then available, most admirable and informative. H. L. Hopwood, who contributed so much in his way to the early study of railway history; and the Rev. W. J. Scott, whom it was an education to have known, and a real "character" who combined extensive knowledge with a keen sense of humour. I could name many others, such as Rous-Marten, G. A. Sekon, Clement E. Stretton and R. E. Charlewood.

With Charlewood, I served for a time as joint secretary of the Railway Club. He was a man of immense energy. When he accepted the position, he was living at Carnforth, and stipulated that he should not be expected to be in London more than once a week. In actual practice, very few weeks passed when he did not come to the club at least three times, travelling backwards and forwards. I owe the inestimable benefit of a large number of friends with similar interests, to the Railway Club, and to the Railway & Canal Historical Society, of which I am a little proud to have been one of the founders ten years ago.

Among my liveliest recollections is the London Underground, both before and after electrification. In the steam days a journey on this was an interesting —almost eerie—experience, what with the gloom and smoke-filled atmosphere, the grim and spartan carriages and the archaic-looking locomotives (which appeared really older than they were). And then the atmosphere! This was pretty thick all round the Circle, but to get the best effects one had to be on the Metropolitan. I can still recall the smoke—could almost say the taste—at what I still find it difficult not to call Gower Street and Portland Road stations. How often have I waited at these stations, and one often had to wait quite a time (or did it only seem long?), coughing and gasping. There were those who claimed that it was healthy—perhaps it was, but I doubt it.

Then came the electrification which transformed things, but only after prolonged teething troubles, especially on the District Line. In the early days of electric working, travel on the District was a most interesting and amusing experience, always supposing that you did not want to get somewhere in reasonable time. For those who would know what it was like I would recommend a poem in *Punch*, by Owen Seaman, sometime about 1906, describing a journey from Putney to Charing Cross. This, though perhaps somewhat exaggerated, did give an idea of what travel on the District was like then. The irregular service, frequent breakdowns, ramshackle rolling stock—with automatic doors which, as often as not, refused to work—which made an appalling noise coming into the stations (Seaman described it as "a crash like skittle-balls on sheeted lead"), and frequent doubts as to the destination of the train, were all really fascinating, unless, as I said, you wanted to get somewhere.

The doubts as to destinations were partly caused by a traffic controller at Earls Court, who apparently arbitrarily altered them at a moment's notice. I once heard, as a result of this, an official call out the destination of a train as follows—"West Kensington, Hammersmith,—Oh! Damn, No!—Walham Green and Putney Bridge."

In pre-grouping days, the railway enthusiast's Mecca was Carlisle, a place of absorbing interest with the trains of six great railways, not to mention the Maryport & Carlisle, a bright little concern with well-kept engines and carriages. It was well worth missing a night's sleep to stay up and watch the night trains with their variegated rolling stock and engines. In early days there was always the rather morbid interest aroused by the down West Coast trains, observing how much, owing to the waywardness of Mr. Webb's locomotive masterpieces, they got delayed on the way, and indeed what might be pressed into service to work them—almost anything was possible.

For obvious reasons, race traffic nowadays is a much smaller affair than it was. But it used to be on a scale which made it very interesting to watch— Epsom, Ascot, Newmarket and Doncaster especially, but above all at the Grand National. An amazing number of special trains were run to Aintree from all over the country, mostly to the special racecourse station, though a certain number from the North used the Lancashire & Yorkshire station at Sefton Arms, and there were trains to the Cheshire Lines Committee station from the systems of its constituent owners. All these in addition to a very frequent local service from Liverpool, including through trains from the Overhead Railway.

On one occasion in the early 1920s, I travelled down to Aintree with a friend on one of the many specials from Euston, and this was an experience of something really well done in the Good Old Days. Like most other specials, the train by which we went was composed entirely of dining cars, with reserved seats, and one had breakfast and lunch on the outward journey, and dinner coming back (and *very* good meals too), all for somewhere about 25s., I forget the exact figure.

We spent an enthralling, if rather exhausting time, trying to watch the traffic at all the stations at once, and then, in the late afternoon, found our way into our train in the sidings, where we relaxed and, incidentally, managed to snaffle some tea as well. At our table in the diner were two obvious cavalry officers, and I shall never forget their faces when, on the return journey, they asked what we had thought of the race, and were told that we had not gone to see it. I think the poor things were quite uneasy—convinced that they were sitting with a couple of lunatics.

Altogether, I think that I can say that I have been fortunate and have had the best of both worlds. I was born early enough to have known all the great pre-grouping railways in action, and to have seen and travelled on most of the small lines up and down the country; to have seen (and frequently admired) the larger and more prosperous minor railways, such as the Furness; the busy and variegated lines of South Wales; and the North Staffordshire, a remarkably efficient little concern. I always marvelled at the way it handled at the two platforms at Stoke the intensive traffic it had until the L.M.S. came along and killed it. Moreover, I saw something of bygone methods of working, such as the horse-drawn Port Carlisle "dandy", and the rope-haulage on Cowlairs incline in Glasgow.

Later on, I travelled extensively in Scandinavia, and became well acquainted with the wonderful scenic railways of Norway, which are regarded as a social service and are still growing. I was greatly impressed by the Swedish railways, whose watchword seems to be "efficiency without officiousness"; and can only describe the train ferries of Denmark as fascinating.

Now, on British Railways, I am able to travel in comparative comfort, and still enjoy it, and can see the beginnings of the great reorganization and modernization—good and bad. Yes, I have much to be thankful for.

ENTHUSIAST BUYS A SIGNAL BOX

When the Colchester–Clacton line of the Eastern Region was electrified, the signal box at Great Bentley became redundant. It was saved from destruction by a 19-year-old model railway enthusiast, Mr. Winston Cole, of Crow Lane, Tendring. He purchased the box, and with the assistance of his father removed it piecemeal to his home, where it was re-erected.

From the Great Eastern Line Edition of the "*Eastern Region News*"

A SIMIAN PASSENGER

A chimpanzee consigned to a circus escaped from its basket in a King's Cross to Newcastle express. It scampered down the train and threw its arm around a passenger. At York it was taken in charge by the parcels foreman. It jumped into his arms and cried every time he tried to put it down. The ape remained in the care of the York parcels staff for some hours.

From "*The Railway Magazine*" (1960)

"*Railroad travelling is a delightful improvement of human life. Man is become a bird: he can fly longer and quicker than a solan goose.*"
From a letter to the "*Morning Chronicle*" from Sydney Smith, 1842

By Any Other Name

WILLIAM J. SKILLERN

A ROSE, SAID SHAKESPEARE, by any other name would smell as sweet. No doubt the same could be said of a railway—the proper, Parliamentary name of a railway, that is. Someone, somewhere, must have thought up a suitable name under which the undertaking could be incorporated, and by which it would be known to the public at large. Some of these names have been known for five generations—much longer than the multiple shops of today.

Railways were built to connect two or more places, and almost without exception our British railway titles contain the names of towns or geographical areas. In general, the earliest railway companies managed very nicely with short names. They seem to have worked on the principle "the shorter the better", and in many cases they were quite satisfied with single place-names, names like Sirhowy, Oystermouth, Monmouth, Hay, Kington, and Carmarthenshire. These single names were all right up to a point, but they gave no indication of the other end of the line, and therefore no clue as to its length or direction. In 1801, one of these early names added another word to a single place-name and became the Surrey Iron Railway; its continuation was the Croydon, Merstham & Godstone Railway (1802), which was the first example of the use of three place-names. Not until 1837 do we find a railway with four place-names, the Glasgow, Paisley, Kilmarnock & Ayr.

Throughout our railway history, two place-names have provided the most common type of railway name. Such a title was adequate and reasonably accurate, and it produced such early names as Gloucester & Cheltenham, Kilmarnock & Troon, Lydney & Lydbrook, Mansfield & Pinxton, and Plymouth & Dartmoor. Best known of these early lines was the Stockton & Darlington which, as every schoolboy knows, was opened on September 27, 1825.

In the next decade or so, railways with two place-names continued to dominate the list of new undertakings and many familiar names date from that period—names like Canterbury & Whitstable, Liverpool & Manchester, Newcastle & Carlisle, Leicester & Swannington, and Bodmin & Wade-bridge. At the same time there appeared the earliest of the many railways that were to serve the Metropolis—railways which started life as the London & Greenwich, London & Birmingham, London & Southampton, London & Croydon, London & Blackwall, and London & Brighton.

Two companies spurned such prosaic titles as "London &—". There might well have been a London & Yarmouth or London & Bristol Railway, but instead a touch of foresight and acumen resulted in the names Eastern Counties and Great Western. The latter was the first of the "Great" railway companies, and it remained the last of them, for its history was unbroken from its first Act in 1835 until midnight on December 31, 1947. Its territory eventually extended to Birkenhead, Fishguard and Penzance, and the name "Great Western" remained appropriate to the end. Only two other major companies were incorporated with "Great" in their titles—the Great Northern and the Great North of Scotland, both in 1846; two others, the Great Eastern and the Great Central, had greatness thrust upon them, as it were, by a change of name.

The continuation northwards of the London & Birmingham Railway could very well have taken the name of Birmingham & Warrington, but instead adopted the fanciful name of Grand Junction, a name which intrigued me in my younger days, for it gives no indication at all of its location, and is just about the most vague of all our railway names. No other British railway began with the word "Grand", although in 1836 a London Grand Junction Railway was incorporated for the purpose of connecting the London & Birmingham with the city of London itself, but it was not constructed.

With so many independent and isolated railways in existence or authorized, there came a time in the late 1830s and afterwards when connecting lines were required in order to link up these local railways and so provide through services. These connecting lines usually had the word "Junction" in their titles; railways so named were, in general, not intended to reach one or other of the places named but to connect with another railway which did. The Ashton, Stalybridge & Liverpool Junction, the Birmingham & Oxford Junction, and the Huddersfield & Sheffield Junction are typical examples.

By Any Other Name

Some Junction railways tended to give themselves inordinately long names—names like Great North of England, Clarence & Hartlepool Junction, or Ambergate, Nottingham & Boston & Eastern Junction, or Manchester, Buxton, Matlock & Midlands Junction ("Stockport & Ambergate" would have sufficed for the last-named). There were, of course, other railways which were strictly "Junction" railways, although they omitted that word from their titles. The Manchester & Birmingham, for instance, was never intended to get within 30 miles of Birmingham, and in fact did not approach as near as that; the Newport, Abergavenny & Hereford started eight miles from the first town in its title.

In contrast to the earliest railways, the names of some later ones seem to have been chosen to impress the public by their very length. Perhaps the promoters thought that a long title was necessary in order to justify the launching of a new undertaking. This may account for such long-winded names as Hull, Barnsley & West Riding Junction Railway & Dock, or Easton Neston Mineral & Towcester, Roade & Olney Junction (which became part of the even longer East & West Junction & Stratford-upon-Avon, Towcester & Midland Junction Joint Railway!). It is perhaps fitting that Yorkshire, the largest county, should have produced the name containing most place-names, the Sheffield, Rotherham, Barnsley, Wakefield, Huddersfield & Goole, which was incorporated as early as 1846.

Just occasionally, a more "romantic" name made its appearance and shows that the British are not entirely hidebound by tradition. We might have had railways called the Cromford & Whaley Bridge, or Pontrilas & Dorstone, or Brynmawr & Nantyglo Junction, but these would have sounded very ordinary. Instead, we were given names with a dash of glamour to them— Cromford & High Peak, Golden Valley, and Brynmawr & Western Valleys. Railways with such names just cry out to be visited, and the same applies to the Bluebell Railway of today. But for sheer oddness of name one cannot beat Oldham Alliance, which sounds as if it ought to have been a temperance society, or a cotton-workers' trade union, or a pact from the Wars of the Roses.

The Railways Act of 1921 resulted in a curious mixture of names for the four grouped railways which emerged. One was called the Southern Railway, and there seems no reason why the other three compass points should not have been used also. As it was, one railway took the complicated name of London, Midland & Scottish; these three words (surely they should have been London, Midlands and Scotland?) are not at all easy to say, and the railway was invariably known as the L.M.S. The name London Midland was perpetuated as the name of a Region after nationalization in 1948, when we might conveniently have had six single-word Regions—Northern,

A " King " heading west through Reading with the " Cornish Riviera Express " in 1953

A " Castle " nearing Hereford in 1962

Southern, Eastern, Western, Midland and Scottish; Caledonian for the last would have produced six different initials.

With names go nicknames. Some railways may have called themselves the Royal Road or the Premier Line, but real nicknames were made up by a pun on initials. Those in the know will recognize the Money Sunk & Lost, the Old Worse & Worse, the Slow, Easy & Comfortable, and the Slow, Dirty, Jerky as the Manchester, Sheffield & Lincolnshire, the Oxford, Worcester & Wolverhampton, the South Eastern & Chatham, and the Somerset & Dorset Joint. The Great Western Railway became the Great Way Round, or Gentlemen When Required; but it was left to George Behrend to provide the appropriate requiem for it with the title of his recent book, *Gone With Regret*.

AN EEL IN THE PIPE

Seldom if ever has a fish threatened to stop a railway service, yet this almost happened at Downpatrick some thirty years ago. The mystery of a continued lack of water in the engine tank puzzled the railway staff, and was not solved until the water main had been opened up. There was found an eel, 22 in. long and almost 4 in. in circumference. It is believed that the eel had been in the pipe for five or six years, as it must have entered through an opening only half an inch in diameter. Fishery experts were at a loss to know how it obtained sufficient food to remain alive.

From "*The Railway Magazine*"

During the Easter holiday rush, some 35 years ago, a heavy excursion train was held up for several minutes at a station because a lady's shoe had fallen from her foot on to the track, as she was entering the compartment. An agile porter had to get underneath the coach to retrieve it, to avoid the lady having to enjoy (or endure) her day's holiday with one shoe.

On Tuesday afternoon, I reached Liverpool after a flight (for it can be called nothing else) of 34 miles within an hour and a quarter. I was dreadfully frightened before the train started; in the nervous weak state I was in, it seemed to me certain that I should faint, and the impossibility of getting the horrid thing stopt.

From a letter to Thomas Carlyle from his wife, 1836

Early Letters of the Stockton & Darlington Railway

E. H. FOWKES, B.Sc. (Econ.)

THE GENTLEMEN AND MERCHANTS who met in an inn, in 1818, to form what became the Stockton & Darlington Railway little realized theirs was to be one of the great success stories of the nineteenth century. They met under depressing circumstances. The end of the Napoleonic wars had been followed by the failure of several country banks in Durham, causing losses of more than £12,000,000; trade was depressed; and poverty and distress were widespread throughout the county.

The meeting was convened to consider building a canal, but capital was so scarce it was decided that it might be cheaper to build a railway. The pressing need was to reduce the price of coal in the localities of Stockton and Darlington by lowering the cost of moving it from the rich Auckland coalfield. Carriage of coal by horses was slow, costly and inefficient; the River Tees was unnavigable; and a canal seemed to offer the solution of the problem. However, advice obtained from the foremost engineers, including John Rennie, favoured a railway instead of a canal.

By a remarkable historical and geographical coincidence, the noblemen, gentlemen and merchants of Knaresborough also met in 1818 to consider building a canal. Trade was languishing in their district, and they, too, realized the necessity for improved and cheaper transport. The district between

Knaresborough and Pateley Bridge is served by the River Nidd, a turbulent and winding river, suitable for power for mills, but useless for navigation. A representative meeting held at Knaresborough commissioned a report from that other great engineer of the canal age, Thomas Telford. Surprisingly Telford reported against a canal, and in favour of a railway. But here the parallel ends; for the Knaresborough Railway was destined never to be built.

The business men from Stockton and Darlington succeeded where those from Knaresborough failed because they were able to mobilize capital, engineering skill and among themselves to provide organizing ability of exceptional quality. During the formative period the pioneers of the Stockton & Darlington Railway wrote many letters. These letters, written when England was still a feudal country, have survived, despite the salvage drives of war and peace, and richly inform us of their hopes and fears in joining together to build their railway.

This large collection of letters, re-discovered in an old book room in Newcastle, are now in the custody of the Historical Records Office of British Railways Board at York. Little did the writers realize that they would, one day, be brought together to form a remarkable source of contemporary transport history. Though many of the several thousands of letters concern ordinary routine affairs some have special historical significance.

The letters clearly show that the objective of the members of the committee in building a railway was to open up the Auckland coalfield, and obtain the rich reward of enterprise by doing so. Some had colliery interests, others realized they would benefit indirectly. As already stated, they were originally interested in building a canal. A printed report of a meeting on September 4, 1818, states "That a Canal or a Rail or a Tram Road from the River Tees to the Collieries and the Interior of the County, will essentially promote as well the Agricultural as the Mining and Commercial Interests of this District". A month earlier Jonathan Backhouse, a Quaker banker of Darlington, who became the first Treasurer for the railway, wrote to Richard Miles, the secretary, about a proposed rival Stockton & Auckland Canal. This was to have connected the coalfield with the sea for the export of coal. Backhouse stated, "the calculations are so erroneous I cannot conceive that the publick will be gulled by them".

A railway was favoured in a letter from Richard Botcherby to Richard Miles, who was convinced of the superiority of a railway to a canal. But he knew it was necessary to make this convincingly clear in what was still the canal age. In this he was firmly supported by Thomas Meynell, a gentleman of Yarm, who became the first chairman of the Stockton & Darlington Railway. Meynell privately urged Miles to engage a Welsh engineer, George Overton, who had experience in laying colliery tramways, adding cautiously "though some of the gentlemen feel a delicacy in appearing to employ any Engineer but Mr. Rennie".

However, John Rennie was also consulted for he wrote on September 23, 1818, shortly after the printed statement had been published, "concerning the probable expense of the Stockton Canal, ———— an Iron Railway, ———— a Canal, ———— a Canal and Iron Railway, ———— the Canal by Darlington and that by Rushyford". Still unable to make a final decision the committee asked Rennie to consult with Robert Stevenson of Edinburgh to give a joint opinion whether a railway was to be preferred. This was too much for Rennie who indignantly replied, "I had been accustomed to thinking for myself in the numerous Publick works in which I had been engaged".

The Committee became convinced of the superior merits of a railway, for Leonard Raisbeck, a leading citizen of Stockton, indignantly wrote Richard Miles, asking him to reply to two press letters favouring a canal. On Boxing Day, Raisbeck also wrote to Miles, confidently and with clear prescience, "inform your neighbours that the committee of the *original* Railway are to meet on Friday".

A private subscription was made to engage George Overton, who prepared a survey and an application was made to Parliament. However, Leonard Raisbeck was prophetically correct when, describing the Bill's progress in the Committee of the House of Commons, he wrote, on March 23, 1819, "My Guess is they don't approve of it".

Then George Stephenson was engaged as Engineer; some modifications were made in Overton's survey; and the Committee decided to make a second application to Parliament. The Rev. W. L. Prattman, owner of Butterknowle and Copley Bent collieries, was rather disturbed, and wrote on December 23, 1819. "I have heard nothing more of the Railway. Is the whole affair gone to sleep?" He need not have been so concerned, for after one failure, when a report alleged that the first application was "a waste of money time and talent", the Committee carefully prepared their second attempt. Leonard Raisbeck's letter of March 30, 1821, was jubilant. "We have passed the Committee in high stile".

This was confirmed by Mrs. Meynell, of Yarm, who wrote to Richard Miles, also of Yarm, "the Bill passed the House of Commons on Thursday without opposition, and was immediately taken to the Lords, where it would be read for the first time that night". As prophesised the Bill was passed by Parliament, and unlike the first application no one grudged the cost.

The railway opened on September 25, 1825, with large crowds to celebrate; but in the intervening four years there had been many difficulties. Although there were no major engineering problems, there was no standard practice to follow. Advice was offered from many quarters but much of it was conflicting.

Edward Pease received a letter from his cousin advising against the use of malleable iron for rails. "I must strongly urge the Committee," he wrote, "going over to Lord Stewart's, where it has been in use and found not to answer." A similar warning against wrought iron rails was received from William Jessop of Butterley, who offered to supply cast iron rails. Fortunately, the Committee was more convinced by Michael Longridge of Bedlington, who was so confident of the quality of his patent malleable iron rails that he offered to supply them on payment "of one half of what they save by using these rails".

At that time, the steam locomotive had still to prove itself against horse traction, and when the railway was opened it had only one engine, *Locomotion*. The words of George Stephenson after the trial of *Locomotion* are well worth recording. It was 12 days before the opening of the railway when he wrote "the Improved Travelling Engine was tried here last night and fully answered my expectations".

More cautionary advice was received from Fenton & Murray of Leeds on October 26, 1825, one month after the opening of the railway. This letter recommended "to have the Engine upon one Carriage with four wheels and the boiler upon another Carriage ──── connected together by a Jointed Steam Pipe, this would reduce the weight of the Engine one half, and would be a great saving of the Rails. Till this is done we would recommend you to use Horses, at any rate not to make *any more* Engines above four Tons." In the following month there is another letter from the same firm which could be interpreted that they had no great faith in the future of the steam locomotive. This states "It does not suit with the present arrangement of our Business to take orders for High Pressure or Locomotive Engines, we have not made any this 8 years". However, it may be that the firm was too fully occupied in making machinery for the textile industry.

The Stockton & Darlington management wanted more locomotives, but was cautious in not wanting to place all orders with Stephenson's. An order had been placed with Robert Wilson of Newcastle, but on Christmas Eve, 1825, he wrote distressfully, "I cannot possibly have the Locomotive Engine ready for delivery before December 31st on account of your Railway being $\frac{3}{4}$ inch narrower than suits the engine". The days of precision engineering still lay in the future. This engine, nicknamed *Chittaprat* by workmen on account of the peculiar sound it made, was later reconstructed by Timothy Hackworth to become the very successful *Royal George*. There were many early troubles with locomotives before they became more reliable than horses. Years later, John Harris, the engineer, complaining of damage to the track, wrote that "the *Meteor* engine is too strait," and "the *Tory* engine throws so much fire".

The initial engineering problems were not confined to locomotives and rails. Laying the track with stone sleepers, which were available from Brusselton and other quarries for 7d. each, involved costly cartage. It was therefore decided to use stone blocks for sleepers only in the district accessible to the stone quarries. Oak blocks, brought by sea to Stockton, supplied by Holmes & Pushman of Portsea, were used as an alternative. These were bought for 6d. each from the shipbreakers' yard and so the new locomotives rode along an iron way upheld by England's hearts of oak. In the choice of track the cautious Quaker management chose cast iron rails from Neath Abbey Ironworks as well as malleable iron rails from Michael Longridge's Bedlington Works.

The Stockton & Darlington Railway had its management difficulties too. Authority was exercised by means of a committee which led to excessive interference in management. Those who had money invested wished too ardently and too personally to make it a success. In 1830, it was suggested that a manager should be appointed, but this was not acted upon. The Committee (or Directors as we would call them today) made decisions on matters of principle, leaving enforcement by a sub-committee. The latter gave instructions and enforced decisions.

In 1837, there were complaints about the accounts, and the accountant resigned. His main function was the issue of stock and the payment of dividends. The Engineer was responsible for personally checking all other accounts, and an additional check was made each month by two cautious committee members. In 1836, a report on the accounts stated "they are imperfect, and such as the Committee ought by no means to be content with". John Harris succeeded Thomas Storey as Engineer, and disliked being burdened with accounts as a routine part of his duties. He wrote to the Committee "it would be to the advantage of the Company that I should be freed entirely from keeping accounts", but it was some time later before this was done.

The Stockton & Darlington Railway has frequently been called the "Quaker Line" because so many of its management were of that sect. Among them were some extremely able men who combined great talents with the ability to induce other Quakers to invest their money with confidence. The railway was also blessed with the services of three engineers who were Quakers, Thomas Storey, John Dixon and John Harris. It is to these men, and to Joseph Pease, that the main credit for success of the railway is due.

Joseph Pease was outstanding and very much overworked. He obtained the finance required for the expansion of the line, piloted the various Bills through Parliament, and yet found time to deal with the most trivial and detailed affairs of management as the large number of his surviving letters show. His office was nominally that of Treasurer, to which he succeeded after the resignation of Jonathan Backhouse, but was akin to that of General Manager. Wise, understanding, liberal in outlook, though stern in manner, he was trusted and easily approached by those suffering from injustice. Yet he imposed a strict if just discipline. Declaring before a Select Committee, in 1839, that the Stockton & Darlington Railway had no disciplinary difficulties he stated "we warn once, and dismiss on a second lapse".

Despite its ultimate success and extraordinary influence on the development of railways, the Stockton & Darlington had its failures. It is not surprising that these were mainly in engineering. One of the earliest failures was the bridge across the Tees to Middlesbrough. This bridge sagged 9 in. when bearing a loaded coal train and although a method was adapted of using chains between sets of wagons to distribute the weight this was rather ineffective. One of the members of the Committee, Jeremiah Cairns, had his doubts before the bridge was open. He wrote on the day before it was opened, "I wish you all safely over the bridge". Shildon Tunnel was also a disappointment. Built by a nominally-independent company it cost more than anticipated, and has always been a source of expense. Still in use, it has required very heavy maintenance expenditure, and now carries only a single track.

Another disappointment was the receipts from passenger traffic. The *Experiment* coach, horse-drawn, commenced its daily service in each direction between Stockton and Darlington on October 10, 1825, and the receipts averaged little more than £1 a day. In consequence, the coach was let on contract after nine months, and passenger services were operated by innkeepers for the next seven years. There were no intermediate stations, but only termini and halting places. The first waiting room was a rented room in the "Masons Arms", Shildon.

Success was due to the improvement of the steam locomotive for drawing loaded coal trains. The result was in doubt for a number of years, during which both horses and locomotives were used. The railway was fortunate in having a falling gradient for loaded coal wagons, and in commanding the services of Timothy Hackworth, a mechanic of genius, who won the hard struggle to keep the engines in traffic. The engine drivers, called "leaders" in those early days, were frequently fined for travelling too fast, high speeds being responsible for damage to the track, and for heavy maintenance on the engines.

The fines box was always well filled, for discipline was severe. The instructions of the Committee were enforced by the Police Superintendent, Thomas Manton, who kept the Committee well informed of any failures or malpractices. It is fair to say that the accumulated fines did not find their way into the company's coffers but were donated to employees suffering from injury or misfortune. Among Thomas Manton's many reports is one, dated March 1, 1848, which states "Geo. Watkinson was sent to transportation for 14 years for breaking open a cabin and stealing a coat"—a savage sentence on a man for taking an old coat in a bitterly cold winter.

It requires a lot of imagination today to visualize how dangerous railways were when brakes were either rudimentary or non-existent. Accidents were all too frequent, and caused great suffering when hospitals were few. Without telephones, and before the telegraph was invented, some time elapsed before medical assistance could be obtained. The regulation for dealing with accidents provided for a workman to be taken home if he lived within two miles of the accident. Otherwise he was taken to the nearest inn, the company paying the innkeeper. To obtain medical assistance, a system of relay runners was worked. In this way details of the accident were passed on from one permanent way gang to another to the nearest doctor. The latter would then ride on horseback to the inn where the injured man lay. Accounts submitted by doctors and innkeepers for their services make most interesting reading.

The Quaker Committee were opposed to Sunday trains, and there were no Sunday services on the Stockton & Darlington Railway until the mail was carried in 1843. Passengers were not booked on the train carrying the mail until two years later. Earlier, permission was given to members of the public to walk along the railway line if going to church or chapel. Otherwise the Company was very keen on preventing trespass. In 1843, William Holberry and Thomas Ingledew petitioned the Committee stating "they continue to suffer pecuniary losses from the high rate of mileages they are charged with, and from allowing Foot Passengers to travel the Line on Sundays". Evidently the horse coach service they operated at that time between Middlesbrough and Stockton was not lucrative to them.

Petitions were the usual mode of indicating a grievance in the early days of railways, and the Stockton & Darlington Committee received many from employees and the public. Among the petitions was one, in 1844, from the gatekeepers (signalmen) asking for the restoration of wages cuts made during the Pitmen's strike when traffic had fallen off. An outstanding petition was that of enginemen beaten in a strike in 1867. Their humble petition asking for reinstatement stated: "We repent what we have done, and promise the act will never be repeated. . . . We cast ourselves entirely upon your mercy."

The gentlemen, merchants, solicitors and bankers formed themselves into a railway committee solely to exploit a rich coalfield. They had no intention of building stations, houses, schools, and supporting provident societies. Force of circumstance compelled them to widen their activities, providing a pattern followed by many of Britain's railways.

It was soon realized that safe working depended on employees being readily available and houses were early provided on the Brusselton and Etherley Inclines. In 1840, a writer described the houses provided: "On one side of the railway small cots are erected for the use of the workmen employed on the line, a plan which will no doubt, very soon be followed on all the chief lines in the kingdom. These buildings are erected at small expense, and are very convenient for the waymen, and others who work on the line, who ought to be always near their work, and are thus prevented from frequenting the country ale house."

Being the tenant of a railway house had distinct drawbacks as John West found to his annoyance, when, on wet days, his kitchen at Fighting Cocks, one of England's earliest country stations, served also as a waiting room for passengers. At Waskerley, the railway was laid across high and wild moorland, where it was necessary not only to house the entire railway community but also to provide a school for their children. The schoolmaster, John Langbone, appears to have carried out his duties very efficiently for a weekly wage of 15s. 7d. Children paid 2d. a week, and the Stockton & Darlington Railway made up the balance, after a very careful check of the attendances.

Having become involved with social welfare by accident rather than design, the Stockton & Darlington Railway formed a Provident Society to encourage thrift among its employees. This caused some dissension, for a petition from the Traffic Department reads: "If the men of the Stockton and Darlington shops continue draining the funds of the club as they have done the last six years . . . the society will be entirely ruined."

Besides encouraging thrift the Stockton and Darlington Committee tried to promote sobriety. They did not pay wages in public houses as was then frequently the practice. However, all their efforts were not too successful, for in 1853, they were asked to provide a scripture reader at Shildon, because "large wages are being earned and too rapidly squandered".

A collection of several thousands of letters contains much that is mundane. Very few were written by women, most of which concern dividends. Letters relating to materials, organization, and complaints against railway servants are numerous. Complaints are mainly concerning shortage of wagons, working of coal, lime and iron traffics. Among them are occasional revelations, such as a letter from Joseph Pease. This alleges that George Hudson, the "Railway King", had stated he had got all the concessions he wanted from Gladstone on the Railway Bill, in 1844.

Nowhere among the letters is there any expressed intention to ruin the turnpikes. Easier and cheaper haulage of coal and freight was the goal, little importance being attached to passenger traffic. It was not intended to carry mail nor was it until the railway had been working for 18 years that it did so after correspondence with the postal authorities.

Early Letters of the Stockton & Darlington Railway

At the outset, the railway had no rule book and no signalling system, though an interesting account reads "to paid Bellman calling notices as to Trespassers at Stockton". Indeed until the middle 1840s, the railway was a very local affair, except for its shareholders who were spread throughout the country. Its clocks registered local time, and it was unconcerned at the difference of seven minutes with the clocks of the Darlington station of the Great North of England Railway, which maintained Greenwich mean time.

Yet its success was vitally important, not only for the Durham coal trade but for the future prosperity of Britain. This was realized by Thomas Hill of Leeds, a carrier by road and canal. On the eve of the opening of the railway he wrote: "the expectation from railroads has fallen in public estimation very much these last 4–6 weeks. . . . The revived good opinion of them . . . will a good deal depend upon the performance and success of the Darlington Railway." When on the threshold of success internal dissension almost ruined its prospects. Jeremiah Cairnes, a member of the Railway Committee, had been responsible for securing the services of George Overton for the original survey. He alarmed Francis Mewburn, the first railway solicitor, who wrote to Richard Miles: "Cairnes proposes applying Mr. Meynell's £100 in discharge of his balance, ———— this, however, will produce uproar, and lay the seeds of disunion which may be fatal to our project."

CRY FROM THE HEART

Seen at Charing Cross Station at the morning rush hour: young man on a platform seat, all but swept away by the tide of commuters, and by his side a briefcase to which was attached a notice saying "Why don't you emigrate or something?"

"Peterborough", in "The Daily Telegraph"

DIGGING UP THE PAST

While clearing out a creek under a railway bridge on his land, in 1935, a Texas farmer uncovered an old Texas & Pacific Railroad engine which had been buried for nearly sixty years. In 1876, a cloudburst washed away the bridge, and the engine plunged into the river where it had lain forgotten.

From "The Railway Magazine"

Southern Occasions

J. N. FAULKNER

THE SOUTH OF ENGLAND is usually associated with the more pleasurable opportunities for rail travel; possibly the seaside holiday, or the day in the country, or an afternoon's sport, or some public celebration. For the railways south of the Thames have long been specialists in the business of carrying large numbers of people on great occasions.

The racing calendar plays an important part in Southern schedules, with 14 racecourses active within the Region, despite closures which have reduced their numbers in recent years. Other sporting interests catered for by the S.R. include rowing men to the Boat Race, yachtsmen to Cowes, riflemen to Bisley, rugger types to Twickenham, and even motor racing enthusiasts to Goodwood now, or to Brooklands in pre-war days. The Southern lines have always been involved in military displays, from the Wimbledon Common Volunteer camps of Victorian days to the Tidworth and Aldershot Tattoos of the 'thirties, the Navy Weeks at Chatham and Portsmouth, the occasional spectacular Spithead Naval Reviews, and in the air the regular Farnborough shows.

The London & Southampton Railway had a rapid and rude introduction to the business of handling crowds. Its line from Nine Elms to Woking was opened a week before the Derby Day of 1838, and the company announced that eight trains were to be run to the Kingston Station (the present Surbiton) for the accommodation of the racing public. Most of the racegoers would then have had to make the seven-mile journey to Epsom Downs on foot, but some of the more affluent were to be conveyed to the course by four-horse coaches for an inclusive return fare from Nine Elms of a guinea—surely the earliest example of a rail/road combined excursion.

The early morning of Derby Day found a crowd of 5,000 waiting outside Nine Elms terminus, and as fast as the loaded trains were despatched more people arrived. The station doors were closed to keep out the impatient throng, but eventually the pressure of the crowd carried the doors off their hinges and the mob poured over the booking counter and climbed through the windows to invade the special train reserved for the guinea ticketholders. Some of these did succeed in reaching Kingston station, only to find that no conveyance to the course awaited them. Back at Nine Elms the harassed officials sent for the Metropolitan Police to clear the station, and at noon a notice was posted that no more trains to the races would leave that day.

Undaunted by this fiasco, the Southampton Company a few days later ran special trains to its Woking Common Station to cater for Ascot racegoers, again entailing a formidable walk to and from the course. It was not until 1856 that L.S.W.R. served Ascot directly, and a revealing account of how race traffic was handled in the 'sixties can be obtained from the evidence at the inquest and manslaughter proceedings following the Egham accident of June 7, 1864. This involved an overtaking collision between two of the specials returning from Ascot in which seven passengers lost their lives.

The return traffic after the races was being despatched from Ascot under the authority of Archibald Scott, the Traffic Manager—no timetable had been issued for the 14 specials, and station-masters were told to expect trains at any and every minute. The usual fixed signals were supplemented by 11 plate-layers stationed at intervals along the line between Ascot and Egham with instructions to exhibit the red danger hand signal for five minutes after the passage of a train, then the green caution flag for a further five minutes followed by the all clear signal. However, enginemen were not to stop their trains at the danger flag, but could proceed cautiously prepared to halt short of any obstruction. In evidence it was found that the platelayer stationed near the Egham auxiliary (distant) signal had no watch and "could read but little", and that the Rusham level crossing signals were being worked entirely on the time interval as calculated by the crossing-keeper's watch (which had stopped and was not showing the correct time) without reference to the nearby Egham auxiliary signal.

A special train to Waterloo was despatched from Ascot at 7.9 p.m. with instructions to stop at Egham, Twickenham, Barnes, Clapham Junction and Vauxhall. This consisted of 14 coaches and two vans, hauled by the Gooch 2-4-0 *Alaric*. It was followed six minutes later by another train, which was to run non-stop to Staines, also formed of 14 carriages behind the early Beattie

Southern Occasions

2-4-0 *Milo* working tender first; most of the return specials were worked in this manner as there was no turntable at Ascot, although this arrangement interrupted the communication chain between driver and guard. The first special was delayed at Egham Station for a few minutes because of a dispute among some cardsharpers. Meanwhile the second train had been running at speed under clear signals until the Rusham crossing semaphore was sighted at caution, followed immediately by the danger signals being exhibited by the Egham auxiliary and by platelayer Drew. Driver Lee then whistled for his brakes, but although the front guard responded the second guard was not attending to his duties and speed was still between 15 and 20 m.p.h. when his train collided with the first special, which had just restarted.

At the inquest a verdict of manslaughter was returned against Driver Lee and his fireman, who were committed for trial at the Surrey assizes. Undoubtedly they had run their train much faster than was prudent in the circumstances, and had not observed the caution required by the special instructions for the race traffic. However, defending counsel succeeded in diverting attention to the casual operating methods—much was made of the fact that the telegraph was used only to signal the departure of the Royal Train and not for the protection of ordinary traffic. Company officials were roughly handled in cross-examination, and the trial developed into an indictment of the L.S.W.R. Eventually the judge interposed and invited the jury to return a verdict of Not Guilty.

These primitive operating methods soon gave way to safe and efficient practice, and at the turn of the century the L.S.W.R. was obtaining a lucrative traffic from Ascot week, with specials leaving Waterloo at four-minute intervals on race days. But even before 1914 this monopoly was threatened, and a feature of several of the chairman's annual speeches was the growing number of motor-cars counted at the course. While Society adopted the new form of transport some of the popular traffic was also being abstracted by the Great Western Railway's motor buses from Windsor Station. However, the first post-war Ascot, in 1919, found the South Western's depleted rolling stock inadequate for the traffic, and for the first and only time a system of regulated booking was introduced, and special offices at Waterloo issued 10,000 tickets in advance for the 25 trains which were available each day. Rolling stock had evidently been pooled, as a contemporary illustration shows racegoers in their finery strolling along No. 14 platform at Waterloo towards a train of vintage G.W.R. clerestory coaches coupled to a class M7 0-4-4 tank.

The inter-war years brought Pullmans and luncheon cars on Ascot specials, and for the railway enthusiast Ascot week was one of the highlights of the year. Much of the freight traffic through Feltham yard was suspended or

173

retimed and the Urie class H16 4-6-2 tanks made their annual appearance on passenger trains. During the 'thirties Ascot week usually coincided with the Aldershot Tattoo, and the homegoing race specials passed excursions bound for the nightly spectacle in the Rushmoor Arena. To meet the demand for extra motive power, engines were borrowed from sheds as far afield as Exmouth Junction. Even after the Alton electrification of 1937, steam-hauled specials to the Tattoo would come from the L.M.S.R. and L.N.E.R. systems, as well as those from south-east London which were usually worked through by L or L1 class 4-4-0s. There was also a supper car train from Waterloo direct to Aldershot Government Siding which necessarily remained steam-hauled.

To revert to the subject of Ascot Races, electrification of the Reading line in 1939 simplified the operating problems on race days. There is only limited siding accommodation at Ascot, and many of the empty specials had to be stabled on running lines in the neighbourhood, with drastic effects on the ordinary train services. One difficulty did arise with the electric trains—how to cater for the first-class-only specials—but this was solved by the attachment of antimacassars (that symbol of first-class status) to all the seats in some Portsmouth corridor sets, and by segregating these trains on the return journey to depart from the racecourse platform. Exceptionally, a genuine first-class-only restaurant car special was run for the Coronation year of 1953, with a West Country Pacific in charge of a motley collection of L.M.S.R. and L.N.E.R. open saloons interspersed by Great Central kitchen cars.

Post-war Ascot Weeks have seen a decline in the number of specials from Waterloo, but if the residents of Mayfair and Belgravia no longer travel by train, social change has brought more traffic to the popular side of the course with long-distance excursions arriving from such unlikely places as Llanelly, Merthyr and Sutton-in-Ashfield. These specials mostly approach Ascot from the Reading direction, and are dealt with at Ascot west platform, but in 1963 there was also a first-class special from Manchester Piccadilly to Ascot main station at a fare of eight guineas, including grandstand ticket, smoked salmon lunch and chicken dinner.

The greatest event in the racing calendar has always been the Derby, and after the South Western's pioneer efforts, the London, Brighton & South Coast Railway secured a firm hold on this traffic with the opening of its line to Epsom Town in 1847, and to Epsom Downs in 1865. But the Brighton's monopoly was broken in 1901 when the South Eastern & Chatham Railway opened the Chipstead Valley line to Tattenham Corner in time for Derby Day, and handled 50 specials at the new terminus on top of the Downs alongside the course. Tattenham Corner Station was laid out even more spaciously than Epsom Downs had been. It had seven long platforms, extensive sidings, a turntable and locomotive servicing facilities. Only on the wooden station buildings was expense spared; these were said to be temporary but they survive today.

A feature of both the L.B.S.C.R. and S.E.C.R. routes used to be the tiny lineside signal cabins, some of them not even distinguished with names, which were manned for two or three days in the year merely to handle the intensive services provided for the big races. In 1937, as an example, 54 trains ran to Epsom Downs and 68 to Tattenham Corner during the morning and early afternoon of Derby Day, the customary electrics being supplemented by steam-hauled specials from Kent, and by Pullman trains from Victoria, Charing Cross and Cannon Street, which brought business men from their offices in time for the afternoon's racing. The steam-worked specials to Epsom Downs were usually double-headed by two tank engines while Moguls were used on the Tattenham Corner trains. Since the war the Pullman specials have sometimes been worked by electric locomotives, but rail traffic has declined in recent years, until only the Royal Train from Victoria to Tattenham Corner remained to break the electrified uniformity of Derby Day. For a number of years this was hauled by a resplendent Schools class 4-4-0, and latterly a light Pacific from Nine Elms was employed.

Epsom races found the three pre-grouping companies in accord for once— they all fixed their fares according to the principle of "charging what the traffic will bear". A 1922 L.B.S.C.R. leaflet quotes a return fare of 8s. 6d. on Derby Day with "no particular class of carriage guaranteed". Even at today's fares the Southern Region will take you to Epsom Downs for 6s. 6d. return.

To turn now from the racecourse to the football field, the Southern does not carry much soccer traffic unless Portsmouth or Southampton has a lucky run in the F.A. Cup competition, but before the Second World War an intensive shuttle service used to be run over the West London Extension line from Clapham Junction to Chelsea & Fulham Station whenever there was a home match at Stamford Bridge. But it is the followers of the Rugby Union code flocking to Twickenham who bring the Southern Region its best football business—on International match days the concourse at Waterloo is alive with hearty crowds waiting for the electric trains which leave every three or four minutes from the main-line arrival platforms Nos. 12 to 15. There is reason in this central point of departure, for one of the attractions of the journey to Twickenham, for those who have other thoughts than Rugger, is the choice of route to be followed. The everyday traveller to Twickenham goes there direct *via* Richmond, but the Rugger enthusiast is more likely to be taken for a circuit of the Hounslow Loop or of the Kingston Roundabout, so that his train will arrive at Twickenham facing back towards London, ready to return for another load or to shunt to the up sidings to await the return traffic.

If Twickenham is the centre of the Rugger world, Bisley is the Mecca of the rifleman, and in 1890 the National Rifle Association opened a light railway (officially a tramway) linking its Bisley ranges with Brookwood station on the L.S.W.R. main line. Normally the branch was open only during the periods of rifle meetings, when the S.R. would provide a frequent service of pull-and-push trains for the two-mile journey. Inevitably, such an occasional service was condemned as uneconomic, and in 1952 the Southern Region announced that the branch would be closed permanently after the end of that year's meeting and replaced by a special bus service.

The final day of operation was Saturday, July 19, also the climax of the rifle meeting when the Queen's Cup competition was decided, and to mark the occasion the branch train was decorated with bunting and its engine, M7 tank No. 30027, adorned with dummy rifles. There was the usual gathering of railway enthusiasts attracted by a closure, and as the day advanced increasing numbers of passengers were travelling. Towards eight o'clock, the time for the final journey from Bisley arrived, and with the week's sport over many of the competitors joined the enthusiasts for a ride on the last train. Eventually it left Bisley in the gathering dusk, its two coaches packed solid with humanity, and the overflow clinging to the outside by any available hand or foothold or even riding on the roof. The engine footplate accommodated another half a dozen travellers, while other passengers rode out in front or stood on top of the side tanks of 30027 and waved Union Jacks in celebration. So the convoy steamed into the bay platform at Brookwood to the accompaniment of the customary fusillade of detonators looking more like a refugee special in revolutionary Russia than a train belonging to British Railways.

The Southern's interest in flying as a spectacle now centres on the S.B.A.C. display at Farnborough, when a highly efficient combined operation between the S.R. and the Aldershot & District bus company conveys thousands of sightseers to the airfield *via* Aldershot, North Camp and Farnborough stations.

But in 1929, the Schneider Trophy contest attracted enormous crowds to watch these tiny seaplanes racing at 350 m.p.h. above the waters of the Solent. All shipping traffic was suspended during the period of flying, and most of the railway-owned Isle of Wight steamer fleet was anchored in Spithead to serve as floating grandstands. As the race took place on a busy September Saturday special trains and boats ran all through the previous night between Waterloo, Portsmouth and the Isle of Wight, and on the morning of the races all ordinary traffic was cancelled on the Portsmouth Direct line to allow for the stream of non-stop specials to Portsmouth Harbour. Special excursions also ran

The down "Golden Arrow" approaching Sevenoaks on its way from London to Dover

to Portsmouth from places as far apart as Dover and Plymouth, while other specials brought unwonted activity to the Gosport branch, which had 13 arrivals during the morning, including a remarkable through train from Bulford. Even the Lee-on-Solent branch enjoyed the busiest day of its unprofitable existence, with frequent non-stop trains taking spectators to vantage points on the seashore.

Meanwhile, over in the Isle of Wight the railway system had been busy since the early hours with holidaymakers and spectators. Normal traffic was suspended at Ryde Esplanade and Pierhead stations during most of the day. However, a unique service of what were in every sense of the word relief trains was provided on the railway between these stations to enable the 3,600 spectators assembled in the grandstand enclosures at the Pierhead to supplement the limited toilet facilities there with the use of those at the Esplanade.

These waters around Spithead have been the scene of Coronation Naval Reviews four times during the present century, and the most recent of these, which took place on June 15, 1953, was the occasion of one of the Southern's greatest feats of organization. The conveyance of the spectators and the official guests to their vantage points on land and sea required the despatch of 46 special trains from London on that Monday morning. Thirteen trains were scheduled from Victoria to Portsmouth, Fareham and Gosport, but Waterloo carried the heaviest burden with 33 departures for Portsmouth and Southampton. The departure of the specials was concentrated into a period of about three-and-a-half hours, which coincided with the normal weekday incoming rush hour traffic, but by some ingenious timetabling only one up suburban train was completely cancelled, two more were terminated *en route*, and a few thousand season ticket holders found themselves slightly delayed by making a detour *via* East Putney. The punctuality of the down specials was vital as a margin of only 15 to 20 minutes was allowed for embarkation at Southampton before the spectators' vessels were due to sail for their anchorages according to schedules fixed by the Admiralty. Besides many of the B.T.C.'s cross-channel ships, such veteran paddle steamers as *Consul*, *Embassy*, *Cardiff Queen* and *Medway Queen* awaited their complement of sightseers off the trains from Waterloo.

An unusual feature of the review traffic was the high proportion of firstclass travel, including trains chartered by large industrial and commercial organizations, and others conveying members of both Houses of Parliament and official guests. Additional first-class stock was borrowed from the E.R. and L.M.R., but the demand for Pullman cars (45 in all) could only be met by forming the review day's "Devon Belle" partly from ordinary stock.

The return traffic was less concentrated; some spectators came home as soon as the review was over while others stayed for the illumination of the fleet.

A Saturdays-only express from North Devon to London, headed by S.R. Pacific No. 34096, Trevone, emerging from Buckhorn Weston Tunnel, near Templecombe

During the small hours of June 16, Waterloo was kept busy dealing with these later return specials, which arrived at ten-minute intervals. The working of the special and ordinary traffic on the review day and the following day was also complicated by the scheduling of four Royal Train journeys. The spare "Brighton Belle" Pullman set was used for these trips which conveyed members of the Royal Family from Waterloo to Portsmouth and on the return from Portsmouth to Windsor. The Southern Region's printed 140-page instruction covered every possible detail of the review arrangements and elaborate precautions had been taken against accidents and breakdowns. For example, the signal boxes along the Alton line were manned throughout the night of June 15/16, in case the return traffic had to be diverted from the main line. In the event the whole operation was carried out without any serious hitch, and punctuality on this big occasion for steam traction was well maintained.

Besides the traditional pageantry and military display, the Coronation of King George V in 1911 was celebrated by a vast festival and fête held in the grounds of the Crystal Palace on June 30, to which were invited all the L.C.C. schoolchildren aged 11 and over. Of the 100,000 children attending the fête, nearly all came by train, and though the L.B.S.C.R. and the S.E.C.R. were both accustomed to dealing with large crowds at their respective stations on Cup Final day such a multitude was never attracted to the Final in pre-Wembley days.

A total of 96 special trains were provided to convey the children to the Palace; 56 *via* the L.B.S.C.R. and the balance *via* the S.E.C.R. The heaviest traffic was handled at the Brighton's Crystal Palace (Low Level) Station which dealt with 42 trains in four hours, 29 of them provided by the owning company, seven by the North London Railway, four by the G.W.R., and one each by the L.N.W.R. and the L.S.W.R. Fourteen trains *via* the East London Line arrived at the L.B.S.C.R. Penge Station (now Penge West), five of them worked by the G.E.R., and nine by the Brighton. The S.E.C.R. High Level terminus received 37 specials, including eight Great Northern trains *via* the Widened Lines and Snow Hill, and lastly the three Midland trains which also followed this route ran to Sydenham Hill Station on the Chatham main line.

The list of starting points now reads like a litany of London's bygone stations—Hackney, Homerton, Holloway, Coborn Road, Chelsea & Fulham, Greenwich Park, Walworth Road and Battersea Park Road, besides many others which are still doing business. The whole of the L.C.C. area from West Hampstead to Tooting and from Putney to Woolwich sent contingents. Each train was tightly packed with an average of 15 occupants to each compartment, but even at this density many of the specials must have been long and heavy. In imagination, one can see the Brighton "Terriers" and the

G.E.R. "Buck-Jumpers" struggling through the Thames Tunnel with their heavily-loaded trains, but in fact, whatever the difficulties, the specials achieved almost complete punctuality.

The movement of the schoolchildren was highly organized; every child had an identity badge sewn on its clothing which displayed its starting station and train number, while the shape of the badge indicated the alighting station in the Crystal Palace area. The routes between the stations and the Palace grounds were carefully planned to avoid conflicting movements between columns, and the railway authorities staged a practical demonstration beforehand of the best way to unload a thousand children from a train in three minutes when traditional scholastic procedures threatened to impede the necessary speedy handling of the specials.

Of course this tremendous volume of traffic could not be handled without a major upheaval of ordinary suburban services throughout a wide area. For instance, the G.W.R. cancelled several of its trains to Victoria, but interruptions were prolonged on the lines leading to the Palace. The S.E.C.R. lines to the High Level and to Greenwich Park were closed for most of the day as the special trains were stabled during the afternoon on both roads between Nunhead and Honor Oak. The Brighton managed to handle a little ordinary traffic at the Low Level during the mid-afternoon, but otherwise its newly-inaugurated electric service was suspended from 10.30 a.m. until 8 p.m. One special electric ran for the Press, but all other specials were steam-hauled, and those arriving *via* West Norwood continued empty to Norwood Junction where they were stabled on the down relief line between there and Croydon. In readiness for the return traffic empty trains lined up nose to tail between Norwood Junction and Crystal Palace, and between Norwood Junction and Penge, so that the stopping trains between Croydon and London Bridge had to be cancelled for periods of the day.

The Coronation of King George had been preceded a year earlier by the death and funeral of King Edward VII, which had been the occasion of probably the greatest gathering of crowned heads ever seen in London, an assemblage never repeated since, as war and revolution have toppled half the thrones of Europe. Most of the royalty and other national representatives arrived in Britain *via* the Channel ports, and the task of conveying them to London fell to the S.E.C.R. During the ten-day period preceding the King's funeral this railway carried an Emperor, a Dowager Empress, seven Kings, two Queens, 21 Princes and Princesses, five Archdukes and Grand Dukes, six Dukes and Duchesses, two Oriental potentates, and five other heads of missions. All these dignitaries required suitable and separate accommodation for themselves and their suites—notwithstanding that the S.E.C.R. was not a line that was well endowed with luxurious modern rolling stock. In all, 15 special trains were run from the Channel ports to Victoria, also several local specials from Herne Hill into the departure platforms at Victoria to convey royal saloons detached from ordinary boat trains there.

This illustrious influx reached its peak on May 18, when seven Royal Trains arrived at Victoria. During the mid-afternoon royalty was sailing into Dover at such frequent intervals that both the Admiralty Pier and the Prince of Wales Pier were being used alternately to avoid any need for haste in receiving and entraining the mourners. The Flushing-Queenborough route was a favourite choice with many of the minor German royalty, and also for Mr. Theodore Roosevelt, the American representative, but the rival Medway pier at Port Victoria was used for the arrival of Prince Henry of the Netherlands on the 18th, and of the German Emperor on the 19th. In 1910, long before the construction of the Lewisham loops, the journey from Port Victoria to Victoria could only be made indirectly with a reversal at Blackfriars. After the S.E.C.R. Royal Train had brought the Kaiser into Victoria at about noon it had to be rushed down to Dover to form the 3 p.m. special from the Prince of Wales Pier for the King of the Belgians and the Prince of Montenegro— seldom can a railway's "special" saloons have seen such intensive use as the S.E.C.R. put theirs to for King Edward's funeral.

Turning, in conclusion, from these bygone days of monarchical Europe to the jet age, one finds that the Southern still has a key part to play in the reception of distinguished overseas visitors to this country. If full honour and ceremony is to be paid to State guests, a worthy gateway to Britain is scarcely provided by the windy tarmac at London Airport, the jostling traffic of the Great West Road, and the vistas of the Hammersmith Flyover. Instead the visitor's aircraft is brought into Gatwick Airport, and within a few minutes of landing the foreign royalty or statesman, ensconced in Pullman comfort, is speeding towards Victoria to receive his official welcome to Britain on No. 2 Platform.

MECHANICAL BREAKDOWN

Woman, recently moved from London, to a shopkeeper in a Kent village: "I like it down here myself, but my husband doesn't. He says he hates being a computer."

"Peterborough", in " The Daily Telegraph"

The Trail of '69

JOHN ROBERTS

ON MONDAY, MAY 10, 1869, the Union Pacific pushing westward from Omaha met the Central Pacific Railroad, on its eastward march from Sacramento, at Promontory Point, 50 miles from Ogden, Utah, and established a steel link between the east and west coasts of the United States. Before the railway was built, travellers had the choice of a long and stormy voyage round Cape Horn, a short journey across the fever-ridden Isthmus of Panama, or a long overland journey across the United States.

At sea at this time, *en route* from Sydney to San Francisco, was an Australian determined to be one of the first travellers by the new route. When he left Sydney, 200 miles of the transcontinental railway remained to be built; when he arrived, after a quick sea passage of 60 days, the new route was open, and England was only 20 days away. The Australian made his pioneer trip, and in *Chambers's Journal* for November 20 and 27, 1869, he told his story. When the railway was first opened, the passage from San Francisco to Sacramento was still made by steamer on the Sacramento River, but the extension from Sacramento City to Alameda, on San Francisco Bay, was opened on September 6, 1869, completing the rail link.

The driving force behind the transcontinental railway was an engineer with vision beyond his years, Theodore D. Judah, who believed in a railway such as this, had spent lonely months looking for passes in the mountains, and had found others with the same vision. Sent to Washington to raise money, as the accredited representative of the Central Pacific Railroad Co., which had been formed largely because of his advocacy, he was instrumental in persuading

Congress to take action. In this he was helped by political fears for the future of an isolated California.

On May 8, 1862, the House of Representatives passed an Act to enable a transcontinental line to be built, and a similar Act was passed by the Senate on June 20. Congress agreed to the Central Pacific line, but also decreed that another company, to be called the Union Pacific, should be organized to build westward to meet it. The companies would be granted a right-of-way, other land near the track as a bonus for each mile completed, a 30-year loan to carry out the work, and a substantial subsidy. They left the exact starting point at the eastern end, and the gauge, to be determined by President Lincoln, who signed the Act on July 1, 1862.

The short existing Californian railways, the Sacramento Valley Railroad and the California Central, were of 5 ft. gauge, as were the lines of the South— a fact which proved useful to the Confederates, who had few of the mixed-gauge problems of the Union forces. The older Eastern lines were mostly 4 ft. 8½ in. Lincoln signed an order establishing the 5 ft. gauge, but he was overruled by Congress within a few days, and the 4 ft. 8½ in. gauge was duly established for this and future lines.

The starting point was rather curious. Congress said that it should be on the 100th meridian of west longitude, but branches were to be built from the various towns in the area, such as Sioux City, Leavenworth, Kansas City, and so on. The President was to decide where the central—obviously the main—branch should be built. On November 17, 1863, he issued an order which was so worded as to be capable of being read as either Council Bluffs or Omaha. The Union Pacific naturally did not want to start its labours by bridging the Missouri, so they assumed it meant Omaha, and ground was broken there on December 2, 1863. The decision had been due mostly to the influence on Lincoln of General Dodge, an army engineer who was later to become chief engineer of the Union Pacific. It was a good choice, for at least three railways were already approaching Council Bluffs, across the Missouri from Omaha, from the East, and there would be plenty of choice of routes to carry the transcontinental trains on to the coast.

Before we end this short survey to set the scene for our Australian's commentary, perhaps we may quote from a speech to Congress by Collis P. Huntingdon, one of the leading members of the Central Pacific's first board, and a colleague of Judah's. He said: "There were difficulties from end to end: from high and steep mountains; from snows; from deserts where there was a scarcity of water, and from gorges and flats where there was an excess; difficulties from cold and heat; from a scarcity of timber and from obstructions of rock; difficulties in keeping a large force on a long line; from Indians; and from want of labour."

The Trail of '69

Our Australian (whose narrative is necessarily condensed) wrote: "San Francisco, or 'Friscoe', as it is endearingly termed by its inhabitants, is, as seen from the water, decidedly disappointing. The bay, it is true, is magnificent—the broad expanse of water stretching out full seven miles to the Golden Gate, as the entrance is termed, reminding us a little of Sydney harbour. But then the aridity of the situation of the city is quite distressing to the eye of any one coming from a sea-voyage, who naturally looks for trees, and grass, and herbage. The sand-hills are worse than our Sydney sand-hills and are not compensated by surrounding vegetation, except where small, carefully watered patches of green mark the outside carpet of some villa. Moreover, a chilly white fog hangs over the scene, spoiling everything, and making us long for our bright southern sky.

"Then the arrangements for landing are very behindhand. We found no conveyance of any kind for ourselves, though we soon got an express for our baggage. Fairly arrived, however, in the city, we found the streets well laid out, with fine large buildings and stores on either hand. The presence of well-appointed street-cars gives to these the twang of Americanism which is otherwise not very apparent. When we got to our hotel, we discovered sure proofs of the wealth of California; in truth, the hotels in San Francisco are luxurious and magnificent beyond expectation. The Cosmopolitan, at which I staid, surpasses any hotel with which I am acquainted in any part either of Europe or America.

"Going below, we try to pick up some information about the great Pacific Railroad. The walls of the newsroom are papered with any quantity of those peculiarly American railroad advertisements (not railway, as that Britisher by my side suggests; here, in America, it is rail*road*, if you please), which are constituted as though it were the object of their publishers to give the least possible information in the largest possible variety of print, and colour, and form. Of course the groundwork of all these is 'Atlantic and Pacific', 'from Ocean to Ocean', or words of like effect; but any one who expects to gain any useful information from such puffs is sure to be disappointed. But is not there an American *Bradshaw* to be bought? Well, there is an *Appleton's Railroad Guide*, which *professes* to do the same thing for one here that *Bradshaw* does in England. It is, however, full of inaccuracies, and is so little used, that I was unable to procure a copy of it in San Francisco. Alas, good *Bradshaw*, we don't know how precious you are till we travel to where you are not! I have often called you hard names. I have called you absurd, and confused. If I live to turn over your pages again, I will do so no longer.

"But what is really to be found out from these advertisements? I find that there is an 'Erie Railway' (it was called railway because it is an English institution, I believe), and a 'Lake Shore Line', and a 'Michigan Central',

and a 'Rock Island', and a 'Chicago and Northwestern', and a whole host
of others too numerous to mention. The Erie Railway carries you on the
'broad gauge', and the 'Pennsylvania Central' promises to do all sorts of
things for you. 'Silver palace sleeping-cars' accompany all sorts of trains, and
'lightning expresses' carry you all over the country: and wherever we go, it
is apparently 'without change of cars'; we read all this in red ink, and blue
ink, and black ink, and are directed to ask for tickets by the various routes
indicated; but not one word is said about the times of starting, or the cost of
our tickets, or, in fact, about anything which a real traveller wants to know.

"The fare through to New York is $112.50 in gold, or a little over £23
of our money. The distance is something less than 3,300 miles. The time of
transit is eight days. From Sacramento to Omaha City on the Missouri River,
is a distance of 1,774 miles. The line between these two points was made, and
is owned by two distinct companies. The Central Pacific Company possess
the western portion, which consists of 690 miles; the remainder, or eastern
portion, belongs to the Union Pacific Company. The Central Pacific worked
from the west towards the east, while the Union Pacific worked from
east to west. Promontory was the point at which the lines happened to
meet. By far the more difficult portion of the work was that which was per-
formed by the Central Pacific. They had to ascend the sierras of California,
while they worked under the pecuniary disadvantage of having to bring their
materials round by sea, or across the isthmus from the eastern states. The
greater part of the Central Pacific Railway route was made, I am informed,
by Chinese labour. The quiet and orderly conduct of these much-abused
Asiatics formed a striking contrast to that of the superior race working on the
Union Pacific. Among the latter, indeed, there was not only lawlessness and
every species of ruffianism, but even murder; while such a crime as this last
was, I am told, unknown on the Chinese section.

"As the railroad progressed, temporary settlements or towns were run up
at its temporary terminus. 'As this was changed every 30 or 40 days,' says an
American writer, 'these settlements were of the most perishable materials—
canvas tents, plain board shanties, and turf hovels—pulled down, and sent
forward for a new career, or deserted as worthless at every grand movement
of the railroad company. Only a small proportion of their population had
aught to do with the road, or any legitimate occupation. Most were the
hangers-on around the disbursements of such a gigantic work, catching the
drippings from the feast in any and every form that it was possible to reach
them. Restaurant and saloon keepers, gamblers, desperadoes of every grade,
the vilest of men and of women made up this "hell on wheels", as it was most
aptly termed.'

"The same graphic writer goes on to describe, in terms which one would fain hope exaggerated, that settlement which he himself visited, as being the then westernmost point of the Union Pacific line. 'One to two thousand men, and a dozen or two women, were encamped on the alkali plain, in tents and board shanties; not a tree, not a shrub, not a blade of grass was visible; the dust ankle-deep as we walked through it, and so fine and volatile, that the slightest breeze loaded the air with it, irritating every sense and poisoning half of them; a village of a few variety stores and shops, and many restaurants and grog-shops; by day disgusting, by night dangerous; almost everybody dirty, many filthy, and with the marks of lowest vice, averaging a murder a day, gambling and drinking, hurdy-gurdy dancing, and the vilest of debauchery the chief business and pastime of the hours.'

"Leaving San Francisco in the afternoon, in the beginning of September last, I proceeded by steamer by the Sacramento River. At 6.30 the next morning the cars left Sacramento, and, having secured a berth in a sleeping-car, I felt well prepared for the long hours of railway travelling which lay before me. Not that I was going through the 3,000 miles without stopping—that was not at all my intention. The chance of visiting Salt Lake City, and seeing something of the Mormons, was far too attractive to me to be thrown away. And, accordingly, I was bound for New Jerusalem. It is one of the advantages of American railway law that a through ticket enables you to stop at any station you choose on the line of route, and go on again when you please, without any forfeiture of your ticket.

"As to sleeping-cars, they are a grand institution, a real comfort, and in fact almost a necessity in these long railway journeys. For the payment of a few dollars, you secure a berth which is laid out with clean sheets; and you can, if you please, undress yourself, and, if you are of a sufficiently imaginative turn of mind, and the motion of the cars is not too great, fancy yourself to be arrived at your journey's end, and established in your hotel. As to sleeping, if you are at all of a sleeping disposition, you will certainly be able to do that; and if not, you will get a good rest, and a stretch of your limbs. Next morning, when you get up, you will find your boots blacked, have a wash and brush, and feel reinvigorated for the next day's travel. This arrangement, added to the facility of moving about, and changing place and position in the cars, really makes American railroad travelling far less wearisome than English.

"Our train started with two sleeping-cars, nine day-cars, and two baggage-cars, and was drawn by a couple of engines. There were, as far as I could count them, about seventy through passengers, and many way passengers, among whom were some Chinamen. In San Francisco, I was told that about fifty odd passengers went through to the east daily; but I cannot vouch for the accuracy of this statement.

"At Roseville the line from Oaklands comes in. Here we waited a quarter of an hour or so for breakfast. The meals along the road are generally well arranged, and the fare good. The train, as a rule, delays three times a day for meals, giving twenty minutes for each. As it pulls up at the platform, you hear the welcome sound of the dinner-bell going, and you sit down to your food and begin to eat without further ceremony. The cost of each meal is six *bits*, or three shillings in California and Nevada; while in the regions of paper currency it is $1\frac{1}{4}$ [five shillings]. The fare decidedly deteriorates as you go east.

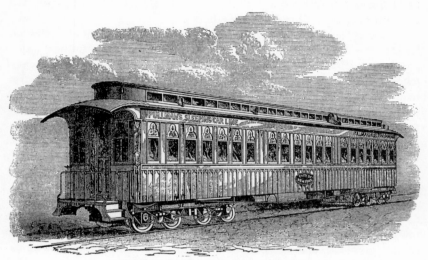

"Pullman's Sleeping Railway-car," 1869

"The line was dusty and disagreeable during the first portion of it; but we were fast ascending. Soon we got to the region of pine trees, and then to a gold-mining district. Some magnificent views were opened up in the sierras; and there was an ever-varying scene as we went swinging about, running right up the gullies, then doubling round, and coming almost straight back again on the other side of the gorges. We passed miles of snow-shedding—strong wooden-work framed to prevent the snow from coming down upon the line and overwhelming it. These sheds have not been, as yet, tried against the snow; but they have found another and an unexpected enemy, which bids fair, as yet, entirely to get the better of them. The heat of the sun dries the woodwork, until it falls an easy prey to the sparks from the engine, which catch on it as on tinder. Whole miles of shedding have been thus destroyed by fire, and some of these fires have been so extensive as to necessitate an entire suspension of the traffic over the blistered rails for days together. Such a fire had occurred a week previously, and we passed the charred remains of the sheds.

"At about 1 p.m., we were on the summit of the sierras, being a little over 7,000 ft. above the sea-level, and 105 miles from Sacramento. Soon afterwards we passed Truckee, a small town made by the railroad, being the chief lumber and wood station of the Central Pacific. Eastward of this point, the scenery gradually becomes tame, and the Central Pacific pursues the remainder of its way over a table-land at levels never descending much below 4,000 or ascending above 6,000 ft. above the sea-level. Reno is the next important stopping-place, being the point of departure of stages for Virginia City, the centre of a large and important mining district in the state of Nevada. The country hereabouts is desert and dreary in the extreme.

"Next morning, being the second day of the railroad journey, I found that we had run as near as possible 400 miles in the 24 hours. Slow as this pace is, it must be remembered that a considerable portion of this distance was up steeply ascending gradients and round sharp curves; though, to say truth, when on the level plains, we did not go much more than 17 m.p.h., including stoppages. I now began to make inquiries as to the stations from whence the stages run up to Salt Lake City. I found it very hard to get any information. Those passengers whom I questioned were not *posted* in the route; while the conductor of the train either did not know, or he did not choose to tell me, and anyhow did not deign to listen to my enquiries. At last I found two Englishmen going up to Salt Lake City, and they informed me that Uintah was the station. It was a new station, and not even marked upon the only time-tables published in California. We were now following up the course of Humboldt River, a small sluggish stream with some vegetation, and patches of cultivated and pasture land in its valley. The only station of importance we passed through that day was Elko, the point of departure for the celebrated 'White Pine' mining district.

"At 10 p.m. we arrived at Promontory, having travelled over the 690 miles in a little less than 40 hours—that is, at the rate of between 17 and 18 m.p.h., inclusive of stoppages. Here we had to wait for a few hours until the arrival of the Union Pacific train, and were, in addition to this, detained after the arrival of that train, while the whole of the baggage was transferred from one car to another. We had ourselves, moreover, to change cars. These very unnecessary and provoking proceedings are, I believe, the result of a jealousy between the two companies, and are about as absurd and unwarrantable an interference with the comfort of passengers as can well be conceived. The result of it all was that four hours were wasted, and we did not get away from Promontory till three o'clock in the morning.

"Promontory is the remains and essence of those 'hells upon wheels' of which mention has been made. Some half-dozen bonfires were burning in the street, and these served to throw light upon the proceedings of certain card-sharpers and gamblers behind them. Each of the former had his table in front of him, around which were congregated about as villainous and black-guard looking a set of men as one may hope to meet with in any single locality. Here one of our passengers was green enough to allow himself to be sharped out of one hundred dollars—all the money he had upon him. According to the account given to me, neither law nor order prevails at Promontory. So great was the terror entertained, that one gentleman, who asserted that his fear was grounded upon his knowledge of the place, refused to go unaccompanied from one train of cars to the other.

"Getting to Uintah about five in the morning, we found a coach just about to start for Salt Lake City. It was, however, full, and we had to wait till eleven o'clock for another coach. At Uintah, and the whole way to Salt Lake City, there are delicious streams of running water, and nice patches of vegetation and cultivation. There is a fine bold mountain above Uintah, which, looking more green than the mountains we have hitherto seen, is refreshing to the eye, and suggests the origin of the water-rivulets. The distance to Salt Lake City is about 30 miles, over a very rough and heavy road. From it are obtained some beautiful views of the Great Salt Lake, peacefully ensconced by the surrounding mountains.

"Salt Lake City is suffering at the present time from a commercial depression, caused, in some measure, by the diversion of the through travel to California, which, before the opening of the Pacific Railroad, used to pass through it. A branch railroad is now in course of construction, which, it is hoped, will serve to right matters.

"But, to return from this digression to the Pacific Railroad. From Uintah the line passes through a gorge, called 'the Devil's Gate', thence up the narrow valley of the Weber, with its refreshing patches of cultivation, and grand red rocks overhead. Echo City is the principal station of this district, which is a mining one. Soon after this, the train passes through a country where there are coal-mines, and leaving Utah, wends its way through the neighbouring territory of Wyoming. We have now left the mountains, and with them all traces of vegetation. There is again the odd sage bush, and the alkali dust of the desert. One or two deep sluggish streams, the water of which looks green and foul, and is, I believe, scarcely fit for drinking purposes, are crossed.

"We were now commencing the fourth day of the railroad journey, and on this day we passed the highest point on the whole line, 8,424 ft. above the sea-level—the highest point reached as yet by any railroad in the world. The ascent to this point is very gradual, and presents few engineering difficulties.

The land bears an even surface, interrupted only by patches of red rock. There are no peaks visible, and nothing but the light mountain air to indicate the great height at which you have arrived. Just below is a forest of pine trees, which serve for supplies of fuel for the line. Sherman, for so the summit is named, is a depot for wood, and it contains a few stores and bar-rooms. From Sherman, the course of the railroad is one unbroken line of descent, the first portion of which is very rapid. There are many walls hereabouts, built to protect the track from the winter's snow-drifts.

"The next station of importance is Cheyenne. This is a real town, and decidedly the most important place we have passed through since leaving Sacramento. From hence stages start for the important and rapidly rising town of Denver, in the state of Colorado. Here we altered our time, taking Omaha clock-time. This is the second alteration of time on the journey—that at Promontory being the first. Soon after leaving Cheyenne, we passed an emigrants' train, or rather a goods-train with emigrant-car attached. These people were, to use a nautical expression, 11 days out from New York, and, at this rate of progress, would take at least 18 days from ocean to ocean. As we proceeded, the country improved rapidly, and there were cattle-stations and patches of cultivation. In the distance, on our right hand, we could clearly trace the course of the river Platte by the trees on its banks. Next day, we were going over the rolling prairies of Nebraska, and had approached close to the Platte, and our country had come within the influence of its fertilizing irrigation.

"From about 60 miles west of Omaha, the rolling of the prairie ceased, and we were passing through the richest and most luxuriant pasture-country conceivable. Herds of cattle on either hand gladdened our eyes; while little boys passed down the cars offering us of the riches of the land—fresh milk and boiled eggs. The track had improved, and so had the pace of our train. All looked cheerful; and as we hastened along, feasting our eyes on the growing maize or the tall grass, I think we should all, if we had been asked, have said that this was the pleasantest two hours of our journey. We arrived at Omaha at about 1 p.m. on this the fifth day of our railroad journey. Thus, including the passage from San Francisco to Sacramento, the journey to Omaha had occupied nearly five days. The time of the journey will probably be soon reduced to four days, and possibly something less; but I think it will not fall below that point, until considerable improvement is made in the track. The present line is very bad in places, especially on the Union Pacific. I did not see much to complain of on the Central Pacific, and this is the more creditable to the latter company, considering that they have had greater difficulties to contend with.

"Omaha is situated upon high land on the right bank of the Missouri

River, being something less than 1,000 ft. above the sea-level. From this point, New York is reached in about three days. There are a great variety of routes. Two rival companies compete for the traffic to Chicago, from which place there are four main lines of travel to New York. The southern and south-eastern states are reached by taking the rail from Omaha to St. Louis, which place may also be reached by steamer down the Missouri River."

LOGICAL SITUATION

A good story of the old Belfast & County Down Railway tells how an English tourist came to a deserted level crossing, one gate of which barred the road and the other the line. He stopped his car, and after waiting 10 minutes he angrily sounded his horn and asked the railwayman who appeared why the gates were in that position.

"Sure," was the reply, "we're half-expecting a train."
Abridged from *"Peterborough"*, in *"The Daily Telegraph"*

ADVICE TO TRAVELLERS

Let someone keep a sharp look-out on your luggage while you take the tickets; carry the tickets of the whole party in your glove or waistcoat pocket, to be ready to show whenever they are asked for. Always anticipate an asking. Hold the tickets like a hand at cards, so that they may easily be counted. When the train comes you must take such seats as are vacant when it arrives, unless you have interest with the stationmaster to secure you a carriage from the starting place, or have one ready to attach when the train arrives. A glove, or book, or anything left on a seat denotes that it is taken. Take yours that way.

See your luggage put on the roof of the carriage you occupy, and book the number of the carriage (which is often in a very indistinct place about the wheels), or you may have difficulty in finding it if you get out of the train after it is lengthened.
Surtees, *"Hints to Railway Travellers"*, 1851

CATERPILLARS STOP A TRAIN

Several years ago, caterpillars gained a victory over a train in Alberta. They crept on to the track, clustered themselves in thick masses, and stopped a mixed train. Other trains made only half their speed because of the slippery conditions of the rails. However, the railway officials found a solution: an engine was equipped with a steam jet blower, to sweep the caterpillars off the track.
From *"The Railway Magazine"*

Railway Circles Round London

CHARLES E. LEE

REFERENCE TO TIMETABLES published in the latter part of the nineteenth century reveals several train services in the London area for which we shall search in vain today. Some of these trains used routes that now appear to be decidedly circuitous, but we must remember that the steam railway was then in its hey-day. The speed and comfort of trains easily offset those rather long journeys, and surpassed anything that could be offered by horse-drawn trams and buses, and even by private carriages.

In the early days of railways, the City of London was thickly populated, and the vast majority of workers—black-coated or otherwise—lived within walking distance of their place of employment. Between 1800 and 1850, the number of people living in the City remained fairly constant at about 129,000, although nearby districts, such as Islington and St. Pancras, expanded rapidly. However, with the continued growth of commerce, the value of land in the central area increased to such an extent that many residents moved outwards to points beyond walking range of their work, and the railway companies tackled the task of building branches and establishing a maze of local services, often in fierce competition with one another.

Among the earliest of these suburban services were those of the North London Railway. Promoted as a route for goods traffic between the London & North Western Railway at Camden Town and the London Docks, this line made a big detour to avoid a heavy outlay for construction in built-up areas. Nevertheless, its passenger traffic began to develop at once, as the new generation of daily traveller preferred "the easy and rapid conveyance by rail to the lumbering roll of an omnibus", even when it involved a longer journey. In 1850, a service every 15 minutes began to run between Islington (Highbury) and Fenchurch Street, *via* Hackney, Bow, and Stepney. Within a few months, the trains had been extended, first to Camden Town, and then to join the L.N.W.R. at Chalk Farm.

In 1853, the North London service was again extended through Kilburn and Acton to Kew, and five years later, the opening of a branch from South Acton to Hammersmith & Chiswick completed a route of 17 miles from Fenchurch Street to Hammersmith. This distance was shortened by about two miles in 1865, when the North London opened its line from Dalston Junction to Broad Street, and the detour through East London to Fenchurch Street was obviated. Today, the distance by the District Line from Tower Hill (near Fenchurch Street) to Stamford Brook (near the terminus of the branch) is about eight miles. Passenger services between South Acton and Hammersmith & Chiswick did not survive the First World War.

With the opening in 1863 of the Metropolitan Railway between Paddington and Farringdon Street, the first underground railway in the world, the initial step was taken towards establishing many services, now long forgotten. The Metropolitan was linked from the outset with the Great Western Railway, and a direct service to Hammersmith over the then new Hammersmith & City Railway was begun in 1864. The London & South Western Railway opened a line from Addison Road to Richmond, *via* Hammersmith and Turnham Green, in 1869, and there was a link at Hammersmith between the two. For some months in 1870, the G.W.R. ran to Richmond by this route. From 1877, Metropolitan trains ran between Aldgate and Richmond *via* Hammersmith, and these survived as a joint Metropolitan and G.W.R. service until the end of 1906, when they had to be withdrawn, because (somewhat amazingly) the short link at Hammersmith was not electrified, although all the other lines concerned had been converted. However, the G.W.R. ran a half-hourly steam service between Notting Hill (now Ladbroke Grove) and Richmond for another four years. The junction at Grove Road, Hammersmith, was removed in 1914.

So-called circular routes seem to have fascinated the later-Victorian railway mind. The original Metropolitan Railway provided the nucleus for the Inner Circle; the company extended its line eastward to Moorgate in 1865 and to Aldgate in 1876, and westward from Paddington to South Kensington in 1868. The District Railway, planned to be complementary, but soon to develop into a bitter rival, built the southern portion of the Inner Circle from South Kensington to Mansion House in 1869–71. The final link between Mansion House and Aldgate was not opened until 1884.

A miscellany of goods wagons ascending Beattock Bank behind a class "5" 4-6-0 locomotive

London scenes of bygone days: (above) Victoria Station, London, Brighton & South Coast Railway, in the 1880s, with a London & North Western train to Willesden at the left-hand platform; (below) London, Tilbury & Southend Railway train leaving Ealing Broadway in 1910, hauled by two District Railway electric locomotives

The other so-called Circles were really horseshoes. The Outer Circle may be traced back to 1865, when the L.N.W.R. began to run trains between Euston and London Bridge, *via* Kilburn, Addison Road, Battersea, Vauxhall, and Waterloo. The connection to the South Eastern Railway at Waterloo extended from two platforms in the L.S.W.R. station, across the circulating area, and over Waterloo Road on the bridge now used as a passenger foot-way. In 1867, Cannon Street replaced London Bridge as the terminus, but the working through Waterloo ceased at the end of that year. A service between Willesden Junction and the L.S.W.R. station at Waterloo was resumed in 1875, and lasted until 1893. Meanwhile, a half-hourly service between Broad Street and Addison Road was begun by the L.N.W.R. in 1867. In 1869, some of the trains were extended *via* Chelsea to the London & Brighton terminus at Victoria, and this lasted for three years, when the service was modified to become the Outer Circle. Instead of crossing the Thames, it was diverted at Addison Road to run over the District Railway from Earls Court to Mansion House.

With the electrification of the District Railway in 1905, the L.N.W.R. trains were hauled by District Railway electric locomotives east of Earls Court, but this ceased in 1908, although steam-hauled L.N.W.R. trains continued to run between Broad Street and Earls Court for another five years. The portion of this route between Earls Court and Willesden Junction was electrified in 1914. Thereafter, by changing at Earls Court and Willesden Junction, it was possible to travel over the Outer Circle until passenger trains were withdrawn between Earls Court and Willesden Junction in 1940. When the Outer Circle service began, although it served Victoria (District Railway), the older link through Chelsea to Victoria (L.B.S.C.R.) was maintained by separate L.N.W.R. trains, which survived until 1917.

The Middle Circle was a G.W.R. enterprise begun in 1872. It ran first from Moorgate, and later from Aldgate, to Mansion House, through Bishops Road (Paddington), Addison Road, and Earls Court. This service was curtailed at Earls Court in 1900, as the result of a dispute between the G.W.R. and the District Railway, and in 1905 Addison Road became the terminus. A shuttle service of Metropolitan trains between Edgware Road and Addison Road survived until part of the line suffered serious damage in an air raid in 1940.

The G.W.R. also had a link through Addison Road with the main-line station at Victoria. When it was opened in 1860, Victoria was intended to become a West-End terminus for numerous railways south of the Thames. However, only the L.B.S.C.R. and the London, Chatham & Dover Railway used it from the south, although the West London Extension Railway, which was opened in 1863 from Addison Road to Battersea, gave both the L.N.W.R. and the G.W.R. access to the station. This route involved crossing

the Thames twice (at Chelsea and at Pimlico) but there was nothing unusual in such journeys in those days.

The G.W.R. arranged for broad-gauge lines to be laid into Victoria, and became joint lessee of that part of the station used by the L.C.D.R. The first G.W.R. service to Victoria began in 1863, and was from Southall, *via* Addison Road. After little more than three years, the service was worked wholly by standard-gauge trains, so that very limited use was made of the broad-gauge tracks, and the cost of their construction was certainly not justified. Great Western trains continued to run into Victoria until 1915. Most of the services were to and from Southall, but some journeys were extended to Uxbridge or Windsor. The company continued to be a lessee of Victoria Station until 1933, and the words "Great Western Railway" were displayed on the main entrance for nearly 20 years after the last G.W.R. train had run. Incidentally, the District Railway worked a through service from Mansion House, *via* the underground station at Victoria and Ealing, to Southall and Windsor, but this lasted only from 1883 to 1885.

At Hammersmith, the links between the Metropolitan, the Great Western, and the South Western were increased in 1877 by a connection with the District Railway, which immediately began a service to Richmond from the southern part of the Inner Circle. These trains still survive. The L.S.W.R., which built the line through Hammersmith to Addison Road that enabled other railways to reach Richmond, last ran its own trains by that route in 1916, and the link between Addison Road and Hammersmith has long been abandoned. Today, the tracks between Hammersmith and Turnham Green are simply part of the London Transport system, and passengers have no thought for L.S.W.R. ownership or G.W.R. trains.

Perhaps the longest example of "circle" technique was a service that was advertised as running between St. Pancras and Mansion House, *via* Cricklewood, Acton, Turnham Green, and Earls Court. Instituted in 1878, and amounting to a "Super-Outer Circle", this was a development of an earlier Midland service, which attracted little support, and was short-lived, but at least caused the North London to admit third-class passengers to its Richmond trains. The 1878 "circle" was a diversion from Acton to Turnham Green and over the District route to Earls Court. Although the timetable showed a service between St. Pancras and Mansion House, the Midland did not run beyond Earls Court, where a change to and from District trains was necessary. This was the shortest-lived of the "circle" workings, as it failed to secure support, and was withdrawn in 1880.

One of the reasons for the circuitous routes of some of the services was the lack of direct north-to-south links in the central area. With the exception of the tube railways, opened early in the present century, the only such link was

Metropolitan Railway: Kensington (afterwards High Street) Station, 1868

(and still is) the line built by the London, Chatham & Dover Railway between Blackfriars and Farringdon Street (Metropolitan Railway), *via* Ludgate Hill, completed in 1866. This line connected the L.C.D.R. with the Great Northern Railway, and from 1868 the Midland Railway also was linked. The South Eastern Railway gained access to this route in 1878, by means of a spur south of Blackfriars goods station. Most other railways were also brought into connection by junctions already existing, and Ludgate Hill became a City station of considerable importance for suburban traffic. Much of its glory had departed by the outbreak of the First World War, and it was closed in 1929. Today, it is almost a forgotten station.

The L.S.W.R. reached Ludgate Hill in 1866, with a service from Kingston, *via* Clapham Junction, Brixton, and Loughborough Junction. With the opening in 1869 of its strategic line between Richmond and Addison Road, *via* Hammersmith, the L.S.W.R. began a service between Richmond and Ludgate Hill taking the circuitous 14¾-mile route through Hammersmith, Addison Road, Battersea, and Brixton. This survived in reduced form until the First World War.

Great Northern trains began to run to the L.C.D.R. *via* the Ludgate Hill link in 1866, and survived until 1907. One particularly interesting service was between Barnet and Victoria, through King's Cross, Farringdon Street, Ludgate Hill, and Loughborough Junction. The first Midland Railway service through Ludgate Hill began in 1869. For some time it was maintained by L.C.D.R. trains, but the Midland participated from 1875. There were services between Finchley Road and Victoria, and between Kentish Town and Herne Hill. All these trains were withdrawn in 1908.

Through services between the Great Northern and the South Eastern were introduced in 1878, but because of the enmity between the South Eastern and the Chatham & Dover, no passengers to or from the South Eastern were allowed to use the stations at Snow Hill (Holborn Viaduct) or Ludgate Hill, and the timetables showed southbound trains as stopping "to set down", and northbound trains as calling "to pick up", only. The through services ceased in 1907.

A third north-to-south link was the East London Railway, from Shoreditch to New Cross. This line, which now has only a local shuttle service, was formerly used for numerous interesting through journeys. It crossed under the Thames in the famous Thames Tunnel, built by Sir Marc Isambard Brunel, father of the even better known engineer of the Great Western Railway. The original intention was to provide a vehicular tunnel, but many serious constructional difficulties were encountered, and the approach roads were never built. Work on the tunnel was begun in 1825, but it was not until 1843 that it was opened to foot passengers.

Twenty years later, the East London Railway was promoted to connect the railways north and south of the Thames, and it took over the pedestrian subway (never very successful) in 1865. A railway service through the tunnel, from New Cross to Wapping, was begun in 1869, and two years later a short branch was opened from Deptford Road (now Surrey Docks) to Old Kent Road (a station on the South London line of the L.B.S.C.R., closed in 1917). This branch was used at first by L.B.S.C.R. trains between Old Kent Road and Wapping, but the service was extended to Liverpool Street

East London Railway: Wapping Station, 1870

(Great Eastern Railway) in 1876, when the East London Railway was completed to a junction with the G.E.R. at Shoreditch. At the other end, the trains were extended to Peckham Rye in 1877, but the Liverpool Street service was curtailed at Shoreditch on the last day of 1885. Trains continued to run between Peckham Rye and Shoreditch until 1911.

Other services long since abandoned used the East London Railway. The L.B.S.C.R. ran trains between Liverpool Street and Croydon from 1876. Like the Peckham Rye service, they were cut back to Shoreditch at the end of 1885, and then continued placidly until 1911. The only variation was in the terminal station at Croydon. For part of the time, this was Croydon Central (a long-abandoned station on what is now the site of Croydon Town Hall), but otherwise the trains ran to and from New Croydon, the name once given to the local line platforms at East Croydon.

The South Eastern Railway maintained a service between Addiscombe Road (Croydon) and Liverpool Street from 1880 to 1884. In the latter year, the trains were diverted to St. Mary's (Whitechapel) for a short time, and then discontinued. St. Mary's Station was later served by frequent London Transport electric trains, but was closed in 1938. The Great Eastern began to work between Liverpool Street and the L.B.S.C.R. station at New Cross in 1886, and some of these trains were extended to Croydon a year later. This Croydon service lasted until 1911.

In 1884, both the Metropolitan and the District Railways were linked with the East London by the opening of a new line from Aldgate to Whitechapel. This brought a large increase of traffic to the East London, as Metropolitan trains began to run between Hammersmith and New Cross (S.E.R.), *via* the northern part of the Inner Circle, and District trains between Hammersmith and New Cross (L.B.S.C.R.), *via* the southern section of that route. When these railways were electrified in 1905–6, both services ceased. In 1913, when the East London Railway was electrified, all passenger trains of the G.E.R., L.B.S.C.R., and S.E.R. were withdrawn, and thereafter the Metropolitan worked the entire service, at first South Kensington, *via* Baker Street, to New Cross, but Hammersmith to New Cross from 1914.

The Aldgate–Whitechapel line later became part of an important east-to-west link, when the District Railway secured a direct connection with the London, Tilbury & Southend Railway. This was in 1902, by means of the two-mile Whitechapel & Bow Railway, built at a cost of nearly £1¼ million as a joint line by the two parent companies. For some years, the only use made of this link was by the District Railway, which extended its services to East Ham and Upminster. With electrification, Barking became the terminus for District trains, but in 1910 a through service between Ealing and Southend was begun by the L.T.S.R. The trains were hauled by District electric locomotives between Ealing and Barking, and thence were steam-operated. This useful through facility was an early casualty of the Second World War, and has never been restored.

Considered in isolation, the disappearance of so many train services in the London area—and those mentioned are a representative, but not a comprehensive list—might appear to be a substantial reduction in travel facilities. In general, this is not the case. At the turn of the century, three new forms of urban transport began to change the pattern of travel, and in little more than a decade had effected a revolution. The electric tram was introduced in the outer London area in 1901, and in the central area in 1903. Within a few years, electricity had not only replaced horse-traction on existing tramways, but new lines had greatly increased the route mileage and extended the area served. From a tentative introduction in 1899, and serious development from 1904, the motor-bus rapidly became an important factor. By 1908, more than a thousand were in service, and the total had risen to some 3,500 by 1913. Both electric trams and motor-buses afforded rapid, direct, and cheap transport against which circuitous steam-operated railway services could not compete.

Another important factor was the construction (largely under American auspices) of tube railways crossing directly under the central area. These were the original sections of the Bakerloo, Northern, and Piccadilly Lines, all of which were opened in 1906 and 1907. Such developments caused the spate of suburban service withdrawals by the main-line companies between the beginning of the century and the outbreak of the First World War. In 1901, the Midland and L.C.D.R. service between Finchley Road and Victoria, with trains covering a 13-mile route in about an hour, was still a useful facility. When it was withdrawn in 1908, the motor-bus could join these two stations by a four-mile route in half an hour.

SAY THAT AGAIN

A lady living in Hampshire rang up her local station to ask about a train connection for a foreign visitor. A clerk answered that he could not be exact about the times and added: "A lot of people are more interested in trains than we are."

"Peterborough", in "The Daily Telegraph"

Soon after the railway was opened from Paris to Rouen, in the 1840s, King Louis Philippe wished to travel by special train on his way to his château at Bizy. Orders were given to this effect, but when the Council of Ministers learned of His Majesty's project, it was decided, at a special sitting, that railway travel was not sufficiently secure to admit of its being used by the King, and the whole journey had to be made by road. A contemporary newspaper made the pointed comment that this was a singular way for the Cabinet to encourage railways.

Middle East Interlude

H. C. HUGHES, M.A.

IN WAR-TIME the railway enthusiast has one marked advantage over most of his fellows; more often than not he is still able to pursue his hobby even in the most bizarre places. This was particularly true during the last war in the area rather loosely described as the "Middle East", where even the most insular enthusiast could hardly fail to find much of interest in his off-duty hours.

The dust of the Alamein battle had scarcely settled when, in November 1942, I paid my first visit to Mersa Matruh, reputed to have been a favourite resort of Cleopatra. I cannot remember now whether I ever saw the place where the Queen of Egypt bathed, but I can certainly recall my first view of the railway "station", and the feeling of nostalgic pleasure at seeing four Stanier-type 2-8-0s simmering gently in the harsh sunlight. Admittedly they were only War Department engines, and one of them (No. 9302) was partly encased in slabs of concrete to protect the boiler from hostile air attack, but a year earlier they had been in service in England, and No. 9326 still carried the letters STJ as a memento of its allocation to Severn Tunnel Junction when, as L.M.S.R. No. 8252, it was on loan to the Great Western Railway. To complete the illusion, the fifth locomotive at Mersa Matruh that afternoon was a six-coupled diesel No. 14 (previously L.M.S.R. No. 7104), with a "Built Derby 1941" plate, one of 12 sent out for service in the Middle East.

Egypt was in fact a happy hunting ground for the railway-minded who found themselves "allocated" to that area through the exigencies of war. Not only were there 42 Stanier 2-8-0s, all of which (except for one which came to grief in 1942) were later absorbed into Egyptian State Railways stock, but there were also 90 Robinson 2-8-os, one of the standard classes of the Railway Operating Department in the First World War, distributed throughout Egypt and Palestine; some of the latter were indeed doing their second spell of war service. Then there were new 2-8-2 War Department locomotives carrying Baldwin, Alco or Lima makers' plates whose typical American features made an interesting contrast with the more familiar British 2-8-os.

The native Egyptian locomotive stud was also full of interest and, although many of the engines were of German, Belgian, French and Italian extraction, the lineage was clearly British. But the construction of the coaching stock was more alien to our eyes, because of the different climatic conditions, and one also had to get used to the habits of the native commuters who, particularly on the crowded Cairo lines, were somewhat prone to enter and leave the carriages by means of the windows.

The general track layout and signalling were British enough and on one occasion, at Cairo Main Station, I was cordially invited into the signal box where, after the usual cups of sweet tea, I was shown how to operate the electro-pneumatic levers in accordance with the illuminated diagram. After despatching a light engine to the sheds without undue incident, I thanked them and went on my way, idly wondering whether an Egyptian officer in England would have received similar hospitality at, say, Victoria; he might perhaps have been offered a cup of railway tea.

The railwaymen were on the whole co-operative, and enthusiasts visited sheds and railway works, both officially and unofficially, without embarrassing Anglo-Egyptian relations. Exiled members of the Railway Correspondence & Travel Society were particularly active in this respect, and used the "Music For All" establishment in Cairo as a regular meeting place for the exchange of railway gossip.

The main E.S.R. workshops were at Abu Zaabal, some way out of Cairo, but I was anxious to visit the site of the old shops at Boulac. This involved a taxi journey, as the area was out of bounds to British troops, and the dilapidated vehicle took me within 100 yards of my objective before the off-side front wheel came adrift and we shuddered to a grinding halt. The driver, muttering "Inshallah", carefully collected my fare before going off to retrieve his wheel from the inevitable crowd of small children.

I made my way to a door in a high wall and, on entering, found myself confronted by an Egyptian sentry who was equally taken aback at my unexpected appearance. The guard commander was summoned, and valuable time was wasted while we found out how little we knew of each other's language. However, my identity card solved all difficulties, and I duly made my tour of the premises accompanied, at a discreet distance, by one of the guard.

Most of the locomotives there were of standard E.S.R. or W.D. types but there was one curiosity; this was No. 278, one of four built by the North British Locomotive Company in 1938, each of which incorporated two two-cylinder Sentinel engine units. With outside frames and small wheels, arranged 2-2-2-2, the general effect was to suggest that the designers had forgotten to put in any driving wheels and it was with an element of surprise that one watched engines of this class moving off under their own power.

They turned out the guard for me when I left; perhaps my "inspection" was a little too enthusiastic, for the commander showed every sign of repeating the performance, and I had to make a hasty, but dignified, exit.

The Railway Museum, in an annexe to Cairo Main Station, was well worth visiting. A quaint 2-2-4 combined engine and saloon built for the personal use of Said Pasha, Viceroy of Egypt, by Robert Stephenson & Company in 1862, with an ornate painted design (but on one side only), and a double-framed 0-6-0 of 1867 by the same makers, looked somewhat dusty and forlorn; but in the main building there was a profusion of models, pictures and documents covering all aspects of Egyptian railway history. In the early days rolling stock had been acquired indiscriminately from Britain, France, Belgium, Germany, Austria and America, and I was particularly interested in some elaborate coloured diagrams dating from the 1880s, which were hidden away in one of the cupboards.

As the museum was open every day until 2 p.m. (entrance fee two piastres, or fivepence) I visited it as often as military commitments allowed, and soon acquired my own private table, complete with ashtray and a screen to hide most of the cigarette smoke from the other visitors.

The journey from Egypt to Palestine was usually timed so that one crossed the Suez Canal in the evening, patronizing the well-stocked Naafi at Qantara East. Heavy baggage was put in the guard's van, after being wired and sealed at Cairo before departure. Our padre, anxious about the safety of his two heavy suitcases, visited the van at Qantara to satisfy himself that all was well. He was relieved, but rather mystified, to find that there were then *three* suitcases labelled with his name and carefully sealed. He returned to his compartment to ponder over the strange ways of the East, but by the time the train reached Haifa the next morning, the surplus baggage had just as mysteriously vanished without attracting any unwelcome attention from the customs authorities.

The motive power of the Palestine Railways could be divided into three clearly defined categories. The London & South Western and London & North Western 0-6-0s that operated on the supply lines pushed steadily forward from Qantara in the rear of the British advance in 1916–18 had been broken up, but the 50 Baldwin 4-6-0s supplied in 1918 were still there— albeit six of them had paid a visit to Armstrong Whitworth at Newcastle in 1926 and had returned as 4-6-2 tank engines, and five others had been similarly converted (but with 4-6-4 wheel arrangement) at the railway workshops in 1937.

Then there were the English designs of the period between the wars, consisting of 4-6-0 tender, and 2-8-4 and 0-6-0 tank engines. Finally there were the inevitable Robinson 2-8-0s and American 2-8-2s that were such a feature of the Middle East lines during the Second World War; later they were joined by some Stanier 2-8-0s transferred from Iran.

During 1943, South African and New Zealand Engineers blasted a route through the rocky headlands of the Lebanon coast, and completed a standard-gauge line from Haifa to Beirut and Tripoli. Thus connection was made with the Syrian system of lines known as the "D.H.P."—prosaic initials for the lilting sound of "Damas, Hamah et Prolongements". At Tripoli, which was the terminus of a small portion of the Taurus Express from Haydar Pasa (on the Bosphorus opposite Istanbul), the D.H.P. locomotives were of the 0-8-0 wheel arrangement. One series had been built by Cail in 1906, although they looked older than that, and the others were of the well-known Prussian G-8 type. All were beautifully kept, with shining brass plates on the cab-sides giving the names of the footplatemen.

Although this connection made it theoretically possible to travel by standard-gauge railway throughout from Haifa to Baghdad, the route passed through neutral Turkey and so the normal procedure was to use the 3 ft. 5 in. (1,050 mm.) gauge line from Haifa to Damascus. Originally built about 1905 as part of the Hedjaz Railway to Medina, financed by the Moslems but constructed by Turkish military labour under German engineers, the portion from Haifa to Samakh was operated by the Palestine Railways after the 1914–18 war, and the rolling stock duly lettered "H.R.". The rest of the line to Damascus was worked by the D.H.P. concern on behalf of the Hedjaz Railway, the rolling stock being lettered "C.F.H.", although of course there was a considerable amount of through running.

It was an interesting little railway, if one was not in a hurry, with the unique distinction of having a station just south of Samakh which was 809 ft. *below* sea-level. From Samakh, the line pursued a steep and tortuous course up the valley of the Yarmuk river and eventually reached Deraa, a name well known to readers of *The Seven Pillars of Wisdom*. There the main line of the Hedjaz Railway ran southwards as far as Maan, the rest of the line to Medina being still derelict after the depredations of T. E. Lawrence and his Arab train-wreckers.

The more important trains were hauled by a series of 2-8-2 locomotives built by Hartmann of Chemnitz in 1918, but there were several other types to be seen, ranging in size from small Krauss 0-6-0 tank engines of 1902 to articulated 2-4-6-0 tender locomotives built by Henschel in 1907. There were also some interesting 2-6-2 and 0-10-0 tank engines built by La Meuse in 1914, which had been captured by the British forces during the First World War and were stationed in the Haifa area.

The passenger stock was adequate, without any unnecessary refinements, and a description of coach No. 101 will serve as a guide to the general standard. This was a wooden bogie vehicle, reddish-brown in colour, with the letters "C.F.H." in yellow in the centre surmounted by the equivalent in Arabic. The number appeared at the left-hand end, just above the solebar, with the prefix AB to indicate first and second class accommodation, the corresponding Arabic inscription being at the right-hand end. A narrow side corridor ran the full length of the vehicle, leading to a small open platform at each end.

There were three first-class compartments, each seating four, and four second class with six seats, separated by a small lavatory; both end compartments were for ladies only, and had frosted glass on the corridor side. At each end of the coach there was a large central buffer, with screw couplings on either side.

A typical train consisted of two such composite coaches together with two or three third class and two baggage vans, the tare weights of the passenger vehicles varying from 17 to 20 tons. As the Yarmuk was the Syria-Trans-Jordan frontier, and the railway crossed the river from time to time, security guards were kept busy checking identity cards and other papers on this stage of the journey.

From Damascus there was a regular service of articulated motor-coaches across the desert to Baghdad. Established by two New Zealanders, the Nairn brothers, this enterprising concern furnished the only direct link between the two cities. From Damascus the road was well defined as far as a French fort which looked as if it could easily have been a film set for *Beau Geste*. Then the coaches, always in pairs, turned straight across the undulating stony desert for well over 100 miles before joining the tarmac road through Rutba. The 540-mile journey from Damascus to Baghdad took approximately 20 hours; a long and monotonous journey which soon began to pall, in spite of the comfortable seats and the provision of a small bar to help to relieve the tedium.

Of all the railway systems in this area none owed more to outside politics than that of Iraq. The standard-gauge Baghdad Railway, instigated by the Kaiser as far back as 1889, was gradually pushed forward through Asia Minor. From the Baghdad end only 74 miles had been completed by the time this section was captured by British forces early in 1917. Meanwhile 2 ft. 6 in.-gauge equipment had been sent from the Indian strategic reserve in 1916 to build supply lines during the Allied advance from Basra; this was supplemented, and in due course replaced, by metre-gauge equipment also supplied from India. After the war, efforts were made to consolidate the system to suit economic requirements, and serious thought was given to a railway westwards through Trans-Jordan to Palestine. In the end, connection with the outside world was accomplished by completing the Baghdad Railway scheme, but this was not achieved until 1940. Then, from 1942 onwards, the whole system was strained to near breaking point by the requirements of the Allied war effort and additional rolling stock had to be acquired hurriedly from any available source.

Thus it was scarcely surprising to find that many of the locomotives looked as though they had been purchased at an auction. On the standard-gauge, the captured German stock of 1917 had soon been augmented by some London & South Western Adams 0-6-0s and six small tank engines that had been used during the construction of Bombay Harbour. There were no further additions for 22 years, but in 1940 four huge streamlined Pacifics were built by Robert Stephenson & Hawthorns for the through "Taurus Express". The last one was sunk en route, and the others looked somewhat out of their element as they jogged through the desert stretches at an average speed of 25 m.p.h.

In 1942, additional standard-gauge engines were difficult to find, and ten Prussian-type 0-8-0s were hired from the D.H.P. Four tender engines were then acquired from a motley collection evacuated from Hong Kong before it was overrun by the Japanese; one still had the legend "Kiao-Tsi Railway" emblazoned on the tender, and another carried the builders' plate of the Tongshan Works of the Pekin-Mukden line. In addition there was a 2-8-2 tank locomotive, ordered for a Mexican oil concern but left on the builders' hands, which duly turned up at Basra in 1942 and was given an old Adams tender to supplement its restricted water capacity; later it was transferred to more congenial surroundings in Palestine. Fortunately, from 1943 onwards, the situation was eased with the arrival of American 2-8-2 tender and 0-6-0 tank engines and, later, some Robinson 2-8-0s transferred from Palestine.

The metre-gauge stock was much more homogeneous, consisting mainly of standard Indian designs of 1903-20. Many of these had arrived during the First World War, and had been the mainstay of the locomotive department ever since. Admittedly a batch of Baldwin 0-6-6-0 Mallet engines destined for Archangel had been diverted to Iraq in 1918-19 for use on the metre-gauge lines, but they had developed an annoying habit of distributing their motion over the desert, and their career had been necessarily brief. Then there

were four 2-6-2 tank engines, originally ordered for India, which had gravi-
tated to Iraq after assisting in the military operations in German East Africa.

In 1942–3 further metre-gauge locomotives were hurriedly acquired from
India, of the same vintage as before, and there must have been touching
scenes as sister engines were reunited after 26 years apart. Then, in 1944, 30
new "MacArthur" 2-8-2 locomotives arrived, much to the relief of the
traffic department, and were promptly put on the heavy passenger and goods
trains on the main line to Basra.

Small wonder, then, that a visit to the Shalchiyah works of the Iraqi State
Railways, four miles north of Baghdad, was of more than usual interest.
Even the Indian engines, which looked more or less "standard", came from
no less than ten different railways, each having its own pet variations of
fittings, and the problems of adequate maintenance must have given night-
mares to those concerned. Add to this a similar conglomeration of carriage
and wagon stock, and it can readily be appreciated that the engineers at
Shalchiyah were not to be envied in their task.

Nevertheless one of the workshop staff was quite unmoved by the agitation
and bustle around him; in a dark corner sat an old man, obviously a close
relative of Methuselah, who did nothing else but cut and bend, entirely by
hand, pieces of wire rod into ticket clips for wagons. No one knew how long
he had been there, but the clips were all perfectly made, and so everyone was
happy; he may be there yet.

I paid a brief visit to Baghdad North Station, east of the Tigris, and at that
time connected with the main part of the railway system only by a wagon
ferry. This was the terminus of the metre-gauge lines to Kirkuk and Khanaqin
"City" (the station board did not have the inverted commas, but anyone who
has been there will know what I mean). There were normally about 24
engines allocated to the shed at Baghdad North, those from the pre-war
period being mostly painted green or a sandy buff colour. Others wore the
sombre black of war-time austerity, relieved by a most distinctive yellow
monogram on the tender or tank sides in an angular form of Arabic
script.

The Iraqi Superintendent, who had done part of his early training at Derby,
was friendly, and offered to show me round the premises. His unexpected
appearance seriously interrupted a card-school innocently going on in a
corner of the shed, but I was able to compliment him, quite truthfully, on the
cleanliness of his engines, and I was given expert instruction in the art of
starting the fire in an oil-burning locomotive.

The main station, Baghdad West, had both standard and metre-gauge
platform lines. From the north came the "Taurus Express", with five through
coaches. Two of these were reddish-brown in colour with the Turkish star

and crescent, one being a first- and second-class composite, and the other third class, both built in Germany in the early part of the century. The other three vehicles were restaurant, sleeping and baggage cars in the dark livery of the Wagon-Lits Company, the first two built in Britain and the baggage car in France.

On the other hand the metre-gauge mail train southwards to Ma'qil, near Basra, consisted of 15 bogie vehicles hauled by a "MacArthur" 2-8-2. Some of the coaches had originally been built at the Ajmer works of the Bombay, Baroda & Central India Railway in 1910–14, but most of the upper class vehicles were of comparatively recent build, and included a dining car and an air-conditioned first- and second-class composite. The newer vehicles were attractively painted in a greyish-brown colour below the waist line, and sandy buff above, with light grey roofs; triple windows were fitted, with slats, wire mesh, and glass in that order from the outside.

From Ma'qil, a metre-gauge line led across the Shatt-al-Arab, using an ingenious road-rail bridge which could be lowered under the water for the passage of boats, to some exchange sidings near Tanuma. From Tanuma a standard-gauge line had been hurriedly laid in 1942 across the desert to the Iran border and on to Hossaniyeh, where it joined another war-time line from the port of Khorramshahr to Ahwaz. The journey from Tanuma to Ahwaz was tedious and uncomfortable; the train consisted of an ambulance vehicle and some American box-cars and kept up a steady 16 m.p.h. over the entire 80 miles.

At Ahwaz, the line joined the main Trans-Iranian Railway, which ran from some jetties called Bandar Shahpur, on a mudflat on the Persian Gulf, to the south-east corner of the Caspian Sea at Bandar Shah. When British Royal Engineers took over the operating of the line late in 1941, the confusion between these names was soon removed by calling them Bandar Gulf and Bandar Caspian, and this was further simplified by the adoption of the code letters BGF and BCP respectively; similar codes were used for all the main stations, both in Iraq and Iran. Early in 1943, the Americans took over the line as far as Tehran, the railway north of that point being under Russian control.

This 860-mile railway, instigated by Shah Reza Pahlevi in 1925, but not completed until 1938, included some spectacular feats of engineering that rivalled anything to be seen elsewhere in the world. It was inevitable that this should be so, as the route chosen lay at right angles to the mountain ranges that run south-east and east from the Armenian massif.

From Bandar Shahpur to Andimeshk the line ran across a flat and desolate plain, the chief work of note being a 3,400-ft.-long bridge over the Karun River just south of Ahwaz. Then suddenly, eight miles north of Andimeshk, north-bound trains were faced with a wicked curving gradient of 1 in 66 for ten miles, followed by a sharp descent to the river Diz. This river had carved itself a narrow, winding and precipitous gorge through the Zagros mountains and the railway followed this route most of the way to Durud. Altogether, in 110 miles, there were 133 tunnels—including one with a length of 2,750 yd.—to say nothing of numerous bridges, sharp curves and heavy gradients. The British Railway Operating Company that first had the task of working heavy trains on this line referred to it, with customary under-statement, as "The Hill"; the American G.I.s called it the "Subway". No doubt there were other less printable names as well.

The section from Durud to Tehran was less spectacular although it in-cluded the summit of the whole line (7,272 ft.) which involved further stretches at 1 in 66 in both directions. But after Tehran the railway had to surmount the huge Elburz range, and in spite of a summit tunnel, 3,150 yd. long, this necessitated more remarkable feats of engineering with long gradients of 1 in 36. Even with these steep inclines a three-tier section, with spiral tunnels, had to be incorporated to achieve the abrupt descent to the narrow plain bordering the Caspian Sea.

It was a very difficult railway to work; unfortunately the Persians had had little experience, or tuition, in locomotive maintenance. Most of the German 2-8-0 and 2-10-0 engines supplied for the opening of the line were in pretty poor shape by the time the Royal Engineers took over the working, and 143 Stanier-type 2-8-0s were hurriedly shipped out from Britain. Most of these were transferred into barges at Abadan and unloaded at Ahwaz with the use of the Anglo-Iranian Oil Company's heavy crane. The first 46 were coal-burners and were restricted to the lines south of Andimeshk. Even so, firing these engines in the blazing heat—with the temperature of the water in the tenders often as high as 110 deg. F.—was certainly no sinecure.

The oil-burning engines worked the line northwards from Andimeshk, and towards the end of 1942 they were joined, and in time replaced, by American 2-8-2 locomotives of the same type as those used in Egypt, Palestine and Iraq. But the real answer to the question of suitable motive power for this difficult section was diesel traction and in 1943 a fleet of 57 large supercharged Alco diesel-electric locomotives were imported. In due course, these worked most of the heavy trains (except the Mails) as far north as Arak, and even Tehran. They were normally used in pairs, or even in threes, but sometimes one diesel was coupled in front of a 2-8-2 steam loco-motive. When, in 1945, the line was handed back to the Persians, these diesels were carefully crated up again and sent back to America, most of them finishing up on the Alaska Railroad.

I got to know this fascinating line quite well during 1943-5, and spent

Among the hills of Wales: a train leaving Commins Coch Halt, on the main line of the former Cambrian Railways from Whitchurch to Aberystwyth

Train from Tripoli approaching Homs in 1950, headed by a o-8-o locomotive

Troop train at Durud, Iran, in 1945. Supplies of drinking water are hung outside the windows in canvas bags to cool

most of my spare time delving into its history and operation. Although the bulk of the work had been directed by a Danish-Swedish consortium, the construction of the line had been sub-let, in sections, to a variety of British, French, Belgian, German, Italian, Austrian, Swedish, Swiss, and Persian contractors, and one needed to be something of a linguist to cope with the accounts in the technical press of the various countries concerned.

I also acquired copies of the annual railway reports—in Persian! Once I had got used to reading everything from right to left, the tabular information was not too difficult to transcribe; but as I could only get hold of a classical dictionary, it required a certain amount of thought to realize that *musāfir haml*, which from the dictionary appeared to indicate a pregnant traveller, meant simply passengers carried by the railway.

Whenever my unit, which was purely infantry, threw an official party I was always careful to ensure that an American officer from the nearest railway camp was invited. He was usually mystified at getting an invitation, but American hospitality was such that this always resulted in profitable reciprocal visits to his establishment. The officer at Arak, when I asked whether he had any records of the earlier operations, pointed gloomily to a large cupboard and said: "Help yourself; you British seem to have run this railway on paper."

The American colonel at Tehran, however, was not quite so co-operative. He was a busy man, with plenty of problems, and he was frankly incredulous that anyone should want to look round the works there for the fun of it. However, my sense of direction is not always reliable; when I left his office I turned the wrong way, and it took me the rest of the afternoon to find the exit. Of particular interest was a large compound, surrounded by a wall and barbed wire to stop the local inhabitants from removing the more attractive accessories, in which most of the pre-war locomotives were stored in various stages of decomposition. These ranged from small 0-6-0 tender engines, which had started their careers on Swedish private railways before being reconditioned by the makers and sent out to work construction trains, to large Beyer Peacock Garratts built especially for the mountain section between Tehran and Bandar Shah.

The passenger train services were, naturally, neither frequent nor particularly speedy. In 1945 the mail train from Tehran to Ahwaz ran five times each week, taking exactly 24 hours for the 510 miles. The normal make-up consisted of eight or nine bogie coaches and two or three baggage vans. Except for a few German four-wheel vehicles, with a very long wheelbase, built in 1929 for the first section of the railway, all the passenger coaches had bogies. Colours were generally brown or brown and yellow, but the most modern vehicles were green, and there were also a few special saloons painted an attractive maroon. In addition there were some Indian broad-gauge coaches, on standard-gauge bogies, brought over during the war.

The enormous goods traffic during 1942–4, especially in connection with Allied supplies for Russia, naturally strained the rolling stock resources to the utmost. The pre-war goods wagons were mostly of German build and included a large number of bogie oil tank vehicles. During 1942–3 over 1,000 War Department and Indian wagons were added, followed by an enormous number of American vehicles of all kinds. Nevertheless, perhaps the most interesting of all the war-time arrivals was a batch of about 50 French-built covered vans, with vacuum and Westinghouse brakes, which had been contentedly operating on the cross-Channel ferry service until they were suddenly transported to the barren wilds of Iran. It must have been rather puzzling for the American G.I.s to read the carefully painted instructions warning them that these vehicles were "not to run between Tonbridge and West St. Leonards or on the Whitstable Harbour branch".

My last few months in the Middle East, towards the end of 1945, were spent at Suez, and the railway workshops and stores there had a long and rather pathetic line of Stanier-type 2-8-0s received in dilapidated condition after their hard service in Iran. Other interesting items included a batch of metre-gauge 4-6-4 tank locomotives with rotary cam poppet valve gear; these had been ordered for the Federated Malay States Railway, but had been diverted to the hurriedly-built line connecting Qena, on the Nile, with Safaga, on the Red Sea. When this war-time line was dismantled, these engines were sent to Suez to recover from their dusty labours; the conditions, and lack of adequate maintenance, had scarcely improved the efficiency of the motion, but after thorough reconditioning they later turned up on the Jordan section of the Hedjaz Railway.

Lastly there were the RAPWI trains at Adabiya docks, near Suez, for the transport of Returned Allied Prisoners of War and Internees from the Far East. Everything possible had been done for their reception and comfort, and someone had had the nice thought to ensure that the engines concerned were suitably decorated. In particular, American 0-6-0 tank No. 71304 was spotless, with gleaming black paint, red coupling rods and white wheel rims. I do not know if there were any railway enthusiasts among those ex-prisoners; if so they must have appreciated this small but rewarding gesture.

The Waverley Route

"LAMMERMOOR"

ONE OF THE MOST interesting and scenically-varied routes from the Scottish capital into England is that of the former North British Railway from Edinburgh (Waverley) to Carlisle, by Galashiels and Hawick, popularly known as the "Waverley Route". This line, 98 miles in length, follows a sinuous and heavily-graded course by river, moor and fell ere crossing the Border Marches, and entering the English city of Carlisle. The railway route crosses the Southern Uplands where they are cut in two by the transverse valley of the River Tweed, and consequently has two watersheds to cross.

Leaving the East Coast Route at Portobello East Junction, the train has first an easy five-mile run over the Midlothian coalfield to Eskbank, by the rich agricultural farmlands of the Lothian plain, dotted by collieries on either side, and with the Pentland Hills rising to nearly 2,000 ft. on the western horizon. Approaching Eskbank Station, the railway crosses the River North Esk by a single-arch stone viaduct of 60-ft. span and 54 ft. above the bed of the stream.

At Hardengreen, immediately south of Eskbank Station, the first long climb commences to reach the 880-ft. summit at Falahill (18 miles from Edinburgh) at the pass on Middleton Moor between the Lammermoor Hills on the left and the Moorfoot Hills on the right. Soon after starting on the ascent, the line crosses the River South Esk by a long masonry viaduct of 22 spans, 388 yd. in length and 75 ft. high, and thereafter follow in turn the valleys of the South Esk, the Gore Water, and the headwaters of the Scottish

River Tyne. More than eight miles of the ascent are on a gradient of 1 in 70.

Borthwick Glen, through which the Gore Water flows, is crossed by a great embankment, 130 ft. high, while near Tynehead Station, Middleton Moor is approached through long and deep cuttings. At the summit, the scenery is of the moorland type, and the country is entirely given over to the grazing of large flocks of sheep.

Then follows a more gradual descent, down the pastoral vale of Gala Water, a tributary of the Tweed, to Galashiels, the line crossing and re-crossing the windings of the Gala no fewer than 15 times between Heriot and Galashiels in a distance of just under 15 miles. Indeed, so acute is one large horseshoe bend of the river between Stow and Bowland that the projecting spur of hillside inside the bend has had to be pierced by a tunnel 219 yd. long, significantly named Bowshank Tunnel. In the course of the run down the valley by Heriot, Fountainhall and Stow, fine views are obtained of the Lammermoor and Moorfoot Hills to east and west respectively.

Then the train arrives at the thriving tweed-manufacturing town of Galashiels, the principal town in Selkirkshire, 33 miles from Edinburgh. A short distance south of Galashiels, the line crosses the Tweed by a five-span masonry viaduct, 278 ft. long, almost within sight of Sir Walter Scott's home at Abbotsford, after whose Waverley Novels the "Waverley Route" is appropriately named. Here, we are in the heart of the Scott Country, and the romantic wooded scenery of the Tweed Valley is followed past Melrose, picturesquely situated at the foot of the triple-peaked Eildon Hills (1,385 ft. high), to St. Boswells.

From St. Boswells, the line continues on an undulating course through several miles of well-wooded agricultural country to Hawick, crossing the Ale Water, a tributary of the Teviot, a short distance north of Belses Station. Passing Hassendean, Minto Crags rise boldly on the left between the railway and the valley of the Teviot, while beyond the valley "Dark Ruberslaw" (1,392 ft.) stands sentinel. Hawick, centre of the hosiery trade, and the largest town in Roxburghshire, is reached, 53 miles from Edinburgh, at the confluence of the River Teviot and its tributary, the Slitrig. Here, while the river valley is heavily wooded, moorland surroundings predominate, giving the town its name "Hawick among the Hills".

The second and longer climb commences at Hawick Station, and involves a steady ten miles at an average of 1 in 75 to 1 in 80 to Whitrope Summit, 970 ft. above sea-level, to surmount the intervening barrier of bleak and desolate moorland which connects the Southern Uplands with the Cheviot Hills. The line crosses the River Teviot by a six-span viaduct, 256 ft. long, at the south end of Hawick Station, and half a mile farther on crosses the Slitrig Water by a similar viaduct, thereafter following the valley of the Slitrig to gain the summit. At Shankend Station, a tributary stream, the Longside Burn, enters the Slitrig from the west, and a 15-span masonry viaduct, 597 ft. long, carries the railway over its wide valley. The country becomes gradually wilder as the summit is approached, with bare moors on every side, and Windburgh Hill, 1,662 ft. high, forming a prominent feature to the east. The final ridge, just before Whitrope Summit, is pierced by a tunnel, 1,216 yd. long.

Beyond the summit, the long steep descent of Liddesdale (the valley of the River Liddel, flowing south to join the Border Esk near Riddings) begins. In the first two miles, the line drops 120 ft. to 850 ft. above sea-level at Riccarton Junction, a village without roads, situated amid great bare hills in the wildest and most desolate of surroundings, dominated by Arnton Fell (1,464 ft.) round the base of which the railway winds in a sweeping curve. South of Riccarton, the line continues to drop steeply for another eight miles at 1 in 75, past Steele Road, still in the heart of the moors of Upper Liddesdale, to the long straggling village of Newcastleton.

Three miles farther on, approaching Kershopefoot Station, the railway crosses the Kershope Burn, which here forms the boundary between the two countries, and enters Cumberland, though still 21 miles from Carlisle; a border sign has been erected on either bank of the stream. The line continues to follow the windings of the Liddel past Riddings, in a country-side less wild in its aspect, with the river banks more thickly wooded, and cultivated fields replacing the barren moors.

The River Esk has now converged on the right from Langholm, and has added the waters of the Liddel to its own. The railway crosses the Esk north of Scotch Dyke Station, and again at Longtown, as it reaches the flat and pastoral Solway Plain. Finally, on entering Carlisle, the River Eden is crossed by a six-span stone viaduct, and its tributary the Caldew, by an iron girder bridge, ere the train draws up at Citadel Station, after a journey of absorbing interest through constantly-changing scenery, alternating between lush and leafy river valleys and bleak and desolate moorlands.

Railway Rarebits

R. C. H. IVES

AT ONE TIME OR ANOTHER there have been nearly 1,300 independent railway companies in Great Britain, among them some whose names are now almost forgotten, like the time-eroded gravestones of important ancestors. Yet these railways completely changed the way of life for our grandfathers. Their histories reveal often the unusual and occasionally the delightful.

One of these small railways of more than a century ago was described by H. S. Thompson to a Select Committee in 1872. Thompson was for many years the able chairman of the North Eastern Railway, and was well acquainted with the East & West Yorkshire Junction Railway. His evidence reads: "The district was covered with a number of short lines, most of which were in embarrassed circumstances. The one nearest to me, and which I regularly used, was perhaps a little worse than the average. It was a line between York and Knaresborough, and had only one set of carriages, and the locomotive was made to do the most work it could, running backwards and forwards to carry passengers, goods and coal, and it often broke down. We used to consider that the speed averaged four miles an hour. They were often stopped by the engine fire being nearly out, and it was obliged to stop to get up steam again. In fact, it was in very bad circumstances and gave very little accommodation to the public. The other railways were not all as bad as that but even the best managed were in great difficulties for want of funds."

Most of the smaller railways had a very short life, and were soon swallowed up by the great railway companies so familiar to our grandparents.

The British have a peculiar attitude towards railways, an attitude which is a curious mixture of affection and cynicism. Railway operation is as subject to differences, difficulties and delays as farming is to the fickleness of the weather. Yet criticism mellows and affection grows, as is particularly demonstrated when a little-used railway, having served its historic purpose, is about to be closed. Closure, imminent or actual, of a local line attracts the attention of the local historian seeking its history or the journalist in quest of information for an obituary.

In the coaching era, a traveller was accustomed to wretched roads, dirty inns and the possibility of robbery. In 1840, one writer stated: "It was the custom about a century and a half ago for persons intending to make a journey from London to York to arrange all their worldly affairs previously to starting on so dangerous and tedious an affair." In 1840, a train journey from York to London took 11½ hours, allowing for half an hour for refreshments at Derby.

Yet, even when railways were a proved success, there was still plenty of criticism. "Whoever," it was asked, "would be prepared to pay anything to be carried from Hexham to Newcastle in something like a coal wagon, upon a dreary wagon way, to be dragged along for the greater part of the way by a roaring steam engine?" Certainly the prospect does not sound very attractive. In 1842, another writer stated: "When the novelty has subsided, we shall seldom hear of a gentleman condescending to travel by this means of transit compatible only with men of business and mercantile travellers."

Ridicule was not confined to the opponents of rail travel. The Leeds & Selby Railway, in 1836, opposed York's first railway, the York & North Midland. At that time, Terry the confectioner was the Lord Mayor of York and also a supporter of the York & North Midland. The Leeds & Selby objection to the proposed railway was that it would have nothing to carry except tarts and cheesecakes. Nine years later when the York & North Midland proposed building a railway to Scarborough the critics ridiculed the idea, stating the proposed railway would commence at Thief Lane (York) and end at Folly Lane (Scarborough).

Not all criticism of railways was light hearted and irresponsible. Ruskin's opposition and that of Wordsworth was aesthetic. They feared the devastation of lovely country by unsightly railway building. Certainly much unattractive development grew around urban railway stations, making entry into our large towns and cities so hideous. In country districts the healing power of nature has often restored pristine freshness to railway banks and cuttings, particularly when spring flowers proliferate. In granting railway companies permission to construct lines, Parliament was little concerned with destruction and drabness, except where large estates were concerned. Yet when the Great Northern Railway received its Act, the objections of the

City of York were acknowledged by the imposition of strict amenity clauses, which were a surprising breach with Parliament's usual attitude of non-interference in the affairs of business undertakings.

The clauses inserted in the Great Northern Act of 1846 stated: "and whereas the line of the said Railway is proposed to pass through the ancient walls of the City of York, Be it therefore Enacted, That in the construction of the said Railway due regard shall be paid to the preservation of a style of architecture consistent with the prevailing architectural character of the said walls, and the said Railway shall be carried through the said walls upon entering and leaving the said city under a stone archway, to be constructed according to such design and in such manner as shall be approved by the architect for the time being of the lord mayor, and the council of the corporation of the city of York."

The Great Northern Railway was destined never to build its railway to York, for it ended, in the words of its Chairman, Edmund Denison, "in a ploughed field, four miles north of Doncaster". Access to York was gained over the lines of the York & North Midland on August 8, 1850, thus obviating the need for the Great Northern to build an independent line to the northern capital.

In the same year as the railway between York and the watering place of Scarborough was opened Disraeli published his novel of the "Hungry Forties" entitled *Sybil, or the Two Nations*. In Chapter VIII Sybil asks her companion, Stephen: "Think you not it would be a fairer lot to bide this night at some kind monastery, than to be hastening to that least picturesque of all creations, a railway station?" Defending the railways, Stephen said: "The railways will do as much for mankind as the monasteries did."

With the coming of railways and the spread of new travel habits, the seaside honeymoon became popular. This made obsolete the dying custom, in the north, of presenting the bride with a wain (or waggon) load of articles of use and luxury. The wain was decorated with flowers and boughs, and the horses or oxen with bride favours. In the North Riding, at the beginning of the nineteenth century, a farmer's daughter, married at Thornton, near Malton, was followed by a bride wain consisting of 20 carts.

It is known that excessive compensation for land was demanded from many railway companies, although it is only fair to add that there are also cases of public-spirited landlords selling land for railways at agricultural values. One case of excessive compensation was that paid to Lord Howden, a matter of £5,000. He objected to the railway going through his land for which the York & North Midland offered £5,000 as compensation. In order to appease him, they re-aligned the route outside his estate, but he still claimed and obtained £5,000 in a successful lawsuit.

"The Waverley Express" leaving Leeds for Edinburgh, with Stanier 4-6-0 No. 45597, Barbados, *working hard on a heavy train*

Railway Rarebits

From time to time, many reasons, some quite genuine, were quoted for high land prices. It would be difficult to state a more absurd reason than that demanded for land owned by Newcastle Infirmary and required by the Newcastle & Carlisle Railway. Regretting their earlier offer to sell at a moderate price an alderman justified the high price because they ought "to take into consideration the sufferings which the poor inmates would endure from the passing and re-passing of locomotives, the annoyance to the sick and dying, to whom the slightest noise is painful".

Railway companies have always been considered fair game for the unscrupulous intent on making false or unjustified claims. No claim less likely to be paid has ever been made than that of a Peter Simpson to the directors of the East & West Yorkshire Junction Railway. The minute book of this little railway between Knaresborough and York records, in 1850, a claim made by this publican for compensation for ale spoiled by blasting. The directors resolved "that such claim cannot be entertained".

Compulsory acquisition of land caused considerable dissatisfaction. When the Sheffield & Rotherham Railway was being built, it was proposed to cut the railway through the lawns and gardens of a house chosen by a Capt. Butler for a well-earned retirement. He petitioned Parliament, protesting: "If an Old Sailor may be allowed to speak in his own language, he would implore the House not to turn him adrift, when he had fondly hoped that, like an old hulk, he was laid up in a quiet harbour for the remainder of his days."

Railway companies have always been subjected to sharp criticism. Throughout the second half of the nineteenth century, and even into the early part of the twentieth, they were frequently attacked for providing Sunday services. Some of the earliest criticism came from *The Railway Times* which suggested there was unnecessary desecration of the Sabbath. In its issue of March 23, 1839, it suggested there was not only a great neglect of the spiritual wants of labourers on most railways in course of construction on this side of the Tweed but an habitual desecration of the Sabbath by the prosecution of work on that day for which there was neither necessity nor apology. It also suggested that many clergymen should be appointed to care for the spiritual wants of the labourers.

Sabbath observance was one of the more important customs affected by opportunities of rail travel. Many, but not all, railway companies refused to operate Sunday services. The Stockton & Darlington did not have any Sunday services until it commenced carrying mail in 1843. Even then it was not until two years later that it carried passengers on the Sunday mail trains, although privately-operated horse omnibuses had been licensed to operate a Sunday service between Stockton and Middlesbrough. Before opening its

A relief train, hauled by a class "5" 4-6-0 crossing the high masonry viaduct at Pinmore, between Girvan and Ayr

railway, the York & North Midland debated whether it should have Sunday services. After lengthy discussion, it was decided to run morning and evening trains for the mail, but all railway servants were to have their hours arranged in order that they could attend a church service.

The Hull & Selby Railway had a clause in its Bill against running trains on Sunday, but this was struck out, and a petition to Parliament for restoration of the clause was rejected. Its neighbour, the Leeds & Selby, had no such sabbatarian qualms, and, on Sunday, August 9, 1840, a train of 40 carriages conveying 1,250 textile operatives from the West Riding arrived at Hull at 8.45 a.m. This was exceptional and, in general, there was little travel on Sundays in Victorian England, because facilities were not provided. An outstanding and unusual case was the opening of the Metropolitan Railway. When opened to the public on Sunday, January 4, 1863, it attracted 10,000 passengers, who travelled largely out of wonder and curiosity.

When Nawton Castle, the home of the Earl of Carlisle, was destroyed by fire the Newcastle & Carlisle Railway ran an excursion on Sunday, July 9, 1844, to allow sightseers to view the blackened ruins. Arrangements were made for the train to arrive at Carlisle in time to allow the excursionists to attend divine service. How many availed themselves of the opportunity is not recorded. An outstanding case of hardship caused by the paucity of trains on Sunday occurred at Perth. The Duchess of Sutherland had received a message that her father, the Earl of Carlisle, was dying at Castle Howard, about 12 miles from York. The Scottish Central Railway refused her a seat in their mail van because the company did not carry passengers on Sundays. When she arrived at Castle Howard, her father was dead.

The Railway Times scorned the opposition to Sunday trains. On February 4, 1842, it stated "Let the men who sit quietly at home on Sunday in the luxuriant enjoyment of their hot joints and well plenished decanters, and yet denounce the poor man's excursion to the country as a Sabbath desecration—who loll in their horse-drawn carriages, yet anathematize the railway train, challenge Mr. Charles Shaw, Chief Constable of Manchester, who wrote 'I am decidedly of the opinion, in which I am supported by the very oldest officers of the force, that the more facilities there are offered to the labouring classes for innocent recreation, the fewer cases of crime are brought before the public.'"

The same periodical openly criticized Dr. Chalmers, a notable sabbatarian, who refused to travel on the Edinburgh & Glasgow Railway on a Tuesday because it also operated a Sunday service. Yet he inconsistently accepted Sunday mail. A *Railway Times* editorial stated in bold black letters: "WE ONCE TRAVELLED WITH HIM IN A CANAL BOAT ON SUNDAY."

One of the later railways, the Tees Valley, provided weekday services only.

The Chairman, a clergyman, announcing the decision not to work a Sunday service, rejoiced that hitherto there was no Sunday mail or newspapers in the valley, and he did not intend to provide facilities for them.

The opposition to Sunday trains, and particularly to excursion trains, came mainly from shareholders. There was a strong minority of shareholders of the North Eastern Railway who persistently organized opposition to Sunday trains, until 1914, when the paramount necessities of national survival overcame their religious scruples. The North Eastern directorate defended their policy contending that they ran fewer Sunday trains in proportion to their weekday trains than any other railway company south of the border.

The main public complaint against railways has always been late running of trains. The York, Newcastle & Berwick Railway's scheme for the avoidance of delays was to impose fines on drivers who arrived late at their destinations. This annoyed the drivers, who petitioned the directors, stating that the reasons for the delays were that platforms were too short and stationmasters too dilatory. On one occasion when a train conveying Edward Fletcher, known as "Old Neddy", who was in charge of the locomotive department, arrived late at its destination he hit the driver over the head with his umbrella.

Petitions on all manner of subjects were very numerous. Among them were petitions to directors from railway employees seeking redress. Civic bodies petitioned when they considered their localities subject to injustices. An interesting individual petition was that of the Rev. E. Shepherdson who was in regular receipt of wayleave payments. These he received for the Durham and Sunderland branch, formerly worked by horse traction, but converted to a locomotive line by the North Eastern Railway. Earlier, the wayleave rents had been reduced by agreement during a period of trade depression. Petitioning for an increased wayleave, Shepherdson stated that his original agreement provided not only for wayleave rents but that he should also have the manure, but by the substitution of locomotives for horses manure is not now bred.

Nowadays there is a disinclination for men to like uniform. This is a reversal of the general attitude in the nineteenth century. Railway directors usually considered, and addressed, their employees as railway servants, and provided uniform akin to livery. When the Leeds & Selby Railway was opened, in 1834, the guards were dressed in suits of green livery, with brass plates on their hats bearing the name of the company. Railwaymen were proud of their uniform. Guard Arnett, of the Stockton & Darlington, was delighted when on being promoted he wrote, in 1839: "Mr. Wilson says I is to have a scarlet coat."

The quality of uniform provided was generally good. In 1843, the uniform for the Stationmaster at York cost £3 13s., and his hat 14s. In terms of modern money this would be about £35 for his suit and coat, and £7 for his hat. Employees not coming into direct contact with the public were less handsomely treated. The Blyth & Tyne Railway merely provided its firemen with eight yards of check flannel which they had to have made up at their own expense. The North Eastern Railway attired its employees quite well, but in its earlier days signalmen had to provide their own watches.

Smoking in railway carriages has always been a source of friction between passengers, and between the railway companies and smokers. Despite having byelaws forbidding smoking in railway carriages and on station platforms, the railway companies fought a steadily losing battle against the smokers from the beginning. Smoking was, of course, dangerous in the early days, when carriages and station platforms were usually constructed of timber. The directors of the Newcastle & North Shields Railway considered it "an evil that had caused injury to the best carriages, the parties getting lights after entering the carriages from phosphorus boxes for the purpose of smoking". They announced that their servants had been instructed in all cases to take proceedings against passengers under the bye-laws, and to expel them from the carriages at any station where they might be found smoking.

Eventually the force of public opinion compelled the railway companies to provide compartments in which passengers were allowed to smoke. But the general public have over the years granted themselves a dispensation to smoke whenever and wherever they wish, and it is with difficulty that the rights of non-smokers have been preserved in the present century. In their early days, because of fire risk, railway companies refused to carry lucifer matches, as they were then called. However they were often tendered surreptitiously described as wooden ware. Ultimately the railway companies decided to carry them at higher rates and under special safeguards.

In the nineteenth century, Britain was divided by class distinctions which was reflected in three classes of railway accommodation. In addition, there were some people whose work was dirty and clothing disagreeable. The North Eastern Railway used to provide special carriages for Irish reapers returning to Ireland after living rough during the English harvest. Chimney sweeps were also a subject of complaint. In 1865, the Traffic Committee decided that "Complaint having been made of Chimney Sweeps travelling by train to the annoyance of the Passengers, Resolved that Station Masters be instructed not to book Chimney Sweeps when in their ordinary dress."

Although this may seem very discriminating against a section of hardworking people it should be realized that standards of cleanliness were very much lower than nowadays. At the half-yearly meeting of the Cockermouth, Keswick & Penrith Railway, in February 1900, Canon Rawnsley, conservator and lover of Lakeland, complained of the dirty condition of the third-class carriages on early morning trains. He suggested that two additional carriages be provided and labelled "Spittoons".

The standard of railway service has always depended on the co-operation of the public and the loyalty of railway servants. Perhaps the earliest example of a helpful report from a member of the public is a rather amusing letter to the Stockton & Darlington Railway concerning a coach accident in 1830. At that time, passengers travelled in horse-drawn coaches, which were privately owned, and merely paid a toll to the Stockton & Darlington Company for the use of the railway, and shared the single track with locomotive or horse-drawn trains of loaded and empty chaldron wagons. At the passing places, the order of precedence for the use of the single line was set out in the byelaws and regulations, which also stated the fines for neglect to take refuge in the sidings. It is said that the old drivers were stubborn and quarrelsome, and held the regulations in very light esteem. The letter, dated December 5, 1830, written in the vernacular and without punctuation, certainly supports this opinion:

Gentellmenn

Not having an opertunity to Call at your office I tacke the Liberty to Lay be fore youre respecktebell Comatee a tru statement of the perticklers of an axcident that toock place on your raill way last Monday Evening I obeserved the Cotchman to be verey tipsey on arriving at the halfway house he lighted his Lamp proceeded on to the next Siding thar was a seet of wagons Cuming up the Coatchman Calld out had on the wagons about 40 or 50 yardes from the other end of the siding the wagon driver running forward aperently with the intention to allter the Switches the Cotch passed the siding the wagon man run back put dowen his bracke but not till the horsess heads were Close togeather Coatch and wagons Came gently together No harme dun . . . horsess one on each side wagon man jumpt off his bracke helld the Coatch horse keept him quiet Coatchman sat still swore like a mad man the wagon man said Cum Dowen and put your Cooch back there is no harme dun and dont sit thare Swareing Year said the Coatchman i will Cum dowen and send you to hell i will send you to the deavell still swareing he got dowen with some difficulty pulled off his Clothes swore he would fighte the wagon man went up to him to fight the wagon man holding the Coatch horse all this time let go the horses when he saw the mad man attempt to sricke him then the mischieff hapened the horses began to kick brocke the Cooach shoved himself dowen passengers pushed the Cooach back horseses footfast in the Wagon harness . . . Coatchman swore at the passengers to let the Coatch a lone or I will send you all to hell wagon man went round the wagons Coatchman following him swaring he would kill him one passenger said you shall not strick him he said if you will not let me

stricke him I will stricke you for I will stricke him the other passengers
requested he would let the man a lone and if the wagon man had not
acted his part as well as he did thare might have beane farther mischieff
the panier man went back the full lenth of the siding tho he had no
right to do so but he apeared to be glad to get out of the mad mans
way I Coulld wright mutch more I am a fraid i shall intrud on your
goodness

I remain yours with Du respect

W.H.A. Passenger on the front of the
Cootch

NB the Coatchman said i will report you for not having a light tru he
   had not But then it was not dark for I Coulld see the wagons more
   than $\frac{1}{4}$ of a mile

No greater tribute has ever been paid to railwaymen than by Charles
Dickens. He was a very frequent traveller by rail, and had a deep appreciation of the services rendered to him on his journeys. Speaking at a
meeting of the Railway Benevolent Institution, he paid this wonderful
tribute:

I would ask you to consider what your experience of the railway
servant is. I know what mine is. Here he is, in velveteen or in a policeman's dress, scaling cabs, storming carriages, finding lost articles by a
kind of instinct, binding up lost umbrellas and walking sticks, wheeling
trucks, counselling old ladies with a wonderful interest in their affairs—
mostly very complicated—and sticking labels on all sorts of articles. I
look around me. There he is again in a station master's uniform,
directing and overseeing with the head of a general and manners of a
courteous host. There he is again in a guard's belt and buckle, with a
handsome figure, inspiring confidence in timid passengers. He is as
gentle to the weak people as he is bold to the strong, and there is not a
single hair in his beard that is not up to its work.

I glide out of the station, there he is again with a flag in his hands.
There he is again in open country at a level crossing. There he is again
at the entrance to a tunnel. At every station that I stop at there he is
again, as alert as usual. There he is again at the arrival platform, getting
me out of the carriage as if I was his only charge on earth. Now, is there
not something in the alacrity, in the ready zeal, in the interest of these
men that is not acknowledged, that is not expressed in mere wages?

And if your experience coincide with mine and enables you to have
this good feeling for, and to say a good word in regard to, railway
servants, then if you take a human interest in them, they will take a
human interest in us. We shall not merely be the 9.30 or the 10.30
rushing by, but we shall be an instalment of the considerable public that
is ready to lend a hand to the poor fellows in the risk of their lives.

Sunday Afternoon in Norway

HUGH STRAVEN

IT HAPPENED ON A SUNDAY in July 1949. Our first post-war holiday in Norway was drawing to its close, and we were on our way home from Oslo *via* Bergen and Newcastle. Our friends had warned us in advance that the Norwegian railways were still suffering from the effects of the war, and that we must not expect too much of them. For instance, Norway has no coal mines, and the only imported fuel then available was of very poor quality. The whole of the steeply-graded line across the mountains from Oslo to Bergen (307 miles) was still steam operated, and serious delays were by no means uncommon. When we reached Oslo East Station, shortly after nine in the morning, we found the Bergen train made up to ten coaches, weighing 350 tons, and hauled by a large 4-8-0, piloted by a 2-10-0. The tenders of both locomotives were piled high with what we could only describe as coarse black dust. We hoped for the best.

Our prospects of a punctual journey gradually faded; for the night train from Denmark and South Sweden, with which our train connected, was running late; and it was not until 10.10 that we got away—35 minutes late. How welcome was the assistance of the big 2-10-0 soon became apparent, as we toiled up the steeply-graded ascent, which begins almost at the station, and carries the railway in a wide sweep round the eastern and northern out-skirts of Oslo. At the suburban station of Grefsen, we made a short stop to pick up passengers and to detach the pilot engine, and the 4-8-0 was left to tackle the remaining, but easier, part of the ascent unaided. As we climbed higher, we were able to look out across the city to the calm waters of Oslo-fjord, stretching away between the hills to the open sea, nearly 60 miles to the south. For the homeward-bound visitor from overseas, this parting glimpse of Oslo is indeed a happy memory.

From the summit of the climb, some 900 ft. above sea-level, and only 12 miles from the start, we ran quite briskly over switchback gradients through the great forest of Nordmark for 20 miles, to a higher summit of 1,200 ft., whence we descended past the south end of the long narrow Randsfjord (one of the freshwater lakes of Norway) to our next stop at the thriving manu-facturing town of Hønefoss, 56 miles from Oslo. Although our train had a restaurant car, which was fully booked for two sittings of an excellent lunch, time was allowed at Hønefoss for passengers to visit the refreshment room. Such stops are a feature of long-distance journeys in Norway, and are adver-tised in the timetables by the letter "S", signifying *spiseopphold* (literally, "food-stop"). The refreshment rooms are of a very high standard, and it soon becomes obvious to a stranger that passengers need not go hungry.

From Hønefoss, the railway runs up Soknadal, and through a long tunnel leading to Hallingdal, a typical Norwegian upland region, with its swift-flowing river, and belts of dense forest, broken here and there by cultivated areas and small villages. Although this part of the journey is by no means severely graded, the bad coal was beginning to have its effect, and we lost time steadily. Shortly before 3.30 p.m. we reached the small station of Gol (71 miles from Hønefoss and 127 from Oslo) about $1\frac{1}{4}$ hours late. We should have made only a brief stop, but several minutes passed by, and then came an announcement over the loudspeaker that there would be a delay, as the engine had broken down. It was really surprising how quickly the train emptied, for within a minute or two many of the passengers were strolling up and down the platform in the hot July sunshine.

We were among those who made their way to the front of the train, and on to the track, where we stood in an admiring group, watching the efforts of the driver and fireman to put things right. The fireman opened the smokebox door, and shovelled out quantities of ash and unburnt slack coal. The per-forated plates round the top of the blast pipe, with which all Norwegian engines are fitted, were then forced apart with a pricker, and there followed much prodding and probing in the blast pipe, in an endeavour to clear away the ash and dust that had found its way through the protective screen. How-ever, all these efforts were of no avail, and eventually the cripple was un-coupled from its train, and limped off into a siding. A telephone call sum-moned a relief engine from the nearest locomotive depot, 16 miles distant, and we resigned ourselves to wait. Not even an eyebrow had been raised at the way in which we had strayed on to the track. That is one of the charms of

A Blackpool-Newcastle train approaching Tebay through the Lune Gorge

railway travel in Norway: within reason, one is not strictly confined to platform limits at country stations.

We strolled back along the platform, to find that the small refreshment room was doing a roaring trade in sandwiches, cakes, lager, soft drinks and coffee. Relays of food and drink were produced without delay, and there was plenty for all, and in variety. No such rush of customers had been expected, but the staff rose nobly to the occasion. We suspect that some of the supplies came from the nearby hotel, but the fact remains that the refreshments were speedily forthcoming when an emergency suddenly arose in the middle of a Sunday afternoon at a roadside station serving a small holiday resort. Yes, there is no doubt that catering has been reduced to a fine art in these northern lands. Although we had had lunch in the restaurant car, we could not resist edging our way into that crowded room for a coffee and a cake. Then we returned to the platform to see both portions of the day train from Bergen to Oslo make a brief stop at Gol, and steam away down the long valley.

It was well after 4.30 before the relief engine (another 4-8-0) arrived, and an announcement over the loudspeaker recalled passengers to the train. We had taken the opportunity of having a quick look at the village. A few minutes later, the long delay at Gol was but a vivid and lasting memory, and we were making quite good speed over the rising gradients of Upper Hallingdal. A run of 16 miles brought us to Ål, where we should have changed engines had things gone normally. Here was another advertised *spiseopphold*, which was not cut short, although the train was nearly three hours late. Many of the passengers made their way to the refreshment room—but no, this time we felt that we just could not!

Beyond Ål, the gradients became steeper, as we climbed towards the Hardanger Mountains, and the pine forests gradually became thinner, giving place to a more hardy type of vegetation, in which birch trees predominated. At the holiday resort of Geilo, 2,600 ft. above sea-level, and magnificently situated at the foot of steep birch-clad slopes, backed by towering peaks, we reached the head of Hallingdal, and the beginning of the mountain section of the line. Climbing steadily, we crossed a bleak plateau, where almost the only signs of habitation were at the stations of Ustaoset and Haugastøl, two popular centres for winter sports. Then came the longest distance between stations on the whole journey—the 16¾ miles from Haugastøl to Finse. We were now well above the tree-line amidst surroundings that became increasingly savage and barren; even the hardy dwarf birch disappeared before the summit was reached.

Soon we were passing through a series of short tunnels and snowsheds, interspersed with stretches of open cutting. The side screens of the snowsheds had been removed, to afford momentary glimpses of the mountains. We

Train from Crewe, headed by "Jubilee" class 4-6-0 No. 45600, Bermuda, *standing in Lime Street Station, Liverpool, at the end of its journey*

already had seen snowfields on the higher slopes, but before we reached Finse, we were looking down on to snow, although the season was high-summer. Finse, another noted resort for winter sports, stands more than 4,000 ft. above sea-level, in surroundings that are bare and wild in the extreme. The station is the highest on a main line in northern Europe. Some five miles farther on, we reached the summit of the railway (4,265 ft.) where ice was still floating on the nearby lake, Taugvatn. For several miles beyond the summit, we ran through long snowsheds, one of which completely enclosed Hallingskeid Station, as a precaution against drifting. Then, as we approached Myrdal, 21 miles from Finse, came a most impressive moment, as we looked out through the side windows of another shed down a sheer precipice into the narrow valley of Flåmsdal, more than 1,000 ft. below.

At Myrdal, we changed trains to travel down the branch to Flåm, at the head of one of the southern arms of the Sognefjord, which penetrates more than 100 miles into the land from the west coast. This was new ground to us, as the line had been completed during the war. In contrast to the main Bergen-Oslo Railway, it was electrified from the first. Although it is little more than 12 miles long, the railway to Flåm is one of the most remarkable in Norway, and its engineering works, its gradients, and its scenic attractions are alike outstanding. Myrdal is 2,860 ft. above sea-level, and the railway had to be brought down more than 1,700 ft. in the first six miles. Even with a spiral location, much of it in tunnel, long gradients of 1 in 18 were unavoidable. On the remainder of the descent to the sea at Flåm, the steepest gradient is 1 in 24, and the engineering works are far lighter.

The branch train of two saloon-type coaches was waiting at the side platform when we reached Myrdal, and a few minutes later the last stage of the day's journey had begun. As we wound our tortuous way down the mountainside, tunnels and snowsheds hid much of the magnificent scenery, but by way of compensation the train was stopped specially for a few moments to enable passengers to enjoy a particularly wonderful view. A second special stop was made between two tunnels, where the waterfall of Kjosfoss comes roaring down a steep gorge of black rock beside the line in a welter of white foam. Little touches such as these add so much to the enjoyment of a holiday journey. Beyond the first precipitous descent, the scenery soon lost its savage grandeur, as the lower slopes of the mountains became thickly wooded, and the floor of the sheltered narrow valley green and cultivated.

Quite unexpectedly, the valley opened on to the shore at the head of the fjord, and the train reached Flåm. As we walked down the single platform of the small station in the soft twilight of the northern summer evening, we felt that we had reached the very edge of the world, and the noise and the rush of city streets seemed infinitely far away. A friendly welcome awaited us at the nearby Fretheim Hotel, and although the time was now well after nine o'-clock, we were assured that dinner would be served as soon as we were ready. Here was yet another example of the excellence and flexibility of Norwegian catering arrangements: the train had arrived more than three hours late, but any difficulties that this delay may have caused were overcome with quiet efficiency and a smile.

The years since 1949 have seen many changes in the Norwegian railway scene. On the main line from Oslo to Bergen, electrification has been undertaken in stages, and is now complete. The route has been shortened by a more direct approach to Bergen, through a long tunnel. Journey times have been reduced, and punctuality and reliability greatly improved. New and comfortable coaches, with large windows affording widespread views of the incomparable mountain scenery, have been introduced. Yet, despite all these changes for the better, we still have happy memories of that July Sunday, when we spent 11 hours on the journey of 223 miles from Oslo to Flåm, with an interlude at Gol. We would not have missed it for the world!

TO BE TAKEN SLOWLY

"Due to earlier late running Inner Rail Circles are running late."—From a notice chalked up at Liverpool Street, Metropolitan Station, at the weekend.
"Peterborough", in " The Daily Telegraph"

MY HAT!

While on a test run, a diesel locomotive stopped on the main line, and had to be dragged off ignominiously by a steam locomotive. This was due to no mechanical defect, but because one of the railway inspectors had had his hat sucked up into the fan duct, and the resultant blockage caused a temporary breakdown in air supplies to the engine.

From the *"Eastern Region News"*

Springbok Century

R. LYLE and V. S. HARAM

A HUNDRED YEARS AGO South Africa boasted a mere 55 miles of railway, laid to the 4 ft. 8½ in. gauge. It was in 1873, after the discovery of diamonds near Kimberley, that the railway was converted to the 3 ft. 6 in. gauge, and commenced its progress inland, to reach Kimberley, some 650 miles from Cape Town, in 1885. Kimberley stands at an altitude of 4,000 ft., but on the journey the total rise is 14,000 ft.—in other words, there is 10,000 ft. of false rise and fall. The coast is separated from the innermost plateau by successive mountain ranges, which impose sharp curvature and steep gradients. It was these adverse conditions which influenced a decision to convert the then existing lines to the 3 ft. 6 in. gauge.

The lines subsequently built from the ports at Port Elizabeth, East London, Durban and Delagoa Bay to Johannesburg comprise the backbone of the railway network of today. As the whole system has developed from the line commencing at Cape Town, the adoption of the 3 ft. 6 in. gauge as standard was the obvious choice. In 1915, in the First World War, South-West Africa, previously a German colony, passed, by mandate, to the control of South Africa, and its metre-gauge system was converted to 3 ft. 6 in., and was extended to connect with the South African railways.

Some 350 miles in the northern part of South-West Africa remained as a 2 ft.-gauge system. The expansion of livestock and mineral traffic in this vast area rendered transhipment at the break-of-gauge station, Usakos, on the Windhoek-Walvis Bay line, completely impracticable, and in 1960 these narrow-gauge lines were converted to the 3 ft. 6 in. standard. This conversion of gauge was, perhaps, the biggest undertaken anywhere in the world in recent years, and has greatly facilitated the movement of traffic.

While the rainfall in the Republic of South Africa is relatively low, that in South-West Africa is appreciably lower, and varies from about an inch a year along the coastal belt, up to 6 in. in the south, 12 in. in the centre, and up to 20 in. in the north. The territory is subject to periods of drought, and the climate is hot and dry with a high rate of evaporation. Under such conditions sufficient water suitable for steam locomotives was difficult to maintain, and the time came when a change in traction could not be deferred. There was only one alternative, and a large order was placed in 1960 for 115 diesel loco-motives of 1,980 h.p., which today operate from De Aar Junction to Walvis Bay, and on the Tsumeb and other branch lines. The cost of these locomotives was approximately £9 million. The gauge conversion and change of traction have wrought a revolution in transport conditions in this territory.

With the advent of railway electrification in South Africa in 1926, when the first electrified section—between Pietermaritzburg and Glencoe, on the Natal main line—came into operation, a new era in railway traction was entered. In the same year, two further sections, Merrivale to Howick, and the old line between Cedara and Boughton, were electrified. In 1928, came the first suburban electrification, the 22½ miles between Cape Town and Simons-town, and this was followed in 1933 by Cape Town to Bellville, on the Cape Western main line, and in 1934 by Maitland to Heathfield, known as the Cape Flats line. Electrification entered the Orange Free State in 1935 with the section between Van Reenen and Harrismith. In the Transvaal, the Wit-watersrand interurban area was electrified in 1937. The Second World War interrupted progress, but after 1945 many new schemes were undertaken as part of a comprehensive £20 million scheme.

In many countries, the steam locomotive is losing ground to electric and diesel traction, but in view of the abundance of coal in South Africa and the low production cost, the administration regards steam power, and steam-generated electricity, as its main source of energy. These advantages led to the policy of having electric traction on all lines where the traffic is heavy and gradients are steep, diesel traction on those sections which are farthest from the coalfields and where water shortage occurs, and steam traction on routes where coal is easily obtainable and water supplies assured. The average cost of coal purchased by the railways in South Africa is 14s. 3d. a ton.

Under the present electrification scheme, the main line between Bellville and Touws River, including the Stellenbosch loop, a total of 174 route miles, was completed in 1954, and the Orange Free State main line between Vereeniging and Kroonstad, 86 miles, in 1959. The most notable expansion, however, took place in the Transvaal where the total electrified route mileage increased from 132 in 1946 to 521 at the end of March 1961. The lines in the Transvaal included such major sections as Randfontein to Klerksdorp, 89½ route miles, and Midway to Vereeniging, 32¾ route miles. In 1961 electrification of the Cape Western main line from Touws River to Beaufort West was completed, and a continuous distance of 339 miles from Cape Town to the North is now operated electrically. Between Cape Town and Pretoria, a distance of 1,038 miles, there are no less than 497 miles of electrified track.

During 1961, approval was given for electrification from Union to Volksrust, in the Southern Transvaal, a distance of 145 miles, at an estimated cost of approximately £2½ million. This work was completed as recently as April 1, 1964, and the whole route from Johannesburg to Durban, 485 miles, is now electrified. With the completion of this project, the electrified route mileage of the South African railways is more than 12 per cent of the total route mileage.

Two further major electrification schemes must be mentioned—the line from Klerksdorp to Beaconsfield (near Kimberley), 191 miles, was completed by the end of 1964; and from Witbank, in the Eastern Transvaal, to Komatipoort, on the border of Portuguese East Africa, 222 miles, which is expected to be completed about the middle of 1966. The electrified system will then total 2,100 miles, comprising about 18 per cent of the system (excluding the lines in South-West Africa) but carrying well over 50 per cent of the total traffic.

Where a change to electric traction to increase track capacity is not possible, because power for traction is not available, one of the alternatives is centralized traffic control. The section of line between Kamfersdam (near Kimberley) and Postmasburg serves very big manganese and iron deposits which are intensively exploited. Gross traffic on this single-line section of 128 miles has reached 30,000 tons daily, and is now moved under control of a panel at Kimberley, operating electrical signalling. The installation was brought into operation between July 1960 and June 1961. A second installation, between Hamilton (near Bloemfontein) and Springfontein, an 88-mile section of the Orange Free State main line, was completed in July 1962.

These installations for the remote control of signalling and point operation on long stretches of single track replace mechanical signalling and token control instruments at a succession of stations five to ten miles apart. The results can be compared with the benefits obtained from heavy capital investment in other works, such as doubling of track or change of traction, designed to increase the capacity of the railway. The Planning Council examine these results to determine the nature of future improvements, based on local conditions and other relevant factors.

In 1956 the Railway Administration sent a mission to the United States of America to study the mechanization of track maintenance and renewal. The heavy ballast tamping and other machines have been considerably improved, and it has been found possible with one machine to undertake the maintenance of track surface over 200 miles of single line. The most important advances in track maintenance are the introduction of automatic lifting and cross levelling which enables the machine to produce a running top correct to within two millimetres. Today an ever-increasing mileage of track, consisting of long rails up to and over 500 ft. in length, on concrete sleepers with special fastening, gives near perfect travelling comfort.

The South African Railways have in service some 2,550 steam, 565 electric and 174 diesel locomotives, and about 6,700 passenger and 112,000 goods vehicles. No further steam locomotives are on order for lines now being electrified. During the past five years, some hundreds of main-line electric locomotives, motor coaches and trailers for suburban operation, and modern main-line coaches have been built at new plants in South Africa. Nearly 10,000 new goods vehicles are on order. These include high-sided and drop-sided steel wagons, iron ore hoppers, grain wagons, refrigerators, petrol tank wagons, cement carriers, and fruit trucks. Today, almost all locomotives and rolling stock are built in the Republic.

The rapid industrial expansion brought many problems which are common in similar circumstances elsewhere. It has been necessary for the Government to plan and finance vast housing schemes for resettlement, particularly of Coloured and Bantu workers. Such housing schemes require facilities for daily travel to and from work of over 300,000 factory, office and domestic workers. New railway lines and other facilities to serve these new residential areas have been provided at Johannesburg, Pretoria, Durban, Germiston and Cape Town. The transport charges are below the economic level, and workers travel once daily in each direction at a maximum cost of 10 cents (1 shilling).

The Johannesburg–Pretoria area embraces the greatest economic concentration in South Africa, if not in the whole continent. Suburban passenger traffic centring on Johannesburg has increased from 16 million passengers in 1932 to 177 million in 1963. The growth of the City has been such as to make essential facilities commensurate with its importance, and a large new through station has been provided at a cost of £11 million.

On April 21, 1963, the main-line platforms of the new station at Cape Town were opened to traffic. A further stage was reached a year later, when it began to handle suburban services. The old station, which had served the City for over 90 years, saw its last train leave (for the southern suburbs and Simonstown) on the afternoon of Saturday, June 13, 1964. When the new station is completed, it will have cost £7½ million. The final six platforms, making a total of 24, will be brought into use in 1966.

The new stations at Johannesburg and Cape Town are considered to be the most up to date on the African continent; and visitors from overseas consider the former as unsurpassed throughout the world. Such comparisons indicate the high degree of efficiency and modernization of railway facilities and emphasize how closely these are geared to the economic development of South Africa.

New works at present authorized are estimated to cost over £300 million. This figure includes £62 million for additional track facilities, £50 million for relaying and strengthening permanent way, £111 million for station improvements and new sidings, £20 million for regrading and deviations of track and £30 million for electrification. In addition, over £25 million has been authorized for new locomotives and rolling stock. With the continued expansion of the national economy, and the basic importance of railway transport, the progressive provision of improved facilities is essential.

Today, the South African Railway Administration controls some 13,680 route miles of railway, and 31,500 route miles of road motor services, the major harbours and air services, and catering and publicity services. To permit of positive advance planning of these services, a Planning Council was inaugurated in 1954, under the chairmanship of a Deputy General Manager. Heads of technical, financial and operating departments are members of the Council, whose activities cover a wide field. Investigations range from the improvements necessary to expand the carrying capacity of main lines, the relative advantages of different forms of traction, the additional locomotives, passenger coaches and goods vehicles required to cope with an ever-increasing traffic, to improved communications and signalling systems.

To achieve adequate and balanced planning, information is obtained annually from about 50 of the large outside organizations in the national economy, such as mining, agriculture, finance, and industry. These institutions include the Reserve Bank and other financial institutions, Government departments, including Control Boards ranging from fruit and cereals to meat, the Chambers of Mines, Industries and Commerce, and the Industrial Development and other Corporations. The data obtained indicate the business climate and the future levels of production for agriculture, mining and industry. From this summary it is possible to assess accurately the turnover of trade and of imports and exports.

The data also assist in estimating the traffic volume over various sections of railway and the extent to which additional facilities are required. By these means and the closest contact with other Government Departments, it is fairly certain that transport facilities will keep pace with needs in a developing country which has a high potential for growth in all phases of its national economy.

In South Africa, the Ministry of Transport embraces two completely separate departments—the Department of Transport, and the South African Railways and Harbours Administration. Whereas the Railway Administration is a State undertaking, the functions of the Department of Transport are to regulate the control of the various forms of transport except railways and shipping.

Under the Act constituting the Republic of South Africa, the control and management of the railways, ports and harbours is vested in the Minister of Transport and a Board consisting of three Commissioners. An Act passed in 1916 had placed the management and working of the Railways and Harbours under the General Manager, subject to control by the Minister in consultation with the Board.

The General Manager has his headquarters in Johannesburg and is assisted by two Deputy and five Assistant General Managers, a Financial Manager and the Head of the Planning & Productivity Department. There are also a Chief Civil Engineer, Chief Mechanical Engineer, Chief Electrical Engineer, Chief Accountant, Chief Airways Manager and Chief Stores Superintendent. The railways are divided on a geographical basis into nine areas, known as Systems, with head offices at Cape Town, Port Elizabeth, East London, Durban, Bloemfontein, Johannesburg, Pretoria, Kimberley and Windhoek. Each System Manager is assisted by a technical, commercial and operating staff, and has autonomous control in his area, subject to general supervision from headquarters.

The Act constituting the Republic provides for the administration of the railways, ports and harbours on business principles, with due regard to agricultural and industrial development within the Country and the promotion, by means of cheap transport, of the settlement of an agricultural and industrial population in the inland regions. As far as possible the total earnings must not be more than sufficient to cover outlays for working, maintenance, betterment, depreciation and interest.

Railways in Law

A. J. F. WROTTESLEY

RAILWAY LAW is both fascinating and far-reaching. It has distinct aspects for passengers and consignors and consignees of goods, for the staff, for contractors, tenants of railway property, railway enthusiasts, and many others. In fact, so diverse is the subject that it would be impossible within the limits of a single article to touch on more than a few of its branches.

In Great Britain, a railway is in itself a creation of the law; for an ordinary line requires an Act of Parliament to authorize its construction. Land is required for the tracks and stations, so Parliament has to consider carefully the rights of landowners whose property is taken compulsorily, and what compensation they are to receive. In practice, when a railway Bill comes before Parliament, it is referred to a House of Commons Committee. If this Committee approves of it, that is, "finds the preamble proved", the Bill goes to the Lords, who may refer it to a House of Lords Committee. If the Lords give the Bill "leave to proceed", it usually is passed. Bills for new lines are not numerous nowadays. In recent years, they have been required only for the Victoria tube line, in London, and for colliery branches in Nottinghamshire.

The opening of a new railway must be sanctioned by the Minister of Transport, after he has been satisfied by his Inspector's report that it has been safely and properly constructed. A new light railway, or the operation of an existing line as a light railway, does not require an Act, but must have the sanction of the Minister of Transport, after he has held a public enquiry on the subject. A light railway, which may be of standard or narrow gauge, is lightly-constructed, is free from some of the regulations affecting the operation of ordinary railways, particularly in relation to signalling and level crossings, and is subject to severe restrictions of speed. The Minister's inquiry, sanction, and "light railway order" are of special interest nowadays, because preservation societies have undertaken the operation of light railways.

Before the days of railways, travel, and even the despatch of goods, was still regarded by many as something unusual and dangerous. The law then said that the "common carrier" of passengers and goods (that is a coach proprietor or a wagoner) was like an insurer. He had to convey safely what was offered to him, except in very exceptional circumstances, arising from an "Act of God" (such as a very severe storm or flood), an "Act of the King's Enemies", an inherent vice or fault of the goods, or the fault of the passenger or consignor.

Even before the days of railways, some Acts had been passed to protect carriers from dishonest claims, but in the early days, railways were mainly "common carriers". These rights and liabilities were soon more precisely defined by the Railway & Canal Traffic Act of 1854. Later, goods were mainly carried, subject to special agreements, on what were called the "standard conditions", which received statutory authority from the Railways Act of 1921 (the Act that amalgamated the railways into four large groups). However, in some respects, the railways continued to be "common carriers" (substantially, for example, of passengers' luggage) for many years.

The nationalization of 1948 made comparatively little difference to the rights and liabilities of the railways as carriers, but the Transport Act of 1962 has given the railways very considerable freedom to decide on what conditions they will carry passengers and goods. It was only then that what little was left of the common carriers' liability was formally abolished.

When a passenger travels, there is a "contract" (that is, a legal agreement) between the passenger and the Railways Board to carry him to his destination "for reward", in other words, for the payment of the fare. The contract is, of course, generally made by the passenger at the booking office. The ticket has on it the names of the stations from and to which the journey is to be made and the date. In the early days, the passenger really was "booked"—his name had to be given when the ticket was issued.

From its nature, a ticket cannot contain all the conditions. Some are mentioned on the ticket, and others by reference (usually printed on the ticket) to the words "issued subject to the conditions and regulations in the Board's publications and notices". The conditions bind the passenger if he expressly, or by implication, agrees to them. Few people ask about the conditions when they travel, although they often do so when they are sending off goods and parcels. The law says that generally if a passenger accepts the ticket without comment, he is considered to have agreed to the conditions.

On the whole, the liability to carry the passenger safely is a high one. Engines, carriages, track, bridges, signalling and electrical equipment, and so on, must be efficiently constructed, properly maintained, and regularly inspected. Stations must be properly lighted, and made reasonably safe for the use of passengers. Special precautions must be taken in fog and other exceptional circumstances.

On the other hand, the Board will not generally be liable if a passenger suffers loss or damage in circumstances over which they have no control. A good example would be if a privately-owned lorry crashed through level crossing gates and collided with a train, where no fault could be attributed to the Railway Board or its staff. In one well-known case, a corporation crane fell on a train coming out of a tunnel, and the railway company was not held liable for the injury of a passenger. But if the railway staff are aware of such dangers caused by others, and fail to take reasonable steps to protect passengers, the Board may be liable.

If the Board issues a through ticket to and from places outside British Railways, or if the journey is made partly by rail and partly by some other undertaking (such as a bus or a shipping company) the conditions specifically restrict the liability of the railways to loss or damage occurring on their own trains or premises. There is an exception to this exception, as the condition states that it does not preclude liability if the loss or damage occurs on London Transport trains, vehicles or premises. This is important because so many passengers travel through between London Transport and British Railways stations.

Liability may be avoided if the cause of the accident is some "latent" or hidden defect in machinery or property, which reasonable and regular inspection could not have discovered. Many years ago, an action for damages for injury against the Manchester, Sheffield & Lincolnshire Railway (later part of the Great Central) failed for this reason. A bad accident at Penistone was caused by an axle breaking, but the company showed that the axle had been carefully examined before the train left Manchester, and no defect could then be found. However, great care is required in such cases, because it must be proved that up-to-date methods of inspection were used.

Besides the duty in "contract" to carry the passenger safely, there is a duty in law to people who come on to railway property. This is a liability in what the law calls "tort", a civil liability not to cause people injury or loss. There are many examples of people to whom this duty is owed: they include passengers before they have bought their tickets, people who have come to a station to see-off or meet passengers, people despatching parcels or luggage in advance, and those who come to a goods station to despatch or collect goods. Before 1957, the law drew a distinction between persons (known as "invitees") who were on the premises on some business with the railways, and others (known as "licensees") with only bare permission to be on the property, such as people watching the trains, or calling on the stationmaster with no business interest.

The liability to the "invitee" was much greater that it was to the "licensee". However, it was not easy to draw the distinction. For example, it is very difficult to define the man who walks on to the station to buy a paper; he has no business with the railway, but only with its tenant, the bookstall keeper. But the Occupiers' Liability Act of 1957 says that it is the duty of the Railway Board, as occupiers of the property, to make the place concerned reasonably safe for persons lawfully using it, without the former distinction of "business interest" and "bare permission", save that it can extend, restrict, modify or exclude the liability by agreement or otherwise. Examples of such modifications are platform tickets, long established at very many stations, where access to the platforms and liability are regulated by special conditions, and also "train-spotter notices", which exclude people specifically.

It must be borne in mind that the passengers, and others who are lawfully on railway property, must take reasonable care of themselves. For example, if there is a prominent notice "Passengers cross the line by the bridge", and the passenger uses one of the crossings intended for the staff, he is not taking proper care. In two recent cases, some oil had been upset on one of the platforms of a large terminus. In one instance, no attempt was made to warn a passenger, who recovered damages for injuries sustained when he slipped on the oil; but in the other, the staff had put a barrier round the patch of oil, and a passenger who slipped and was injured, after disregarding a warning shout, failed to recover damages.

Two cases, both concerned with stations in North-East London, well illustrate the duty of the railway towards the passenger and the person who is lawfully on a station. The first was brought against the London, Tilbury & Southend Company, shortly before it was absorbed by the Midland in 1912. The second was in 1936, and was against the London & North Eastern Railway, in respect of a former Great Eastern station. In each case, a woman bought her ticket at a booking office at road level, and had to reach the platform down pitch-dark steps which made right-angled turns. On both occasions, fog was so thick that the platform lamps could not be seen; and in the second case, the whitened edge of the platform could not be distinguished. The second station was the more dangerous, because the flight of steps ended half-way across the platform, and at right-angles to the line. The fog appliances were working properly—indeed the passenger in the second case gave, in evidence, the opinion that the train would be safer than the bus in such a fog—but this did not help if the station was dangerous. In neither case was the passenger warned by the booking clerk, or by anybody else, of the dangers of the dark steps. Both women fell on the line and were injured. In the second case, the passenger, although her leg was broken, managed to drag herself to one side, and was only touched by an approaching train.

In each case, the company was held liable for not providing a station that was reasonably safe because of their servant's failure to warn passengers of dangers, and not taking special precautions in fog. In the first case, the company's appeal to the House of Lords was dismissed; in the second, the judge, after the facts had been established in evidence, gave judgment in favour of the plaintiff on the authority of the earlier case.

The proper handling of carriage doors and windows involves both the railway and passengers in duties and responsibilities. It is the duty of the platform staff to see that doors are properly shut before the train leaves, taking care that people standing inside are not hurt by the door shutting suddenly. The passenger who opens the door before the train stops, and jumps out leaving the door swinging, can be successfully prosecuted, but he is the despair of the Railway Board, because he can cause injuries to other passengers and the staff, besides himself, if he falls over. In one case, not long ago, a passenger was held liable for the injuries to a porter who was hit by a swinging door.

A person with no right or permission to be on railway property is a trespasser, and can be prosecuted accordingly. There is no duty or liability to him, save that he must not be injured deliberately, such as by shunting a truck at him, or by using more than reasonable force to remove him if he will not leave on request.

There is, however, an important exception, if the trespasser is a child. The law recognizes that a child does not appreciate dangers or take care of himself as an adult can, and that many things on private property attract a child's interest—that is, that they are what the law calls "allurements" to children. The Occupiers' Liability Act emphasizes that a particular duty arises for these reasons if the child is lawfully on the property. If the child is a trespasser, the law holds that the Railways Board is bound to refrain from acting in wilful or reckless disregard of his presence.

In one case, brought many years ago in Ireland against the Midland Great Western Railway, and decided by the House of Lords on appeal, children got through a hole in a fence and played on an old turntable, with the result that one was seriously injured. The company was held liable, because the turntable was dangerous and an "allurement", and there was not sufficient evidence that the company's servants had ever driven the children away or mended the fence.

In another case (in England) about 12 years ago, a young boy got on the line and was injured. The evidence showed that other boys had broken the fence and made a slide down the bank; but the fence had been repaired by the railway staff, after they had learnt what was going on, and the injured boy had got through it. The Railway Executive (as it was then) won the case, because, although it was stated that it had to take reasonable action by mending the fence regularly, to prevent something it knew was happening, omission or failure to take every possible precaution did not mean liability.

Escalators at underground stations are a very attractive "allurement" to children, who are apt to run up and down, or slide on the side and catch their hands in the moving handrail. In one case against the Central London Railway (when it was a separate company) the evidence showed that the children always ran away when a policeman, ticket collector or booking clerk chased them off, but had come back. They were old enough to realize, and admitted, that they had no right to be there. The company was held not liable.

Some Acts of Parliament, and regulations issued by the Minister of Transport (by the President of the Board of Trade before 1919) provide for various safety precautions and appliances. For example, every passenger train running more than 20 miles without stopping must have sufficient means of communication between the passengers and the people in charge of the train. In practice, this means the alarm signal chain in the carriages, the pulling of which partly applies the brakes, and attracts the attention of the guard.

Safety rules are laid down for the staff. If there is an accident, an Inspector, appointed by the Minister of Transport, holds an enquiry. In his report to the Minister, the Inspector may suggest amendments or clarification of the rules and regulations to provide against such an accident.

The railways convey free of charge 150 lb. of luggage for first-class passengers, and 100 lb. for second-class passengers. They will generally accept liability for loss, damage or delay to luggage if it is properly labelled and put in the guard's van, or is "otherwise in the control of the Board", or is deposited in the "cloak room" (left luggage office) in accordance with the left luggage conditions. If it is in the luggage van on the train, the conditions state that liability will not be accepted if it can be proved (that is, if the Board can substantially satisfy the court) that the loss was not caused by the negligence or wilful misconduct of the railway staff. The expression "otherwise in their control" is of great importance, because it refers to the occasion when, as so often happens, a passenger hands a suitcase to a porter with instructions to put it in the compartment. If a passenger does this a reasonably short time before the train starts, the luggage will be held to be in the Board's control.

In what lawyers call the "leading case" on the subject, Bunch *versus* the Great Western Railway (which began in the Marylebone County Court and ended in the Lords), it was held reasonable for a woman passenger to hand a bag to a porter to be put in the compartment 40 minutes before the train started on Christmas Eve, when Paddington Station was thronged with travellers.

In a later case, a bag was put into a sleeping car at St. Pancras, on the instructions of an inspector, an hour before departure time. It was stolen before the train started, and the company was held liable. On a more recent occasion, on the "Cornish Riviera Express", a porter had put a suitcase in a compartment at a passenger's request, but it was stolen while the passenger was having lunch in the restaurant car, or was with friends in another compartment. It was held that the suitcase was still in the company's control.

However, if the luggage is at the station, but not "in control", that is, if the passenger is standing about with his luggage on the platform, or leaves it lying on a platform seat, the Board's conditions say that they will not be liable, except on proof that the loss was caused by the negligence or wilful misconduct of their servants. Moreover, the Board will not accept liability if the passenger was not on the same train as his luggage, unless it has been properly despatched as "luggage in advance", in accordance with the conditions on the consignment note, or the passenger was on the wrong train as the result of the neglect or default of a railway servant or agent.

It is important to remember that when luggage in transit is lost, damaged or delayed, the conditions emphasize that the liability is limited to £50 per passenger. If the luggage is lost or damaged after being put in the left luggage office, the Board will not accept liability for more than £25 per depositor.

It is not always appreciated that if a passenger holds only what the conditions call an "excursion ticket", no more than small handbags or similar articles are carried free. An excursion ticket is a day, half-day, or evening ticket, issued at a reduced fare, and available by specified ordinary trains, or a special excursion train. At one time, cheap-day and excursion tickets were often issued subject to a condition that the company would not be liable for injury to the passenger in any circumstances. Several cases came before the courts turning on the question whether such a condition had been sufficiently brought to the passenger's notice. However, since 1947, the law has provided that conditions purporting to exclude or limit liability for death or bodily injury to such a passenger (other than the holder of a free pass) were of no effect.

As we have already seen, the standard conditions under which the railways had to carry goods no longer apply. Carriage of goods is now dependent only on the contract between the Board and the consignor. The Board, substantially, has power to provide this service on such conditions as it thinks fit. A new set of conditions, under which the Board accepts goods for carriage,

Deep Winter on the Somerset & Dorset: 2-8-0 No. 53807 approaching Midford, near Bath, in January 1963

A stern view of life: a cleaner shovelling ash from the smokebox of a Stanier 4-6-0 at Holbeck Sheds, Leeds

was issued in 1963. These conditions provide various exceptions to the Board's liability for loss, misdelivery or damage to goods. There are the old exceptions of an "Act of God", an "Act of a Foreign Enemy", and similar consequences of war or rebellion, including requisition or destruction by an "Act of Government, or Public or Local Authority", seizure of goods by legal process, act of omission by the consignor or his servants or agents, inherent liability to waste or deterioration of the goods, and "casualty", such as wreck, fire or explosion.

But conditions further provide that the Board must, if necessary, prove that it used reasonable care and foresight in carrying the goods. Liability will not be accepted if there has been fraud by the consignor, nor if it can be proved that the loss or damage occurred through insufficient or improper packing of the goods, or as the result of riots or strikes, or because the consignee did not take delivery in a reasonable time.

Criminal liability of passengers who avoid paying the proper fare, or who commit similar offences, is of great importance. Unfortunately, a large number of people in many walks of life, who are scrupulously honest in other ways, regard the railway as "fair game", and try to avoid paying a few shillings, or even pence. In other cases, people do not appreciate what the law is, although it is well defined. Some offences, such as travelling with intent to avoid payment of the proper fare, are created by statute. Others, such as deliberately altering the date on a ticket with intent to avoid paying the fare, are provided for under the bye-laws made by the Board (formerly by the companies) with parliamentary authority. Byelaws are approved by the Ministry of Transport, and posted up at stations. It is also an offence if a passenger who has bought a ticket travels further than his ticket allows with intent to avoid payment of the additional fare.

The essence of these offences is: did the passenger *intend* to avoid payment of the proper fare? It does not matter when the passenger formed the intent. He may have decided to cheat when he started his journey, or only when the collector asked him for his ticket at the exit barrier. A common practice is for a passenger to approach the collector with no ticket, and offer the fare from a station a short distance away, but later admit that he had travelled from a station much further off. It will not avail the passenger if he then offers the proper fare. The law says that if a passenger does not produce a ticket on request, he must either pay the fare from the station from which he started, or give his name and address. Many passengers who have genuinely lost their tickets do not understand this.

A passenger who has lost his ticket should tell the collector and give his name and address. He can be arrested only if he refuses to pay his fare or to give his name and address, and he cannot be detained while his name and address are being checked. If after failing to pay the fare (even though no intent to avoid is shown) he gives a false name or address, that in itself is an offence. The maximum penalty which a magistrate can now impose for travelling with intent to avoid the payment of the fare is a fine of £25, and for a second offence it can be up to three months' imprisonment.

If a passenger travels first class with a second-class ticket, with intent to avoid payment of the proper fare, he has committed an offence. He is not entitled to travel first class if there is insufficient second-class accommodation. But if that difficulty arises, the Board's chief officials, such as stationmasters, inspectors and guards, have authority to permit passengers holding second-class tickets to travel in first-class compartments without paying first-class fares.

THE JIM CROW CAR

As the train drew across the border between New Mexico and Texas, I was surprised to see all the negroes in the coach get up and begin to make preparations to sit together. When the train stopped at El Paso, they moved in a body along the platform to a coach at the end of the train. Then I realized what it was all about. Texas stands for segregation—for Jim Crow Cars, for eating in separate restaurants, for sitting in separate rail coaches, for doing all the things which make white and black people in the United States realize how different they are.

From "*John O' London's Weekly,*" 1950

The utter absence of discipline at important stations defies description or explanation. The arrival or departure of a through train seems to be the signal for a general paralysis of common sense amongst all the station staff, who, instead of organising themselves to grapple with the crowd, at once lose heads or temper, and stiffen into philosophic apathy, until time, of whom they are never weary, brings their trouble to an end. Why should we embark in our orderly thousands at Euston to be re-embarked as a rabble in Edinburgh, Perth or Inverness?

Professor Foxwell, 1889

From London to
Inverness by Day

H. A. VALLANCE

THIS JOURNEY really began more than 30 years ago. I had been asked to read
a paper on the Highland Railway to the Railway Club, and was delving into
a file of *Bradshaw* to trace the development of the train services. At that time,
it was impossible to travel from London to Inverness without break of journey unless one was prepared to spend a night in the train, and I had supposed
that this had always been the case. However, my search through the timetables revealed that for a few years at the turn of the century the journey
could be made by day, during the summer holiday season, by both the East
Coast route from King's Cross and the West Coast route from Euston.

Through coaches were run by both routes, and between London and Perth
these were attached to the old-established Anglo-Scottish expresses starting
at 10 a.m. The only feature of the service that was entirely new was the connecting train on the Highland Railway, leaving Perth at 8.15 p.m., and
reaching Inverness at 11.30. It was a long day's journey, with a late arrival in
Inverness, but the overall speed of rather more than 40 m.p.h. for the 568
miles from Euston, and 558 miles from King's Cross, was by no means bad
going for that type of service in those days. Unfortunately, this facility was
not well supported, and lasted only from 1900 to 1903.

The primary reason for the failure of the service appears to have been the
refusal of the Highland Railway to guarantee the connection at Perth when

the trains from the south were late—a by no means uncommon occurrence 60 odd years ago. If the connection was missed, passengers had to wait at Perth until after midnight before they could continue their journey in a night train that called at many stations. Inverness was reached at about 5 a.m., after a journey that had lasted 19 hours, and with breakfast-time still a long way off.

As he walked down the platform, disgruntled by this depressing start to his holiday, the passenger may well have reflected bitterly that it would have been better if he had caught the night train leaving London in the early evening, and reached Inverness in time for a rather late breakfast. But in those days there were only first-class sleeping berths; that amenity was not extended to third- (now second-) class passengers until the autumn of 1928. It was to avoid the discomforts of "sitting up all night" that the tourist had been lured on to the day service—and it just hadn't worked on that occasion. It is only fair to add that the southbound day service survived, in winter and in summer, after 1903. The train left Inverness shortly before 9 a.m., to connect at Perth with the midday trains on the East and West Coast routes, which reached London at 10.45 p.m.

After the failure of this rather unattractive service, there was an interval of more than 30 years before it again became possible to travel from London to the heart of the Highlands by day, even at the height of the summer holiday season. Meantime, the grouping of 1923 had placed the whole West Coast route from Euston to Perth and Inverness in the hands of the London, Midland & Scottish Railway, and the East Coast route from King's Cross to Edinburgh and Perth had become part of the London & North Eastern Railway.

At long last, in the summer of 1936, there came an improvement of a sort. The coaches for York detached at Doncaster from the early morning train leaving King's Cross at 7.25 for Leeds were extended to Edinburgh. This new Anglo-Scottish service reached Edinburgh (Waverley) at 3.50 p.m., to connect with a stopping train leaving at 4.10, and reaching Perth at 5.50. After another change into a train that had started from Glasgow, the northward journey was continued from Perth at 6.5, and Inverness was reached at 9.40.

It was not a very good service. Indeed, the overall speed was slightly slower than that attempted in 1900. Moreover, passengers from London to Inverness had to change twice. However, there was at least one big improvement: a restaurant car was available throughout the journey. Perhaps the most serious criticism of the service was the early hour of departure, even for those living in Central London. For many people living in the outer suburbs, or beyond, it was just tantalizing; they could not reach King's Cross by 7.25. Nevertheless, the L.N.E.R. hailed the service as a novelty—perhaps it was as well not to recall the past! The L.M.S.R. provided no corresponding service from Euston, but by starting early, and changing at least once, passengers from places as far south as Birmingham could reach Perth in time to join the 6.5 for Inverness.

Suspended during the Second World War, as an economy measure, the evening train from Perth to Inverness did not reappear until 1955; and another two years elapsed before an early morning service from London to Edinburgh, leaving King's Cross shortly before eight o'clock, was restored. Once again, it was exasperating for those who lived well outside London; the improved service was not for them. But with the introduction of six-hour schedules between London and Edinburgh in 1962, there came a great change—the departure time from King's Cross became first 9.30, and in the autumn 10 a.m. Needless to say, many of us promptly noted the improved service as a "must". My wife and I were among the unlucky ones; the "must" had to remain outstanding for two years.

The opportunity came at last, and eight o'clock on a sunny morning in early June found us on the platform of our home station, in South-West Surrey, at the start of the first stage of our journey, 35 miles on the "Southern Electric" to Waterloo. An hour later we were crossing the Thames in a taxi on our way to King's Cross. There, awaiting us, was "The Flying Scotsman", made up to 11 coaches, a 400-ton load for the diesel locomotive that was to haul us throughout the 393 miles to Edinburgh, with only one intermediate stop, at Newcastle. Punctually at ten o'clock we drew slowly out of the station, with its arched roof and severely plain brick walls, and were soon in the first of the seven tunnels which are the outstanding feature of the London end of the East Coast main line to the North.

Potters Bar, 12¼ miles from King's Cross, is a short distance beyond the last of these tunnels, and is at the summit of the climb across the ridge of hills, known as the Northern Heights, which fringe the valley of the Thames in the London area. From this summit, ten gently-undulating miles took us beyond the outer suburbs, over the long Digswell Viaduct of 40 arches, which carries the line 90 ft. above the valley of the little River Mimram, and to the two tunnels through the chalk of the Chiltern Hills at Welwyn. Then came the descent past Hitchin, and a long run at high speed across the flat country of the South Midlands and the western edge of the Fens. More than 100 years ago, when the railway was under construction, these low-lying fenlands were described as "a quaking bog you could stand on and shake by the acre". A firm foundation for the line was obtained by building continuous rafts of brushwood, overlaid with peat sods. An embankment was tipped on this raft gradually, so that the water could escape without seriously disturbing the surrounding soil. As the years passed by, the embankment tended to settle, and in one place near Holme (70 miles from London) the track is now said to be slightly below sea-level.

So smoothly did the train ride that the miles were slipping away almost unnoticed, and it was hard to realise that at 11 o'clock we had covered 73 miles since leaving King's Cross. Four minutes later, we passed Peterborough (76¼ miles) one minute ahead of schedule. As we approached the station at greatly reduced speed, we caught a glimpse of the cathedral, the most southerly of the great churches which have earned for the East Coast main line the name of "The Cathedrals Route". Recovering quickly from the speed restriction, we were soon climbing the long gentle rise to the summit of the line, 345 ft. above sea-level, at the 100th milepost, a short distance on the London side of Stoke Tunnel. We had gained another minute since passing Peterborough, and had covered the first 100 miles of the journey in 85 min. at an average speed of 70 m.p.h.

A long descent took us through Grantham and out into the flat country bordering the Trent, which we crossed just north of Newark. Less than 20 miles farther on, a severe speed restriction over the site of a new under-bridge at Retford more than robbed us of the two minutes we had gained on schedule, but we made a good recovery, and passed Doncaster, 156 miles from London, punctually at 12.17. Although many miles of sustained high speed and rapid acceleration after slowings had provided ample proof of the capabilities of diesel traction, our thoughts were tinged with wistful regret as we recalled some of the outstanding achievements of steam engines built at the locomotive works established at Doncaster by the Great Northern Railway in 1853.

At Shaftholme, four miles north of Doncaster, we crossed one of those un-seen railway boundaries, which have long since ceased to have any practical significance, whatever may have been their importance in the past. Here, in what was once officially described as "the middle of a ploughed field", the Great Northern made an end-on junction with the North Eastern Railway, and until the grouping of 1923, the Anglo-Scottish expresses ran over the lines of the latter company for the next 174 miles, to the border town of Berwick-upon-Tweed. The tendency to gain time continued over the next 20 miles, past Selby, where the fine old abbey church stands in full view of the railway, and we were again rather more than two minutes early when we passed York, having covered the 188 miles from London in almost exactly 2¾ hr. York is one of the most impressive points on the journey from London to Edinburgh. First comes a glimpse of the Minster, and then the station, with its glazed all-over roof, and impressively-curved main-line plat-forms, more than a quarter of a mile in length.

Between York and Darlington lie 44 easily-graded miles, for the most part through the broad Vale of York, for which "The Flying Scotsman" is allowed only 36 minutes (73 m.p.h.). We improved on this schedule by a full minute, but, once again, the train rode so smoothly that we did not realize the sustained high speed that we had attained, although by this time we were having lunch in the restaurant car. Darlington holds a special place in British railway annals, for it was one terminus of the Stockton & Darlington, the first public railway to use steam traction. The 0-4-0 locomotive No. 1, *Locomotion*, built by George Stephenson for the opening of the line in 1825, has been preserved, and occupies a place of honour on a pedestal in Bank Top Station. The East Coast main line crosses the track of the pioneer railway on the level, to the north of the station.

The outstanding features of the 36 miles from Darlington to Newcastle are the ancient cathedral and castle of Durham, both of which are seen to advantage as the train crosses the high viaduct near the station. Through this increasingly industrialized area we ran at appreciably reduced speed, and a severe slowing for engineering works caused us to lose most of the time that we had gained. However, we were still nearly a minute early as we crossed the Tyne on the King Edward VII Bridge, and drew slowly to a stop in Newcastle Central Station. The 268 miles from King's Cross had been covered within the four-hour schedule, and our driver had given an excellent exhibition of accurate timekeeping.

Punctually at 2.5 we left Newcastle on the non-stop run of 125 miles to Edinburgh, for which 1 hr. 55 min. are allowed. The start was not promising, for a severe signal check was followed by a speed restriction for engineering works, and we lost some precious minutes. However, we soon ceased to think about this setback as we once more gathered speed, and emerged from the Tyneside industrial area into rural surroundings. We even missed the half-way point in our journey, the 279th milepost from London (11 miles north of Newcastle) which we passed at about 2.20. Distant views of Bamburgh Castle and Holy Island heralded a delightful run along the Northumberland coast, as we approached Berwick. Unfortunately, we encountered yet another severe speed restriction for track relaying at Tweedmouth, and we were more than five minutes late as we came slowly round the long curve leading to the south bank of the Tweed.

The Royal Border Bridge, which carries the railway over the river at a height of 126 ft., has 28 masonry arches, and is more than 700 yd. long. Designed by Robert Stephenson, and opened by Queen Victoria on August 29, 1850, the bridge was the last link in the East Coast route between London and Edinburgh. Its graceful but impressive outlines contrast sharply with those of the two road bridges—one modern, the other dating from the seventeenth century—a short distance downstream. Berwick Station is at the north end of the bridge, and stands on part of the site once occupied by the castle. In pre-grouping days, it marked the point at which the North Eastern and the North British Railways met.

Although Robert Stephenson referred to the opening of the Border Bridge as the "last Act of Union", the bridge does not link England with Scotland. Berwick is on the north side of the Tweed, but it is an English borough, and the Border is some three miles north of the town. The point at which the railway enters the Northern Kingdom is marked by a lineside sign, displaying the words England and Scotland, and the national emblems of the rose and the thistle. It was 3.15 when we entered Scotland, and with only 45 min. left in which to cover the 55 miles to Edinburgh, our prospects of a punctual arrival were slender in the extreme. Moreover, a nasty little worry began to rear its head: we had only 15 min. in which to change trains; how late should we be, and would the connection be held? If we missed our train, we could not reach Inverness that night—visions of travellers stranded at Perth 60-odd years ago recurred with persistent frequency.

For some miles beyond Berwick, we ran high up on the cliffs, overlooking the rocky coast, along which the incoming tide was breaking in a thin line of white foam. An unforgettable picture was completed by the bright afternoon sunshine sparkling on a myriad ripples off-shore. Then we turned inland, to follow the valley of the Eye Water to a summit, about 330 ft. above sea-level, near Grantshouse, whence we descended steeply to return to the sea. We had made good running time from Berwick, and had recovered fully two minutes of our lost time when we passed Dunbar, 29 miles from Edinburgh, at 3.37. But our luck was out; a speed restriction was followed by a slight signal check, and we were still nearly six miles from Edinburgh at four o'clock. Fortunately, we suffered no more checks, and reached the long arrival platform at Waverley Station at almost exactly 4.8. At first sight, a loss of eight minutes on a six-hour schedule for a journey of nearly 400 miles may appear trifling, but it can be serious when you have to make a quick connection into the last train of the day.

Seven minutes in which to change trains; our memories of those minutes are decidedly sketchy. A porter appeared, as if by magic, and we thrust our luggage into his hands. "The 4.15 to Inverness?—aye, we'll make it," and we scurried after him, right across the huge station, to one of the terminal platforms at its western end. Our reserved seats were in the very front coach of the train, and there were less than three minutes left when we reached them. We were not the only passengers from "The Flying Scotsman" who made that dash across the station, but so far as we could tell, all the others managed to get safely on board when the train started on the dot of 4.15. As soon as we had regained our breath, our first thought was a cup of tea; and it was from the windows of the buffet car that we had a glimpse of Princes Street Gardens, and the Castle, perched on its precipitous rock, as the train ran through the natural trench that was once the bed of the shallow reed-fringed Nor' Loch.

In the outskirts of the city, we diverged from the main line to Glasgow, and ten minutes or so later were rumbling across the Forth Bridge, high above the waters of the firth. Although it is now well over 70 years old, the bridge still ranks as one of the great engineering achievements of the world. From the carriage window, the three main cantilever spans, with a combined length of over a mile, appear to be an intricate maze of huge steel tubes and cross-girders in which the train shrinks into insignificance. Their complicated details contrast sharply with the far simpler outline of the recently-completed suspension bridge for road traffic, a short distance up the firth.

From the north end of the bridge, we ran cautiously down the steep winding descent, through the tunnels, to the junction with the Aberdeen line at Inverkeithing. Then came some three miles of rising gradients to the busy manufacturing town of Dunfermline, with its ancient abbey, and long association with the kings of Scotland. The ascent continued into the Fife Coalfield, where for some ten miles, colliery subsidences have necessitated several long speed restrictions, some of which appear to be permanent. However, the introduction of diesel locomotives has minimized the effects of these obstacles; and our eight-coach train weighing 280 tons accelerated rapidly after these slowings. The rather dreary mining area gave place to rural surroundings as the train entered the county of Kinross, almost the smallest in Scotland, and we were soon within sight of the wide expanse of Loch Leven, and its island-castle in which Mary Queen of Scots was held prisoner.

Beyond the County Town of Kinross, well-cultivated farmlands gradually gave place to moorland scenery as we approached the bold ridge of the Ochil Hills, and climbed to a summit at Glenfarg. The succeeding six-miles descent, largely at 1 in 75, took us through thickly-wooded Glenfarg, where the heavy engineering works include viaducts and tunnels, to the flatter country of Strath Earn, across which we ran to join the main line from Glasgow to the North at Hilton Junction. Two more easily-graded miles took us through the tunnel under Moncrieffe Hill to Perth, where we arrived two minutes early, at 5.47. An average speed of barely 32 m.p.h. for the 48-mile journey from Edinburgh may not appear to be outstanding, but it included seven intermediate stops in addition to the severe restrictions in the colliery area.

A combined train of six coaches, weighing 210 tons, was made up from the 4.15 from Edinburgh and the 4.25 from Glasgow, which arrived a few minutes later, and punctually at 6.8 we set off on the 118-mile journey to

Inverness. The lines of the former Caledonian Railway, which we had joined at Hilton Junction, were followed for seven miles from Perth, but at Stanley we diverged on to the Highland main line, and for the first time on our long journey began to run on single track. Almost at once, the scenery changed completely. The country became more rugged, and it was obvious that we had crossed the invisible boundary between the Lowlands and the Highlands. A short, but rather steep, climb to a summit at the southern end of Kingswood Tunnel was followed by a similar descent to Dunkeld, 15 miles from Perth. Then came some 12 miles of easier gradients through the flatter open country bordering the Tay, which we crossed on a long lattice-girder bridge.

At Ballinluig, the railway leaves the Tay, and follows first the Tummel and then the Garry to reach the holiday resort of Pitlochry, reputed to stand right at the centre of Scotland. Three miles north of Pitlochry, the train threads its way through the famous Pass of Killiecrankie. In the golden sunlight of this June evening, we had a superb view of the narrow thickly-wooded defile as we crossed the curved viaduct of ten masonry arches near the northern end of the pass. However, this wonderful vista was cut short abruptly by the tunnel which immediately follows the viaduct. Although the main line through the Central Highlands is essentially a mountain railway, it has only three short tunnels—one on either side of Dunkeld, and the third at Killiecrankie.

A few minutes after emerging from the pass we reached Blair Atholl, 35 miles from Perth, and 430 ft. above sea-level. Here the country changed completely, as we climbed steadily for 17 miles, largely at 1 in 70, to cross the Grampians by the Druimuachdar Pass, 1,484 ft. above sea-level, the highest summit on British Railways. The well-wooded Vale of Atholl gradually gave place to increasingly desolate surroundings, and the view from the summit extended over a vast expanse of heather and naked rock, utterly devoid of habitation. Snow fences beside the line were a clear indication of the severity of the winter storms in the mountains. Originally, the whole railway was single track, but the section from Blair Atholl to the summit, and down the succeeding descent for six miles, to Dalwhinnie, the half-way point between Perth and Inverness, were doubled in the early years of the present century.

We were enjoying high tea in the buffet car when we topped the summit at 7.45 p.m., exactly 12 hours after leaving home. The ascent from Blair Atholl had taken 31 minutes, which was yet another tribute to the diesel locomotives that had hauled us throughout our journey. We quickly gathered speed on the less severely-graded northern slope, and soon reached the softer country of Strathspey, through which we ran to Kingussie and Aviemore, where the line divides. The older route (completed in 1863) goes north, through Grantown-on-Spey, and climbs to a height of 1,052 ft. at Dava, before falling steeply to the coast of the Moray Firth at Forres, whence it turns sharply to the west to reach Inverness. The newer line, opened in 1898, shortened the distance from Perth to Inverness by 36 miles, by taking a direct course over the intervening mountains. It abounds in steep gradients and heavy engineering works.

Leaving Aviemore, we diverged on to the newer line, to climb steadily through the hills for about 12 miles to a summit of 1,315 ft. at Slochd Mhuic. There are long gradients of 1 in 60 and 1 in 70 on the last five miles of the ascent. We attained some quite high speeds on the descent from Slochd Mhuic, which begins at 1 in 60, before easing for a few miles. At Tomatin, we crossed a curved viaduct of nine girder spans, from which we looked down nearly 150 ft. into the wild mountain-girt valley of the Findhorn. A few miles farther on, at Culloden Moor, came another magnificent vista, as we crossed the wide valley of the River Nairn at a height of well over 100 ft. on a viaduct of 28 stone arches. By this time, we were well on the way down the long descent at 1 in 60 and 1 in 70 from the hills almost to sea-level at Inverness. The last 11 miles are double track.

As we neared the coast we looked out in the soft light of the evening sun across the waters of the Beauly Firth, to the distant outlines of the mountains of Ross-shire and Sutherland. A few minutes later we curved sharply round to join the line from Aviemore *via* Forres, in the outskirts of Inverness. The approach to Inverness by rail can be confusing to a stranger. The station is a terminus, and is divided into separate sections for northbound and southbound traffic. To facilitate the interchange of passengers to and from connecting trains, it is usual for trains from the south to run past the station, and then reverse into the northern platforms. A similar procedure is adopted with arrivals from the north. Although our train had no connections to make, it was reversed into the northern part of the station. As we stepped out on to the platform, the time was 9.16 p.m. We had arrived four minutes early, after a journey of 558 miles from London. We were fortunate in getting a taxi almost at once, and we reached our hotel, looking out over the swift-flowing River Ness, before half past nine.

Half an hour later, as we took a late evening stroll beside the Ness, we looked back over the day with a feeling of satisfaction. Yes, it had been a really good day, for we had at last made the journey that had evaded us for so long.

Had we any complaints?—No, not one. We had had a most enjoyable and comfortable journey.

Any suggestions?—Yes, just this: could rather more time be allowed for changing trains in Edinburgh, even at the expense of a slightly later arrival in

From London to Inverness by Day

Inverness, and minor adjustments to the schedules of other trains? It does make such a difference if passengers can rest assured that they will make their connection into the last train of the day without a wild rush.

Postscript: Since this account of our journey was written, the summer time-table for 1965 has appeared, and our grounds for criticism have been removed. "The Flying Scotsman" now reaches Edinburgh in 5 hr. 55 min., and 38 min. are allowed for changing trains. An acceleration on the final stages of the journey has made the arrival time in Inverness 9.15 p.m.

HOPE IT WAS ON TIME

"The bride made her own wedding gown—a classic style in white brocade. Her train was the 6.15 p.m. from Redhill—held by a diamanté tiara."—Surrey newspaper.

"Peterborough", in "The Daily Telegraph"

GEORGE STEPHENSON

When my father came about the office he sometimes did not know what to do with himself. So he used to invite Bidder to have a wrestle with him, for old acquaintance sake. And the two wrestled together so often, and had so many "falls"—sometimes I thought they would bring the house down between them—that they broke half the chairs in my outer office. I remember once sending my father in a joiner's bill of about £2 10s. 0d. for mending broken chairs.

Robert Stephenson

TICKETS, PLEASE!

A ticket inspector in Bohemia informed several passengers that they were in the wrong train, and must change at once. As his progress along the carriage continued, he found still more passengers who had made the same mistake. Then one of them had a bright idea, and asked the inspector whether he was not in the wrong train. He was!

From the *"Evening News"*

264